I0042180

Reconstructing Social Justice

The rhetoric of social justice is commonplace, but increasingly it means little more than a tag line or a punctuation point. *Reconstructing Social Justice for a More Social and Less Political World* presents a new framework for social justice that will change the way people think about social justice and change the way people implement social justice. This book carves out an intellectual and practical space for social justice that is distinct from political, legal, and economic spheres. While emphasizing a distinct domain for social justice, the author then makes sense of its healing role in terms of polity, economy, technology, and religion.

Drawing from a rich supply of classroom experiences, including research on mosque controversies after September 11, 2001 and the global examples of truth and reconciliation commissions, Frederking invites the reader to think about the relevance of social justice from the micro to the macro level. Rather than a set of policy outcomes or ideological positions, social justice is a process of social accountability that demands honest and transparent engagement. While disagreement is likely and controversy inevitable, this social justice process reaffirms our connectedness and moves us forward as a collective.

Lauretta Conklin Frederking is an Associate Professor of Political Science at the University of Portland. Research interests include the politics of terrorism and cases of social justice across the United States, including mosque controversies after September 11, 2001. Previous research on literature and politics was published with Routledge in an edited volume, *Hemingway on Politics and Rebellion*. Currently, Frederking is writing a book on Steinbeck and the enduring themes in American politics and society.

Routledge Studies in Social and Political Thought

For a full list of titles in this series, please visit www.routledge.com

Reconstructing Social Justice

Lauretta Conklin Frederking

Routledge
Taylor & Francis Group

NEW YORK AND LONDON

First published 2014
by Routledge
711 Third Avenue, New York, NY 10017

and by Routledge
2 Park Square, Milton Park, Abingdon, Oxfordshire OX14 4RN

*Routledge is an imprint of the Taylor and Francis Group,
an informa business*

First issued in paperback 2015

Library of Congress Cataloging-in-Publication Data

Frederking, Lauretta Conklin, 1969–
Reconstructing social justice / by Lauretta Conklin Frederking. — First
    edition.
        pages cm. — (Routledge Studies in Social and Political Thought)
    1. Social justice.   2. Social justice—Study and teaching.   I. Title.
    HM671.F74 2013
    303.3'72—dc23
    2013023392

ISBN 978-0-415-83238-0 (hbk)
ISBN 978-1-138-19402-1 (pbk)
ISBN 978-0-203-49970-2 (ebk)

Typeset in Sabon
by Apex CoVantage, LLC

For Clete and Amelia and Nathanael
who taught me that social justice begins at home.
Every day you remind me that life is far better "together."

Contents

Preface

The Founding Fathers of the United States left their indelible mark on its foundation, and their profound choices continue to inform American society today. At the same time, this country has demonstrated its remarkable capacity to reinvent and to reinvigorate itself.

The United States is a robust democratic capitalist system. Its democracy guarantees fundamental individual rights and provides the institutional checks and balances to preserve many equalities of opportunity. The capitalism system is an emblem of opportunity, reinforcing individual freedoms and celebrating choice. Technological advances continue to push the production possibilities and intellectual innovations that make this country great. Finally, the institutional and cultural respect for religious autonomy affirms an overriding respect for the necessary limits of government.

This book is not a condemnation of the United States, nor is it a condemnation of democratic capitalism more generally. However, it is a critical study of the weaknesses that currently undermine U.S. democratic capitalism, and likely other democratic countries as well. The chapters lay out the conceptual and empirical possibilities that are not necessarily unique to the United States but carry particular potential to be realized in the United States. With its entrenched rule of law, fundamental rights, robust civil liberties, and unassailable economic progress, social justice is the next step to reorient our foundation for a better America. The extent to which, and the specific ways that the systemic malaise is generalizable, is beyond the scope of this book, but it is an important question, which will require study of other countries.

Social justice as it is reconceptualized in this book, can launch the United States into the next era of political, economic, and social development. It is the way to invigorate and rebuild from the roots of stronger community engagement. Social justice is not meant to undermine individualism but to enrich the foundation upon which we thrive as individuals and thrive as a collective. Through some significant but not impossible effort and commitment, social justice can cultivate a more virtuous cycle of individual and collective prosperity.

In addition to the reviewers who offered critical insights, I thank David Conklin for reading and re-reading drafts and providing countless helpful suggestions. Beyond guiding me to understand the importance of the good life, he inspires me as a teacher, thinker, and writer. I thank my students, especially Kevin Hershey for his inspiring curiosity and compassion, and Elizabeth Romero for her research assistance during the summer 2012. Finally, I thank my colleagues at the University of Portland, who continue to stimulate my ideas through conversation, challenge, and friendship.

1 Introduction

This book presents an analytical framework for thinking about social justice. I carve out an intellectual and practical space for social justice that is distinct from political, legal, economic, and religious spheres. With a strong reassertion of collective identity, social justice can become a healthy foundation to strengthen and enhance individualism. The central claim throughout the book is that there is systemic malaise eating away at democracy, capitalism, technology, and religion. Currently, these systems reinforce a pathological individualism that we tend to celebrate in terms of its freedom, choice, competition, and creativity. However, without the balance of a strong collective identity to coexist with individualism, our systems dangerously cultivate isolation, unyielding consumerism, and polarization. My reconceptualization of social justice involves a distinct shift away from a liberal political agenda that is the common association today. Instead, social justice is the sphere within which we engage each other in transparent, reiterative dialogue and debates. The content of our dialogue and debate is much less relevant than the connections we forge because of our reiterated meeting and communication. Rather than advocating particular policy outcomes, reconceptualized social justice focuses on a space within which we rediscover and then nurture our authentic identities as socially bound individuals.

The rhetoric of social justice is commonplace, but increasingly it means little more than a tag line or a punctuation point. Leaders, academics, and activists invoke social justice to convey fundamental significance to a cause. When you really care about something, it's beyond political; it must be social justice or the platitudinous "common good." While it typically refers to some version of civil rights legislation, legal recourse, or economic opportunities for the disadvantaged, these vehicles for today's social justice are well-worn domains that call into question the legitimacy of social justice as a separate practice. If social justice means civil rights legislation, then it is political mobilization, if it is legal recourse, then it is judicial activism, and if it is economic opportunities, then it can be either political or judicial or some other version of economic mobilization—but there is really nothing special to define social justice as content or process that is distinctively *social* justice. Today, the umbrella of common references to social justice covers a wide range of issues, including gender, economic development, race, the environment, and human development issues like civil rights, education, and healthcare. While possibly laudable from a sentimental perspective, it is very difficult to locate consensus around the intellectual concepts and practical experiences of social justice.[1] In fact, individuals who cloak themselves with the social justice mantle often sit on different sides of each of these issues. As much as these issues sometimes overlap and tap into similar opinions or preferences from a citizenry, it has become a slippery slope to welcome all these causes and issues and goals within the expansive space of social justice.

Given such a pervasive social justice agenda, we have to pause and wonder why rigorous academic analyses of social justice are so *un*common. Certainly, political scientists address a range of relevant issues, like interest group mobilization and legislative change, economists study inequality, and legal scholars study progressive civil rights laws, for example. But we don't really have any social justice social scientists. I would argue that the lack of social science analysis in the social justice field comes from the fact that social justice does not conjure concepts or theories independent of these traditional fields. Likely, most academics understand whether subconsciously or not, that the uncertainty within the social justice project make it both a politically loaded and an intellectually empty concept.

My reconceptualized social justice is a process of social engagement and accountability that reaffirms our connectedness and moves us forward as a collective. Social justice is a process of discourse and negotiation around a set of principles, including transparency, accountability, and repeated engagement. While it operates around these principles familiar in discussions of justice, its priority is the engagement of opposing perspectives. Social justice stands apart from political justice or legal activism. It needs to be distinctly *social* from an empirical perspective, and then social justice can offer distinct concepts, procedures, and outcomes from an intellectual perspective. Social justice is about the engagement between people rather than the success of legislation, and it is about the challenge of creating solidarity among a broader collective society. Solidarity from the social justice process preserves, and even fosters, diversity at the same time as it nurtures a shared commitment to the collective.

Each chapter outlines how the current trends in politics, the economy, technology, and religion damage and degenerate a collective will. I argue that the process of social justice heals societies that are increasingly defined by disassociated and disaggregated selves. According to Charles Taylor, "[T]he notion that each one of us has an original way of being human entails that each of us has to discover what it is to be ourselves."[2] While social justice fosters collective harmony, it is also a process through which we can discover what it is to be ourselves authentically and in a highly conscious, more comprehensive way. Rather than the prominent Rawlsian perspective of "justice as fairness,"[3] my presentation of social justice precedes fairness and is a reinvigorated foundation for the other spheres of our lives. Underlying interactions in the political arena, the market place, technology spaces, and within religion, social justice reconciles individual liberty and our collective identity for healthier interactions.

Much of the book places social justice in conversation with other social science disciplines, but through its liberation from their spheres, it can become more distinct and more relevant. The book provides a new agenda for social justice in a way that can be practiced, and it is meant to be highly accessible to all those participating in the social justice project or advocating social justice perspectives. The book provides an analytical framework that sets up social justice as a set of practices that can be empirically tested with identifiable and enduring concepts. It draws on academic conversations that I believe are also accessible. To elucidate the possibilities, the introduction provides a map of the examples expanded in Chapter 6, highlighting what social justice looks like as a practice away from the political arena, apart from the courtroom, removed from the economy, distinct from technology, and separated from religious activities.

Great philosophers like Plato, Aristotle, and Rousseau oriented many of the enduring social problems around the central tension between individual interests and social interests. In their independent terms, they agree that politics is an arena that acknowledges individual interests. At the same time, the political sphere binds individuals to social commitments. For these thinkers, politics may preserve the individual while also preserving and cultivating a harmonious collective. Perhaps it is more a reflection of current reality rather than an essential condition, but politics today has not realized the collective possibilities presented by the great philosophers. From rhetoric to legislative deadlock, politics now fosters less in terms of social commitments. In fact, it isn't just that politics seems unable to fulfill its ideal role, but the political arena today seems to have become an increasing barrier to social commitments.

One might celebrate that individual interests thrive, especially without the hindrance of collective responsibility. While there is an intellectual handiness around the zero-sum description of the individual and the collective, this conceptualization is a monumental error. There is an essential tension between the individual and his or her society, but the vitality of either depends not only on the tension but also on the strength of each. Taylor captures the relationship in his discussion of politics: "Recognizing difference, like self-choosing, requires a horizon of significance, in this case a shared one."[4] Individual self-actualization and authenticity struggles with, but also depends upon, social engagement. From this perspective, even the most egocentric, self-interested individuals *need* social justice as a process of social engagement. This social justice puts forward a framework to restore a type of social engagement for *individual* fulfillment as much as for society in its collective interests.

It is legitimate but also very important to frame the individual in relation to social justice. This book calls upon individuals to realize the value of social justice, but not as an add-on luxury or "kum-ba-ya" motivation. Rather than requiring individuals to surrender themselves and their interests, social justice is the process integral to identity and to individual interest formation. Social justice restores humanity as collective responsibility, but it does so motivated by the interests of the individual and his or her drive toward self-realization and individualization.

While agreeing with Taylor about the importance of social connection in order to realize individual authenticity, my vision is different from Taylor's insofar as I don't see politics as the solution. Political justice today is much more about distribution and managing difference than collective harmony. Apart from politics, social justice can fulfill the unrealized expectations identified by Plato, Aristotle, and Rousseau. As a new foundation, social justice can heal and motivate a healthier politics. Rather than cultivating cohesion and collective responsibility, politics today perpetuates trends of divisiveness, violence, and corruption. This book carves a legitimate space for thinking, studying, and writing about social justice in ways that are both intellectually meaningful and relevant for activists as well. From the more refined understanding of social justice, this book can contribute to the debates in traditional disciplines in very interesting ways. Ultimately, the ideas may bring a few more academics into the study of concepts and theories that are specifically attached to an intellectual field of social justice, and the ideas may then also alert current activists to realize a very different, more credible agenda implied by social justice.

In addition to providing an outline for each of the chapters, the introduction describes the problems that motivate this effort to provide an analytical framework for social justice. The United States is a contextual case for identifying problems and possibilities. While specifically located, the problems and possibilities can be generalized to other democratic capitalist countries. These problems are troublesome from the perspectives of a wide range of disciplines, and they can be taken up as central issues to be discussed in their own books. Here, the burning problems are presented to justify a new study of social justice. Social justice can be developed as a unique practice and conceptual approach, not in competition with traditional academic disciplines as much as a complement that these disciplines never intended to be a central focus. As I develop it here, social justice is not politics, it is not legal activism, it is not religion or technology, and it is not an economic agenda.

Today, the term social justice has its broadest reach in regard to action and policy, and as long as social justice embodies all articulations and perceptions of unfairness, it is much more of a feeling rather than a concept. It is much more of a rallying cry, without substance, than an intellectual discipline with concepts that can be operationalized and distinguished from other social science concepts. There have been real problems created by this slide toward social justice becoming the flash words for anything perceived to be unfair, and it is worthwhile to explore some of these trends in order to make sense of my push toward a very different path.

1. Nonacademic

Far too many issues, and even those with opposing views on issues, fit under the social justice umbrella. Most of these issues are tied to the political arena. The recent Occupy Movement embodied the loosely formulated agenda and widely applied rhetoric of social justice;[5] yet even the most seasoned analysts found it hard to pinpoint a shared vision or shared tactics, ranging from peaceful to violent, even within occupy protests.[6] While espousing "social justice," there was a widespread advocacy for *policy* changes with far-reaching implications for political participation and economic opportunities. As exemplified by the Occupy Movement, even while activists put forward social justice claims that are politically focused, the concept doesn't articulate too much in terms of identifiable and reliable policies. Nor does social justice connote unique scholarly studies in any meaningful way.

At best, political scientists might add social justice to the cacophony of political rhetoric—meaningless except as rhetoric.[7] But there is a problem, because while political scientists can dismiss social justice as a rhetorical device, colleges and universities across the country are introducing social justice as a coherent academic program. With the propagation of social justice programs, we are inviting students to take it seriously, but I am not sure that many administrators, faculty, or students know what they mean by social justice. For ten years, I have been part of inventing and reinventing a social justice academic minor at a liberal arts university in the United States, and my anecdotal evidence suggests that at its most coherent, it elides far too easily with a liberal political agenda. Faculty and students tend to think about social justice in "rights" language with a clear bent toward an American liberal, political agenda. While universities can be rich hubs for generating activist groups through student clubs or guest speakers, an activist agenda can't define an academic program, certainly not an academic program worthy of intellectual respect and participation. I suppose even universities are subject to sexy trends, and since social justice sounds good to everyone, it is very appealing. Nevertheless, after ten years in the trenches of implementing a social justice program, I believe that we can do better. This book lays out a framework to reinforce the belief that social justice can be a worthwhile academic program, but a significant step needs to be its conceptual liberation from a policy agenda.

2. Compartmentalizing Complexity

One vexing trend has been the increasing prevalence of individuals and institutions being "caught" as self-proclaimed actors of social justice but also harboring activities or views of social injustice. Calling out individuals and institutions for hypocrisy has become a favorite tactic of media and proponents of the current cause celebre. Targets include states and foreign policies,[8] aid organizations, and individuals whose lives exude competing goals within the current social justice movement. For example, historically, the Catholic Church offers traditional and institutional support for "social justice" across a range of issues, but it also adheres to practices that rub against social justice advocates for a range of other issues.[9] Does the breadth of Catholic social teachings and practices preserve the Catholic Church as an institution of social justice, or does the hierarchy and aspects of exclusion position the Catholic Church as an institution of social injustice? Of course, it depends what "side" you are on and for what issue. By the seemingly infinite boundaries of social justice, far too often either the individual or the institution can be accused of injustice almost as soon as they sit at the table of social justice. For example, if one is gay, and a practicing Catholic, then one is caught up in the complexity of accusing the Church of hypocrisy, or else acknowledging that he or she is a hypocrite for practicing faith within the Church while simultaneously fighting for gay rights. If one is a corporate watchdog, do you accept a company's social initiatives, or do you scrutinize the many websites calling out sweatshops measuring social justice and injustice on these terms?[10]

Compartmentalizing complexity is a common challenge around social justice today. Perhaps most generally, we lobby for peace at the macro political level but malign others or escalate hostility in our more pedestrian one-on-one daily interactions. Too often, social justice becomes compartmentalized around the set of issues that suits our own purposes. So in a peculiar trend, social justice has become both ubiquitous and strategic. It is utilized by everybody, regardless of competing causes, but it is dragged out often merely in order to shore up support for a cause. It no longer defines a particular cause or approach or understanding. It has lost its calling as a way of viewing the world and acting in the world, and it has become little more than an addendum or self-proclaimed badge of honor to whatever issue is being pursued. This trend is chiseling away at the legitimacy of social justice in the university and in practice, and increasingly social justice sounds like white noise moving us further away from resolutions rather than toward them.

3. Hypocrisy

Another current trend in social justice is that it is increasingly used by both sides on the same issue. To pick just one of the stirring political conflicts in the world today: which side in the Palestinian-Israeli conflict carries legitimacy in terms of social justice? This problem became apparent recently when I attended a social justice young artists' exhibition. One of the conveners began a conversation that ended in an inflamed diatribe. First, he railed against me for "claiming" to be an advocate of social justice, and then he railed against my university for "claiming" to be an institution of social justice. In a paraphrase of his comments: how could I and my institution propound leadership of social justice when our retirement fund investments contributed to funding the wrong side? I assured him that I couldn't be so certain that one side had the moral authority of social justice. Accepting both sides of this polarized political issue obviously doesn't fit well with most individuals who have an opinion about which side is "right" and legitimate in terms of this crisis. While I was uncomfortable with either side being authorized as *the* socially just side, as a social scientist, I was equally perturbed by a concept that allows both sides to maintain a claim on social justice. In terms of intellectual rigor, it is a significant conceptual weakness if the same concept defines two opposing positions on an issue. Likely, we don't see too much writing on social justice from social scientists for precisely this reason. The social justice concept is too blurry, too politicized, and it no longer serves as an intellectual marker of meaningful debate. If we really care about learning how social justice works across communities and countries, then the nonparticipation of the social science academic community significantly limits the debates, study, and generalizability. This trend should concern the practitioners of social justice quite significantly.

4. Polarization

The problems of political polarization and economic inequality are well-documented by scholars and journalists alike. However, a simple overview of the Occupy Movements conveys how widespread the disagreements are, and how intractable they appear. At least the most vocal representatives of the 99 percent have lost enthusiasm for electoral cycles and seem ripe for social movements instead. Congress's approval is at a historic low and suggests intractability, and the fragility of citizens' tolerance is at a historic high.[11] Students no longer perceive the possibilities of employment sufficient to pay back student loans,[12] and according to the Organisation for Economic Co-operation and Development (OECD) website in 2012, the United States is plummeting to the bottom of developed countries in terms of education performance. Within the political sphere, escalating expectations dissolve quickly into deepening frustration, and Americans seem less capable than ever of finding creative, nongovernmental solutions.

Problems of inequality in the economic sphere amplify the disconnections between the "haves" and "have-nots." Historically, the "have-nots" rallied for government assistance and benefits, but in this era, even the "haves" of big business readily embrace a historical government bailout. While Americans hold onto the heritage of individualism, they simultaneously direct hopes and complaints toward the state and seek remedies from within the political sphere. At the same time, populism and voting give way to cycles of protest and social movement, both of which challenge and undermine the credibility of the political sphere.

It is enough to let readers determine their own heightened alarm. But clearly there is a "meta" set of issues about how we solve our problems. Should government be the focus for all of this discontent and systemic malaise? In particular, when government is increasingly ineffective from the perspective of those participating in social protest, why not push into different realms with creative possibilities? The question becomes where and how solutions can emerge. Regardless of how severe one perceives the problems, to the extent that there are acknowledged problems, it is worthwhile to think about viable solutions or mechanisms for change. We have become too comfortable venting our expectations and disappointments around political leaders and also the political sphere more generally. A central claim in this book is that change needs to come from outside of the political and economic arenas, and I propose that this reconceptualized framework of social justice is a potential mechanism for effecting change.

5. Politicization or Social Affirmation

My courses on social justice issues introduce the cleavages around gender, sexuality, migration, war, poverty, and the environment. Students have profound stories and opinions, most especially about their personal injustices. Each one of these issues generates enough fireworks from both sides (where there are seemingly two sides) to make one run away or rejoice because of the enthusiastic participation. For the introductory course, my colleague and I determined that it was a good sign that typically both sides were equally angry with us. What struck me again and again was the fact that these students, who were so righteous and so determined to shout the loudest, were also most desperate for affirmation from us, the teachers. What we interpreted as a great success because of their honesty and engagement was actually an intellectual and emotional wreck for them until they were affirmed at the interpersonal level. These young people didn't want political solutions. These students wanted to be approved by their peers, their mentors, and by the community.

I suppose it makes sense at the most basic level of human nature. Acceptance by one's reference group is critical to self-esteem. It reminds me that even though I may be a political scientist legitimately focusing on politics with my research and subsequent solutions, many solutions aren't political and shouldn't be political. This is a central point throughout the book. This reconceptualized social justice relieves the pressure valve on political expectations, and it does so in a way that is more connected with what humans want and need outside of politics. For example, at the end of the day, if I am working in a "man's" privileged world, I want equal pay for work of equal value, sure, but what I really want is affirmation from the men and women with whom I work that I am worthy. I want to hear it and see it in the most informal, casual ways as much as I want everyone to follow the rules that require respect manifest in equal pay. The one type of satisfaction is clearly solved within the political realm, while the other needs something else. Political scientists often adhere to the fact that institutions matter because they change norms—eventually. I argue that we can do better through the vehicle of social justice, as a complement to the political realm or as an instigator for change in the political realm. But most critically, political remedy and social justice are not the same; they do not always coincide, nor should they. Today, we have a politicization that is everywhere, and we have advocates of social justice immersing themselves in the arena of political solutions. Arguably, advocates could reorient around something other than politics as usual. Reconceptualized social justice is at least a step forward in rejuvenating the health of our society and potentially reinvigorating the health of our democracy.

6. Public Tolerance and Private Righteousness

> The demand for certainty is one which is natural to man, but is nevertheless an intellectual vice.
>
> —Bertrand Russell[13]

Another apparent problem is the peculiar combination of public tolerance and private righteousness. By the time students go away to college, they have accepted a very empty or limited version of liberalism that permits everyone to have his or her own opinion about an issue. Rather than engaging others, especially those who don't share the same views, students have absorbed a "live and let live" approach that undermines interpersonal, authentic engagement. It seems insulting to them and to the principle of tolerance to try to persuade someone to think differently. As a result, students don't try to change other people's minds, and they wear their own certainty as a badge of honor. Changing one's mind—and even worse—letting dialogue change one's mind, cuts like a knife of insult or injury. I have been surprised by the visible shock of students when I comfortably admit changing my mind on a number of issues. Somehow, along the education path, students learned that being smart means being certain. So they cling onto certainty but let everyone hold onto their own certainties just as well. They listen politely and then state their own views in a way that the value of human dialogue is missed and the art of persuasion is maligned. Instead of deeper understanding, superficial interactions become strategic weapons of insult to other's certainty.

This phenomenon suggests a trend described by Timur Kuran's theory to explain the fall of the Soviet Union.[14] In his empirical case, individuals maintained both public and private preferences, and while the public preferences displayed support and compliance for the Soviet regime, individuals' private preferences reflected the inevitable revolutionary change in ideology and regime structure. In a similar sort of way, students articulate this public preference for tolerance, while not too deeply below the surface they have profound intransigence toward others' views. To some extent, this layer of civility can be good. It maintains decency and postpones or limits conflict. However, the disconnect between public tolerance and private intolerance suggests potential volatility, like Kuran's description of the communist Soviet Union just prior to its fall. Austere public tolerance is more of a performance than the social outcome of interpersonal exchange, engagement, and reflection. Tolerance has become more of an act—and a flimsy one at best, without the virtuous qualities expected from tolerance in a robust democracy.

Clearly the social justice project has become rife with righteousness and has added confusion as students have personal stakes in some final declaration about who holds legitimacy from the social justice perspective. Students offer and receive the stings of this social justice righteousness in a pervasive way. To the student who is in the military training program, how can he or she be an advocate of social justice? To migrants from Haiti, how is it possible to be denied refugee status in the United States compared to Cubans who are welcomed? To my female student who would like to be a priest, how can she view the same institution that denies her priestly membership as the institution that supports her social justice activities? And to the broader community, as a religious university, how can we maintain leadership around the social justice project and also maintain a robust Reserve Officers' Training Corps (ROTC) program on campus? These few examples are miniature anecdotes of the larger polarizing conflicts in society: Is social justice about minorities or gender? Is social justice about freedom or protection? Is social justice about peace or a just war? Is social justice about U.S. human development or global human development? Is social justice about the job you do or what you do in your job?

If these trends continue, it seems as though we are forced to accept an inevitable hypocrisy around institutions and the individuals that participate in the social justice project. Alternatively, we necessarily embrace social justice as an ideal that is filled with contradictions. More realistically and more significantly, it is time to acknowledge that social justice has become good propaganda to shore up individual advocacy, but it is increasingly defunct as a conceptual tool or as a distinct and definable project. Of course, it sounds much more powerful to be fighting for better family-leave policies in the name of social justice rather than personal or even group interests. Like "greenwashing," where people and products market themselves as advocates for the environmental cause,[15] the veneer of social justice is everywhere, and everyone is somewhere or somehow part of the social justice project. However, these claims to social justice and a common good are often flimsy and a thin disguise for strategic self-interest. While self-interest is an essential part of a healthy political and economic life, social justice needs to be the sphere where we suspend our personal strategic self-interests, not entirely and not permanently, but considerably and consciously.

We have both diluted the relevance of social justice and increasingly tied it to our individual interests rather than making it something distinct from idiosyncratic individual interests. Invoking social justice no longer tells us anything about the content of social justice or the way out of any particular conflict. This book settles most of these questions that currently taint our understanding of social justice because it develops the broader conceptual issue of who gets to wear the mantle of social justice, which social justice programs present a legitimate academic agenda, and what content gets to fit within the social justice paradigm. In the chapters ahead, I develop an intellectual agenda to resurrect social justice from the language of "right" and "wrong" and to defuse the social justice project of its mixed messages and contradictory content.

THE FRAMEWORK OF SOCIAL JUSTICE

This book frames social justice in terms of its relationship with some of the broader trends of modern society: democracy, capitalism, technology, and religion. Ultimately, it carves out an intellectual space for social justice that is unique and distinct from these spheres of activity. In this way, I present the idea that social justice as a concept and practice needs to be more distinctly circumscribed than currently utilized. For example, in the United States, a great deal of the self-identified social justice practice currently focuses on the political system: more rights for gays, more rights for undocumented migrants, more rights for women. It seems appropriate to evaluate the relationship between social justice and the political realm, and then move toward constructing a meaningful conceptual and practical space independent of the political arena. If my ideas carry weight and offer legitimacy for a distinct space for social justice, then it becomes important to articulate both the practical and theoretical agenda for this space. While there is some risk of removing potential allies and advocates from this more narrowly defined social justice agenda and intellectual study, the benefits are significant in terms of removing a lot of the confusion that characterizes social justice today.

In addition to an emphasis on the *social* sphere rather than the political, economic, or religious, the second central theme of the book emphasizes social justice as a *process* rather than a set of outcomes. While there are robust possibilities to link with political causes, economic causes, and environmental causes, this needs to happen through a newly invigorated and more narrowly circumscribed understanding of social justice as a process more than any particular cause. Each chapter expands upon the challenges with social justice as it is practiced and theorized today, and it explores this intellectual shift in conceptualizing social justice more thoroughly. The rest of the introduction is meant to present a broad brushstroke picture of the current problems with the social justice project, around both the practice and study of social justice, and, in order to justify this new conceptual understanding.

The pages ahead unpack much more systematically the associations of social justice in terms of different government types, different types of economic organization, and in terms of technology and religion. A new understanding focuses on social justice as the foundation for political, economic, and religious interaction. It prioritizes process rather than an outcome. It is a process of discourse and negotiation around a set of principles that include fairness, transparency, and equality. While it operates around these principles familiar in discussions of justice, its priority is the engagement, rather than mere proclamation, of opposing perspectives. It stands apart from political justice or legal activism. Social justice needs to be distinctly *social*. It is about the engagement between people rather than the success of legislation. It is about the challenge of creating solidarity among a broader collective society. This solidarity permits diversity in the political, economic, and religious realms but evolves from a robust and shared commitment to the collective. In Chapter 2, I distinguish social justice from a communitarian vision of social organization that replaces the state or that exists independent of the state. In terms of the social justice project, I argue that we don't need to join together in intimate and multisided ways that bind us to extensive informal codes. Rather, we need to engage reiteratively with meaningful transparency and accountability with those we don't know, and those we don't want to join, in a more intimate community. It is easy to find peace and consensus with those who share our views, our policies, and our goals. One of the central powers of social justice should be its orientation around deliberation and engagement with those who don't share our views, our policies, and our goals.

Also in Chapter 2, I explore alternative government structures in terms of social justice. On the basis of efficiency, many authoritarian regimes move forward much more efficiently and effectively in terms of popular "social justice" goals. Nevertheless, my reconceptualization aligns social justice with democracy. But rather than emphasizing outcomes, I draw attention to the deliberative process uniquely fostered within a democracy. Certainly, civil liberties are relevant, but the emphasis here remains in defining social justice as a process rather than as a set of outcomes. Social justice fits very comfortably with the group of political theorists who emphasize deliberative democracy. The key distinction for social justice that sets it apart from these other theories is that it remains independent of the formal political process. It is not about group organization formally oriented around the process of legislative reform. Of course, legislation reflects the most polarizing and most consensus-building opportunities, and these discussions will filter into social justice deliberation. However, an important criterion of this conceptualization of social justice is that it denies the political process as its primary vehicle for engagement and focus. While social justice becomes a foundation from which people participate in politics, social justice cannot be coopted by the political sphere or else it ceases to be social justice.

In Chapter 3, I address anticapitalism as a common theme for social justice advocates. Capitalism brings with it such gaping and growing inequalities that it seems an easy place to find common ground for current social justice advocates. However, this chapter sheds light on the complexity of the market in terms of social justice. After unpacking the many ways in which the market has been part of the solutions as much as the source of the problems, I argue that my conceptualization of social justice as a process makes the market and a capitalist economy the most compatible system. Precisely because social justice as a process relies on diversity and transparency, capitalism is more effective than alternative modes of economic organization. However, the most challenging aspect of capitalism is the yawning inequality it creates, and this feature (typical although not inevitable) continues to frustrate the realization of social justice, even as a process. This chapter also challenges globalization as an ineluctable trend and as a desirable trend. My critique focuses on the tide of globalization in terms of the disaggregation of exchange and the alienation from our productive value, our citizen potential, and our identity from interpersonal exchange.

Technology is another important aspect of modernization, and Chapter 4 lays out the proper place of technology in terms of social justice. Similar to the economy, there are many places where we can point to the benefits of technology. The role of social media in transforming and mobilizing populations across the Middle East to bring down oppressive regimes fits within the mainstream conceptualization of social justice. At the same time, there are many examples where technology is the tool of oppression, where technology reinforces the inequality between populations, and where technology, particularly machines, replaces human value and human dignity. Here, the reconceptualization of social justice does not mean that technology should be reviled, however. Rather, the foundation of social justice needs to be the foundation to evaluate and to make some of our decisions about the limits and uses of technology. The practice of social justice can feed into the practical uses of technology, but social justice must remain a separate sphere of engagement. Likely, this perspective will meet initial reluctance from most readers, especially younger ones caught in the wave of social media. Kony 2012 brought forward controversial and competing claims. However, just watching Kony 2012 unfold, one perceives the virtues of fast networking and "outing" of the enemies of social justice causes. For many who perceive the social justice virtues in the project, moments like Kony 2012 could be crowning moments, exhibiting the height of social justice success. However, it is precisely this outing and mobilizing toward an enemy that is the antithesis of social justice as conceptualized here. This example may be viewed as successful political justice or it may even be considered as a worthy social movement, but it is not *social justice*.

Chapter 5 focuses on social justice and religion. Like technology, religion includes many possibilities for promoting social justice as well as many possibilities for fostering social injustice. Historically, countless wars have been fought in the name of religious causes, and at the same time, religion and religious organizations are typically on the frontline, providing shelter for the homeless, food banks for the hungry,[16] and assistance programs for new immigrants. In this chapter, I systematically outline the theoretical strengths of religion at the center of the social justice project, as well as the core doctrines of several major religions identifying social justice as a priority. These positive qualities include the breadth and depth of social capital, the particular forming of conscience involved in religious development, as well as its efficiencies. The negative tendencies emerge from any religion's exclusivity of membership, albeit to varying degrees. Related to exclusivity is the tendency toward sectarianism. Not only is membership limited but religious group membership is defined in a way that those outside of the group are necessarily perceived by the group to be less than those who are members of it. Ultimately, I argue that the theoretical relevance of religion in terms of social justice depends upon how one views human nature. If the reader perceives that we are fundamentally spiritual, then social justice most likely will involve some sort of concession to a religious dimension. While there is clear potential for religion to fit comfortably within this reconstructed social justice, it is not a necessary part. Chapter 5 presents these limits and possibilities.

Chapter 6 explores the possible mechanisms for implementation. Expanding from the market, to the neighborhood, to the nation state, these examples demonstrate the practice of social justice. Interest groups, social movements, and education make the realization of this type of social justice fathomable. Here, I identify potential sources for change and examples of a redefined social justice. This reconceptualized social justice incorporates the concepts into a redefined, perhaps more plausible, project shared and understood similarly by both academics and practitioners. I draw from my research and empirical examples to highlight optimism and the possibilities for implementing social justice amid economic competition, religious polarization, and in the aftermath of injustice.

My first example is a study of the wine industry in Oregon. Here, it is evident that individuals working against each other in a highly competitive market can come together in community to share ideas, resources, and collective interests. With a focus on the environment, these types of "green niche" communities provide an example of a sharp turn away from solely competitive market forces as the foundation for capitalism. Clearly, capitalism can be more than a sphere dominated by self-interests, profit, and competition. With a social justice foundation, capitalism can become just as much a societal and social phenomenon. It is about connections around productive values that support community relationships. Here my case emphasizes *how* entrepreneurs transform into socially just communities and the collective possibilities for more widespread economic exchange.

A second example presents the constraints, the urgency, and the possibility of social justice. For over a decade, migrant communities in the United States, and especially South Asian migrant communities, have been a focus of my research. Immigrant groups generally confront challenges around adaptation and integration into their host countries. Settlement can often lead to segregated neighborhoods that reinforce stereotypes and seemingly irreconcilable differences. Especially after September 11, mosque controversies have been a salient example of polarizing differences and the difficult engagement between groups that acknowledge the "other" as illegitimate or threatening. However, my research of mosque controversies suggests the possibility of a social justice process, albeit unintended, with benevolent consequences. While these positive outcomes are limited and unintended, they highlight a process of engagement that emerged precisely because of conflict. At times there was hostility between groups, but groups within the neighborhood also experienced learning about their shared identities and the identities that distinguished them. My study of testimonies reveals the articulation of hate-filled views that became muted and then transformed when confronted by new friends and groups articulating a strong opposition. Certainly, some individuals maintained divisive rhetoric, but interviews emphasize a wide circle of learning, changing beliefs, and emerging understanding of the "other" as well as a shared commitment to move forward within the broader community.

Truth and Reconciliation Commissions (TRCs) have been implemented in over twenty countries since 1983, and they are a third example of ideal social justice. While far from perfect, when measured by a political or legal yardstick, they fit the procedures and outcomes associated with this new version of social justice. TRCs were born out of the brutal regimes that institutionalized racism, torture, and arbitrary punishment of minorities. The TRCs did not attempt to punish the individuals who committed atrocities, and they did not attempt to compensate victims. Instead, they provided a public forum for victims and perpetrators to approach each other, to acknowledge pain, to hear, and to engage. They were not designed for unilateral, private confessions or accusations. Rather, TRCs facilitated a social process of engagement, helping individuals to understand opposing perspectives and compelling them to confront truths. Participants didn't walk away with the pillars of formal justice to support them or with punitive vindication, but they made steps forward collectively in a shared understanding of history. Small scale or large scale, there has been social recognition that everyone has to move forward, and the movement forward has to be together. What had been polarizing and vitriolic needed healing.

The TRCs didn't replace justice or politics, but they provided a unique and essential stage in societal recovery and development. While fortunate that our Western society has not experienced these kinds of systemic and violent injustices in our recent past, there is no doubt that our society needs renewal through the social justice process. However, in some senses, we are also too luxurious or too complacent a society to consider the extent to which we could benefit from such interactions. We hurt each other every day with insults that carry societal burdens of injustice. Our response is to return to our homes, licking our wounds privately with self-soothing tricks, like alcohol or drugs, or privately healing in the care of our consoling families, who help us forget how wrong society has become. The social injustices are obvious to everyone, but rather than privatizing recovery or politicizing recovery, this book begins with recognition that a new way of thinking about and practicing social justice is a dramatic and important first step.

Teaching social justice in the classroom is another case and the central theme of Chapter 7. I unpack some common associations with social justice and make them more conceptually and analytically relevant for university study. For each association, I suggest we need to introduce greater scrutiny. Some of the associations seem largely misguided or highly politicized, while others point to the enduring tensions that are often overlooked when we articulate the social justice project. The purpose of this chapter is to make the study of social justice more rigorous in the college classroom, but the themes should resonate as broader trends in society that can be questioned. If we are to move forward with the vision of social justice as distinctly *social* and as a distinct *process* rather than a liberal agenda, or a set of particular outcomes, then many of our current assumptions don't fit comfortably.

Below are ten key ideas around social justice that require some significant demystification or reconsideration. Each one is developed more extensively in Chapter 7, and these ideas should become the analytical starting point as academic hypotheses to be analyzed with empirical evidence. These ten ideas can be the focus for a very different type of social justice program. Each idea proposes concepts and new ideas that can be tested and evaluated from both an empirical and normative perspective. Without a political agenda, social justice can become an academic program that is interdisciplinary but unique, relative to other disciplines, and rigorous.

1. Individual Justice v. Social Justice

Current liberal agendas emphasize the importance of individual rights. However, while individual justice *for all* may be worthy as a goal, it is not the same as social justice. We need to identify the differences systematically and make sense of the unique characteristics of social justice. Similarly, a critical question is how leadership can be part of the social justice project and whether the qualities of leadership are really the qualities that move the social justice project forward.

2. Formal v. Informal

Rules and laws may protect individual rights but disassemble the cohesion of the broader community. Legal change does not always correspond with social acceptance, and usually not acceptance in the ways that may be desired. Similarly, compelling individuals to particular treatment by the law certainly can improve the status of groups, but it can also limit improvements to a minimum standard set by the new law. Gender equality and racial equality need to be analyzed from this perspective. For example, laws for "equal pay for work of equal value" may formally protect women but leave them isolated and frustrated with gender interactions in the workplace. What do laws provide, and then what do they take away in terms of social cohesion?

3. Process v. Outcomes

We love innovation and success, but as a society, we fail to nurture a mainstream understanding that the path of innovation and success is necessarily driven by failures and challenge. This sensibility that failure is an essential part of success is lost in our education standards and social norms. We educate students for the winning outcomes, in particular, rather than the process. This reconceptualized social justice encourages study of the processes of change and exchange, as much more important than any official tally of legislative victories or profit or membership.

4. Local v. Global

When one is alert to the plights of poverty, inequality, and suffering, the geographical reach for social justice seems appropriately vast and demanding. In teaching college students about social justice, it is clear that one of the least scrutinized areas is the prioritization between local and global social justice. College students are oriented to think globally these days. We wear the statistics about student participation in study abroad programs like a badge of honor. However, along the terms of social justice described in this book, we need to evaluate the implications and limits of global social justice.

5. Empathy v. Consensus

Conversations on college campuses today are soaked with political correctness or silence in the name of political correctness. "Live and let live" is the motto that chisels away at authenticity. Students have lost the art of civil discourse, which often demands disagreement as part of cultivating an authentic identity. It isn't enough to have an opinion. Students need to practice and study case studies to unpack different types of disagreement, persuasion, and change. Are there cases when disagreement leads to empathy and shared understanding rather than, or distinct from, consensus? For example, "Kyriarchy"[17] describes intersectionality and the ways in which we have many layers of oppression in society. As a reasonable hypothesis, we can expect that situations where intersectionalities are consciously identified lead to more empathy, not necessarily consensus, around difference.

6. Private Sphere v. Political Sphere

Social justice rhetoric brings the most private issues of identity into the public square. For example, few would disagree that gender and sexual identity are hot-button themes on most academic campuses. However, in an effort to push forward political rights, the current social justice agenda slips into publicizing what could remain private. Are the social costs of the public square for potentially or previously private issues? What are the social justice arguments for avoiding legal action? Are there social costs to political action? Can we be systematic and analytical about process and then these types of consequences?

7. Unintended Heroes of Social Justice

It is hard to fathom but some of our greatest heroes for implementing measures of political, economic, and social justice are often those very leaders who sat on thrones of injustice. In line with thinking about social justice as a "battle" with winners and losers, or thinking about social justice in terms of "heroes" and "villains," we often think in binary terms about the presence or absence of social justice. However, my reconceptualized social justice as a process of engagement cultivates fertile ground for change so that even the most unusual heroes emerge from the fertile environment of social justice. The emergence of unintended heroes may become a reasonable measure of social justice "success" that we can compare across countries and cases.

8. Solidarity v. Diversity

Students and faculty often preach solidarity around liberalism rather than authentic diversity. We need to practice and study contexts and issues around which meaningful diversity thrives. We need to study the boundaries of diversity and when diversity thrives with solidarity or deteriorates into conflict.

9. Emotions

Classrooms need to provide a safe place for students to explore what social justice as a process of engagement feels like—to be vulnerable with strangers, frustrated or angry, but civilized, and to probe and accept alternative positions without feeling defeated. It is not easy. There is something profound in terms of potential learning that emerges from a student's vulnerability and willingness to take a public risk. How do emotions fit into reasoned discourse? How do emotional arguments compare with reasoned arguments in terms of social engagement?

10. Fact v. Fiction

Stories reveal life's complexity. Any position can be thwarted, challenged, and effectively reversed by the emotional potency of a life changing event. Sharing stories opens us up to similar transformations, and reading stories together can be helpful where our personal experiences are limited. Within social justice programs, and as part of an experimental design, we can study the impact of fictional narratives on behavior, preferences, and beliefs.

TEACHING SOCIAL JUSTICE AS PRACTICING SOCIAL JUSTICE

In addition to my research discussed in Chapter 6, which supports the wide and deep possibilities for implementing social justice, the classroom is also an ideal sphere to experience social justice in practice. For two years I have taught a course called "Catholicism and the Theoretical Roots of Social Justice." My co-teacher was a Holy Cross Priest, and the course was the required introduction for students interested in a Catholic studies minor as well as students interested in a social justice minor. Perhaps not surprisingly, several fault lines within the class centered on the implied differences between Catholicism as an organized religion and social justice as usually construed by activists. This tension erupted when one student came out to the class about his homosexuality and the frustrations it presented for his identity as a practicing Catholic. He was emotional without being either sentimental or hypersensitive. He reasoned and articulated the problem in a way that made him a hero of my new version of social justice. After the dramatic and poignant revelation that was emotional but reasoned, several students (in the commonly associated "social justice" camp) aligned themselves with a different type of discourse. They launched vitriolic criticisms about the hypocrisy and inhumanity of the Catholic Church writ large. Just when the conversation was spiraling into a closed space of accusation, with about a quarter of the class nodding their heads and staring wide-eyed, and with the remaining class clearly "tuned out" in their tolerant but righteous indignation and opposition, an equally earnest second student engaged the first student by presenting the view of the Catholic Church. From my perspective, this second student joined the first as a hero participant in this type of social justice. He knew the church doctrine and wanted to dispel the myths to the hostile group, and he wanted to let my initial hero know that practicing Catholicism wasn't as dichotomous as he suggested. "You aren't in or out of the Church based upon obedience." With this honest proclamation, students joined the conversation, and the dialogue became rich with metaphor, frustration, passion, and engagement. Students wanted to persuade the other side why they believed what they believed, why they did what they did, and why it mattered.

It is a curious observation that by far the rudest tones and most cutting accusations came from those self-proclaimed "social justice" activists. In fact, one of the students suggested I should be fired because I didn't defend the "right" side. But after my first hero modeled transparency and offered personal but reasoned dialogue and after my second hero presented an equally personal *and* reasoned role in the dialogue, we experienced a version of social justice emerging. After initial hardliners screamed versions of intolerance, the exchanges settled into a rich multilayered transformative dialogue. Social justice was not complete at the end of the class. In fact, we were in the thick of it by the end of the class with everyone pumped up, uncomfortable, and looking to us, the teachers, to make it better by telling one side they were right while the other must be wrong. For this new version of social justice, it became clear that a critical component of the success was the students' understanding that there would be many iterations of the dialogue. They had to figure the "other" out if they were going to make it through the course. They engaged with me and each other out of their frustration and continued to engage with anger until anger began to transform into something else.

Our Friday hot topics discussion classes came close to 100 percent attendance and approached this ideal version of social justice. My students might be gay rights activists in the political sphere, they might fight for employment justice rights in the economic sphere, but through their dialogue and exchange, they became participants practicing social justice in my classroom. More and more, they listened, and they talked authentically. More and more, they made each other laugh even while they made each other angry. By the end of the course, we had a type of exchange that was healthy in its honesty and respect for the other and rigorous in its intellectual analysis, even while students continued to disagree. Over the course of the semester, students were compelled to share enough to realize that their disagreements didn't reinforce difference. Cross-cutting disagreements became apparent and the foundation for curiosity: "I wonder what that ROTC student thinks about torture as a weapon of war?" The earlier assumption, revulsion, and dismissal that characterized patterns of *dis*engagement at the beginning of the semester began to dissipate.

While examples of my framework of *social* justice are increasingly rare in the developed world, the need for social justice to provide a foundation for our political, legal, and economic spheres is increasingly apparent. This book focuses on framing social justice in a new way, as well as presenting the relevant considerations in the practice of social justice. The overarching theme identifies conceptual problems if we consider social justice in terms of a particular set of outcomes—food stamps, job training, pay equity, the list is endless. In these instances, social justice becomes a placard to shore up one's policy position rather than a concept delineating a unique set of theories, or even a set of distinguishable policies. Republicans and Democrats, democracy and authoritarian regimes, gay rights, religious rights, less government, more government, all claim legitimacy under the umbrella of social justice. This current state makes social justice intellectually problematic, and it makes social justice pragmatically meaningless. Throughout the book, I offer the context and criteria to reframe social justice in a distinctive and meaningful way. In its new form, Republicans and Democrats, those within democracies or authoritarian regimes, those interested in gay rights, religious rights, less government, more government can claim legitimacy under the umbrella of social justice still, but not by their ideological or policy positions. While my particular conceptualization may not appeal to all, across both the academic and practitioner spheres, it is a loud call to all of us involved in the social justice project to establish clearer boundaries and content. Ideally, this will enhance our debate and make our differences more transparent. If this understanding of social justice carries conceptual strength and empirical relevance, it will also serve to push social justice in a very different direction. While it is a sharp departure from the ubiquitous conventional and contradictory uses that have surfaced, this new direction is actually more rather than less inclusive. It invites the same opposing groups, and many more perhaps, to the table but it does so in a very unique, *socially* defined way. It is not more exclusive in terms of who participates, but it is definitely more particularized in terms of how we participate.

NOTES

1. The practice of social justice has been contested from the time of its Thomistic roots, but conceptual criticism has been relatively muted. See Stefano Solari and Daniele Corrado, "Social Justice and Economic Order According to Natural Law," *The Journal of Markets & Morality* 12, no. 1 (2009): 47–62. A notable exception is Hayek, who was an early critic of social justice as a concept because of its breadth and subsequent meaninglessness. See Adam James Tebble, "Hayek and Social Justice: A Critique," *International Social & Political Philosophy* 12, no. 4 (2009): 581–604 and Edward Feser, "Hayek on Social Justice: Reply to Lukes and Johnston," *Critical Review: A Journal of Politics and Society* 11, no. 4 (1997): 581–606.
2. Charles Taylor, *The Ethics of Authenticity* (Cambridge: Harvard University Press, 1991), 61.
3. John Rawls, *A Theory of Justice* (Cambridge: Harvard University Press, 1999). See also Joshua Cohen, "The Importance of Philosophy: Reflections on John Rawls," *South African Journal of Philosophy* 23, no. 2 (2004): 114–19 and Carl L. Bankston, "Social Justice: Cultural Origins of a Perspective and a Theory," *Independent Review* 15, no. 2 (2010): 165–78.
4. Taylor, *Ethics of Authenticity*, 51–52.
5. In the introduction to their edited volume, *Occupy the Future*, Grusky, McAdam, Reich, and Satz acknowledge that "We understood, in other words, what Occupy was against, but what was it for?" David B. Grusky, Doug McAdam, Rob Reich, and Debra Satz, eds., *Occupy the Future* (Cambridge: A Boston Review Book, 2013), 6. Versions of inequality—social, economic, and politics—become their focus.
6. CNN Wire Staff, "Occupy Oakland Protest Muted After Last Week's Arrests," *CNN Cable News*, February 5, 2012; Patrick McGeehan, "Envelopes with White Powder Sent to Mayor and 6 Banks," *New York Times*, May 1, 2012; Kirk Johnson, "Protesters Regroup in Nashville and Denver," *New York Times*, October 31, 2011, A15.
7. See, for example, pro-life activist Peter West, "Social Justice and the Catholic Vote," *American Thinker*, March 16 2012, http://www.americanthinker.com/2012/03/social_justice_and_the_catholic_vote.html. Accessed on July 26, 2013. For strong family rights activists that include abortion as social justice,

see "Strong Families," Forward Together, http://forwardtogether.org/strong
-families. Accessed on July 26, 2013. As another example, the pro-environmentalist
EPA makes social justice claims, but so too does BP oil. See Ronald Sandler
and Phaedra Pezzullo, *Environmental Justice and Environmentalism: The
Social Justice Challenge to the Environmental Movement* (Cambridge: MIT
Press, 2007) for further complications as they lay out the social justice challenges to the environmental movement.

8. The accusations of hypocrisy aren't limited to one party over the other. For
example, while Bush was accused repeatedly of social injustice in terms of
interrogation techniques to obtain terrorist information (See Carrie Johnson and Julie Tate, "New Interrogation Details Emerge," *Washington Post*,
April 17, 2009, A1), Clinton was attacked for inaction in the case of Rwandan genocide. See Barbara Crossette, "Report Says U.S. and Others Allowed
Rwanda Genocide," *New York Times*, July 8, 2000, A4. See also Rory Carroll, "US Chose to Ignore Rwandan Genocide," *Guardian*, March 31, 2004,
14.

9. Gustavo Gutierrez and Richard Shaull, *Liberation and Change* (Atlanta: John
Knox Press, 1977) and the debates around "liberation theology" offer an
example of a social justice cleavage within the Church community.

10. For a good example, see "Primary Nike/Anti-Sweatshop Campaign Network Sites," Center for Communication and Civic Engagement, http://depts
.washington.edu/ccce/polcommcampaigns/nikecampaignsites.htm. Accessed
July 26, 2013.

11. See Gallup Poll in Jeffrey M. Jones, "U.S. Congress' Approval Rating at 21%
Ahead of Elections," GALLUP Politics, http://www.gallup.com/poll/158372/
congress-approval-rating-ahead-elections.aspx. Accessed on July 26, 2013.

12. A recent article in the *Oregonian* catalogued that fewer than half of law
school graduates across the country have been able to find employment. See
Jeff Manning, "Legally Bound," *Oregonian*, August 5, 2012, 1.

13. Bertrand Russell, "Philosophy for Laymen," *Unpopular Essays* (London and
New York: Routledge, 1950), 27.

14. Timur Kuran, *Private Truths, Public Lies. The Social Consequences of Preference Falsification* (Boston: Harvard University Press, 1997).

15. Lauretta Conklin Frederking, "Getting to Green: Niche-driven or Government-
led Entrepreneurship and Sustainability in the Wine Industry," *New England
Journal of Entrepreneurship* 14, no. 1 (2011): 47–61.

16. A 1999 study from the Department of Housing and Urban Development
found that approximately one-third of homeless providers in the United
States were religiously affiliated. See "Homelessness: Programs and the
People They Serve," U.S. Department of Housing and Urban Development,
Posted October 20, 1999. Accessed July 26, 2013. http://www.huduser.org/
portal/publications/homeless/homeless_tech.html.

17. For the origins and description of the term, see "Word of the Day: Kyriarchy," *Feminist Philosophers* (blog), May 1, 2008. Accessed July 26, 2013.
http://feministphilosophers.wordpress.com/2008/05/01/word-of-the-day
-kyriarchy/.

2 Democracy and Social Justice

Remember, democracy never lasts long.
It soon wastes, exhausts, and murders itself.

—John Adams[1]

INTRODUCTION

As one of the Founding Fathers of the United States, John Adams acknowledged that democracy's own pathological characteristics lead to its demise. Even nations with strong political constitutions that protect rights and set up institutions of representation cannot entirely protect against problems associated with the very strengths of democracy. Participation, compromise, and accountability fall into corresponding crises of disengagement, inefficiency, and polarization. These inherent weaknesses of the state and of democracy need to be addressed, just as the virtues of the state and democracy are undeniable. While the strengths and ideals of democracy can coexist with their weaknesses and even compensate for many of their outcomes, democracy is not self-correcting.[2] Rather, with democracy's self-reinforcing incentives and outcomes, the remedy and repair needs to emerge from outside of the political sphere. I offer social justice as the mechanism for correcting these pathologies. As a new and necessary *social* constitution for democracies, it can become a foundation for healthier political engagement. The banter and contradictions that surround social justice as it prevails today are merely symptoms of democratic crisis. Currently, social justice is not a solution. However, my reconceptualized social justice includes the processes and community value outcomes that can make democracy work well.

Social justice needs to remain independent of the political process in order to be an effective mechanism for political change. Because of this separation from politics, my conceptualization of social justice raises the question of whether or not this is a version of communitarianism, which rejects the state as a benevolent structure for managing social relations. In this chapter, I distinguish social justice from communitarianism, and in particular, I address the important role of the state in terms of social justice. Also relevant,

I distinguish between different regime types and how democracy is privileged in terms of the social justice project. While my vision of social justice is critical of the current practice of democracy, and while I insist on its distinctiveness from political democracy, social justice is clearly amenable to the procedures and institutions of democracy.

Analyses of capitalism in Chapter 3, technology in Chapter 4, and religion in Chapter 5 follow the organization of this chapter on democracy and social justice. After summarizing the strengths of the state and democracy, and then the accompanying weaknesses, I introduce social justice as a remedy. The end of this chapter outlines how social justice works and how it can be implemented in liberal democratic capitalist societies. While Chapter 6 develops more specific examples and the processes of implementation, this chapter presents an outline for the reader to understand social justice as a unique, viable foundation for systemic change.

At the same time that the reconceptualized social justice remains distinct from politics, those who study political democracy contribute greatly to my framework of social justice. A departure from their work is my driving goal: to think about social justice as a project to nurture civil society independent of political society. The argument for social justice denies the possibility of positive systemic change from within the political system. Rather than focusing directly and immediately on reforming formal political institutions, social justice needs to precede, and then inform, political reform. Social justice focuses on our ways of being together in society, and it becomes the foundation for healthier ways of engaging in politics, economics, technology, and religion. Conceptually, this reconstructed understanding of social justice can contribute to current theoretical discussions of political democracy and the possibilities of reform. Empirically, social justice can become a foundation from which healthier political interactions emerge.

Attempts at reform from within the U.S. political system have not been successful in reducing the gap between voter expectations and policy outcomes, or in reducing the trends of polarization that limit compromise. As a potential foundation that is focused on social interaction, social justice can be a vehicle for coordination and learning in ways that contribute to positive change in the political sphere. Social justice is about cultivating a collective responsibility. However, it is not necessarily about cultivating consensus, and in fact, it has mechanisms to protect and to incorporate dissent more systematically and more effectively. Scholars of democracy emphasize the value of diversity. The difficult challenge that remains is the preservation of diversity without the exacerbation or escalation of diversity into conflict, especially violent conflict. Knight and Johnson present the importance of *structuring* disagreements in order to ease potential intransigence or the intractability that characterizes many democracies today.[3] The puzzle of nurturing diversity within a structure of shared consensus has been the focus of great political theorists. Commitment to democracy, whether through an initial social contract or the ongoing practice of voting, is often identified as the emblem of this shared consensus. However, these theorists focus their remedy on the political sphere, whereas I suggest that a restructured social justice can become an effective meta-framework or collective foundation within which diversity, including political diversity, can thrive.

There is another important aspect of social justice that serves the political system precisely because it exists as an entirely different sphere of activity. Social justice can digest and resolve many of society's most volatile issues without channeling them into the political system. As described in the introduction, people don't always want political solutions to some of the most vulnerable aspects of their lives. When victimized, people often need societal affirmation, sometimes even more than retribution. In discussing South Africa and the truth and reconciliation process that paved the way forward from apartheid, Desmund Tutu distinguished between restorative justice and retributive justice.[4] The former embraces testimony, witnesses, and judgment, but denies punishment. It assumes that moving forward collectively may be at least as important as the assessment and attribution of blame. In the absence of social justice, people may look for solutions in the political realm. But political solutions are not ideal in all cases for the individual, for the collective, or for the stability of political institutions. While the ubiquitous plague of apartheid made revolutionary change desirable, leaders across society recognized the need to limit the punishment process. From the perspective of human capital, but also the limits of the existing political and legal systems to digest the widespread crisis, South Africans pursued a Truth and Reconciliation Commission (TRC) simultaneously with political and legal changes as a different mechanism to transform society.

This chapter offers the foundation of social justice as a remedy for some of the weaknesses apparent in modern democracies today. Rather than visionary political heroes, democracies like the United States require the commitment of citizens to social justice independent of the political system, precisely in order to allow for potential changes within the political system. Along with specific case examples in Chapter 6, I address mechanisms for implementing social justice, and I offer the broader institutional reforms and possibilities for change. However, social justice is not merely a catalyst for political change. It shouldn't go away once a healthier democracy is in place. It can become the permanent foundation for maintaining values that become relevant for good democratic practice.

DEMOCRACY AND ITS VIRTUES

1. Institutions

Apart from the democratic regime-type, the state itself is a set of institutions that provides important functions for its population. The state offers its own essential virtues, many of which contribute to the development of policies and principles that facilitate the social justice process. For many, community is an ideal form of social order, but without the state, and so this chapter considers both alternatives of community and state from a social justice perspective. While the foundation of social justice exists apart from the state, it does so precisely in ways that can nurture state capacity. In a reciprocal way, credible commitments, coordination, and communication are among the virtues of a state that facilitate social justice.

Institutions facilitate interaction.[5] As a set of institutions, the state reduces uncertainty in ways that are critical for the context of social engagement. By reducing uncertainty, institutions increase human interaction and provide potential for greater efficiencies. Institutions make up the state, and the state structures more informal organizations in ways that determine both long-run change and also stability. Douglass North's analysis admits that institutional arrangements vary, and his focus on economic development is addressed more in the next chapter, but the argument that institutions reduce uncertainty is a compelling vindication of any state. From this perspective, and in terms of initial conditions, the state becomes an integral part of laying the foundation for social justice. State institutions also provide communication structures and financial capabilities that can reinforce beliefs in the social justice process as well as institutional mechanisms of accountability.

Coordination is another virtue of the state. Schelling constructs models to articulate how individuals with relatively benign preferences make decisions that unravel collective outcomes.[6] Initial conditions of racial integration without prejudice quickly evolve into outcomes of racial segregation through simple decision rules. In this way, micro-motives or individual self-interest lead to inefficient, even destructive, social outcomes. State strength and strong state capacity can contribute to shifts and reorientation away from collectively inefficient and destructive outcomes. A state, in particular, has the concentration of power sufficient enough to be able to redistribute and reorient conditions for a more equitable distribution of opportunity. In addition to administrative responsibilities, social justice requires coordination of individuals and communities. The potential for social justice to affect systemic change does not depend upon the strength and capacity of the state, but social justice can still be enhanced by support within state institutions.

2. Transparency

Transparency refers to the public availability of information, credibility of information, and also the authenticity of individual ideas and beliefs. Each of these aspects of transparency is a critical characteristic of democracy, but the authenticity of individual ideas and beliefs is particularly essential to the progress of social justice. Transparency contributes to the social justice type of engagement. If we are to develop our own thinking, we need to hear ourselves articulate beliefs and challenge these beliefs in the context of opposition. For social justice, transparency is much more important than consensus.

Essential to the premise of social justice is the idea that many of our problems and possibilities are better handled by informal institutions rather than enforced uniformly by the state. However, like the state structure, there *are* characteristics of democracies that are particularly compatible with social justice and make democracy the most reasonable regime-type for social justice. The prevalent virtues of democracy include transparency, formal accountability, competition of ideas and people, and opportunity for change. While the Founding Fathers identified these virtues, our current political system has outrun its ability to rejuvenate, to cultivate creativity, and to protect diversity.

As highlighted in the introduction, Timur Kuran's claim about preference falsification emphasizes that individuals in Eastern Europe and the Soviet Union held dichotomous beliefs.[7] Public beliefs shored up support for the regime and affirmed the prevailing communist ideology, while private beliefs revealed the surging support for a revolution. These types of public lies and private truths lead to disconnected individuals and surprising political, economic, and social upheavals. While Kuran's argument is historically and geographically located in communist societies to explain the unpredicted, tidal-wave shift away from communism, this level of public and private disconnect is also more prevalent among individuals in developed societies today. In so many ways, we have digested liberalism as "live and let live" rather than maintaining parameters for engagement that push us forward to figure out ways to live better. Tolerance is interpreted as a passive acceptance of behaviors and attitudes rather than an active exercise to weigh these behaviors and attitudes. Social justice demands interpersonal engagement to affirm a minimum foundation of solidarity, with or without consensus, and to orient society to consider alternatives. While our current democracy preserves the availability of information and the credibility of information well, it is increasingly less successful at fostering the authenticity of individual ideas and beliefs. Our formal institutions of democracy channel existing interests into polarized alternatives, so often moving individuals into more isolated camps. Here, interests feed into more intransigent conflicts. Social justice emphasizes deliberation and trusts the power of dialogue, in terms of outcomes, when the dialogue is characterized by both diversity and transparency. In line with Gutmann and Thompson:

> the better arguments become revealed through deliberation. And while there are risks of increasing polarization, the outcomes likely include clarifying the nature of the moral conflict and cultivating mutual respect as individuals continue to disagree.[8]

Through the process of social justice, individuals share their beliefs transparently, and more importantly, they perceive where their beliefs coincide and diverge with others. Critically, social justice does not offer outcomes that reward strategic incentives, and beliefs shared through the social justice process may be independent of formalized interests. Also critically, the goal is not necessarily consensus. Rather, the focus is mutual understanding of shared beliefs and unshared beliefs, and strengthening solidarity specifically around commitments to each other independent of strategic goals.

Social justice is a space where we accept collective responsibility for problems, and we heal as a community to go forward. Reiterated play, or repeated engagement, is an essential component of this social justice program. Individuals are held accountable for their dialogue without punishment in terms of the state. However, they are fully accountable to their social communities as well as informed by alternative views. While mutual respect is the ideal outcome, several other consequences are likely and fit into the relevance of social justice for political activity. Social justice makes meaningful deliberation in other spheres more possible and more likely. A citizenry practiced in social justice is less likely to shift to polarized intransigence. Social justice provides both a meta-framework for conflict resolution as well as a viable alternative sphere for conflict resolution.

3. Deliberation

Both Knight and Johnson's *The Priority of Democracy*,[9] and Gutmann and Thompson's *Democracy and Disagreement*,[10] assume the importance of democracy as a mechanism for dealing with conflict. Contrary to many democratic theories that emphasize consensus building, they focus legitimacy for democracy around the idea that it is the best system for managing disagreements. In the context of this focus on social justice and injustice, a theory that acknowledges diversity and that is located in understanding disagreement is particularly helpful. These scholars center their normative argument on pragmatism and include three central characteristics, of which fallibilism is most relevant for social justice. Fallibilism recognizes the contingency and indeterminacy of our beliefs. Not only do we recognize the fallibility of our beliefs, but we commit to engage these beliefs with contrary beliefs in order to test them. For Knight and Johnson:

> This commitment has two implications. It means that pragmatists recognize that even those beliefs about which we are most convinced may turn out to be false. It also means that whatever certainty we may attain requires that we actively organize experience in such a way that our beliefs are challenged.[11]

In social justice, it is not likely, nor is it ideal, for individuals to merge toward uniform beliefs as some democratic theorists advocate; structured disagreement can be equally optimal in terms of social justice outcomes.[12] The process of social justice invites individuals to share beliefs but also demands that individuals are accountable for those beliefs to their communities and then also to those outside of their communities. While pragmatism and its associated version of fallibilism cannot be tied singularly to democracy, Knight and Johnson argue that the consequences of pragmatism are most amenable with democracy and contribute to the legitimacy of democratic outcomes. I also argue that democracy is most compatible with the social justice project, but my argument focuses on fostering social justice, independent of the political arena.

From my perspective, the claims of pragmatism, like the seminal writing of Dewey, that democracy is a social idea as much as a set of political institutions, become very important.[13] Social justice on the one hand, and democracy as political institutions on the other, may reinforce each other but the distinction is conceptually relevant. Perhaps Dewey's statement about democracy as a social idea suggests something similar to what I am calling social justice, which needs to be separated in practice from the more formal institutions of democracy. The characteristic of fallibilism is helpful in this social sphere and perhaps a critical foundation for the commitment to political participation in the first place.

4. Opportunity

Concentration of power brings coercion over individuals. Compared to other regime types, like monarchy or dictatorship, democracy maximizes freedom by preventing concentrations of power. Friedrich Hayek advocated democracy by these terms, but he recognized the need for limits on any government, including democracy. The principle of majority-rule in democracies could lead to inefficient and coercive outcomes, but at the same time, democracy's institutionalized freedoms support the greatest possibilities. According to Hayek: "What a free society offers to the individual is more than what he would be able to do if only he were free."[14] A free society is the most fertile context for new ideas, collective synergy, and productive innovation. In terms of politics, the economy, or the sphere of technological innovation more generally, society benefits from a free competition of ideas. Democracy is the political regime that best preserves freedom of expression, opposition, and opportunity.

On many levels, communist, democratic, or authoritarian types of governments vary, but not significantly. Anthony Downs argues that "a democratic government and communist government face the same conceptual problems and handle them in the same way, but. . . . In a democracy, everyone's preferences receive the same weight; whereas in a communist state, the preferences of Politburo members are weighted much more heavily than those of nonmembers."[15] Political representatives can be likened to entrepreneurs, and because of the democratic process, which is based upon the competitive struggle for each individual vote, these representatives cultivate new ideas that they hope will "sell." Conceptualizing political candidates as entrepreneurs suggests that the political sphere with votes is comparable to the economic marketplace with profits, and both generate the ideal, most efficient outcomes because of competition. Democracies cultivate free thinking through education and then preserve the value of free thinking through constitutional protections for the freedom of association and opposition.

While it is theoretically sensible to connect democracy and freedom, maximizing freedom may require a bridled version of limited government, even democratic governments. As Milton Friedman said:

> I'm not in favor of no government. You do need a government. But by doing so many things that the government has no business doing, it cannot do those things which it alone can do well. There's no other institution in my opinion that can provide us with protection of our life and liberty. However, the government performs that basic function poorly today, precisely because it is devoting too much of its efforts and spending too much of our income on things which are harmful. So I have no doubt that that's the major single problem we face.[16]

Since most democracies do not fit the minimalist ideal, an essential exercise of freedom and preservation of freedom becomes the process of holding government representatives accountable through the competitive, democratic process.

CRITICISMS OF DEMOCRACY

1. Disengagement

While voting is an important part of maintaining solidarity, the practice of democracy has not been able to sustain this shared commitment to the collective. Today, the political sphere is charged with a lack of civility that threatens stability as well as people's engagement. A 2010 survey reveals that 48 percent of Americans perceive a decline in civility with a subsequent rise in apathy and disengagement. The study reports that "[I]t pushes people away from politics and from paying attention to politics and lessens their willingness to be engaged."[17] Both apathy and polarization have become pathologies of contemporary democracy, affirming the need for something else to provide self-correcting mechanisms to accompany healthy diversity. By structuring disagreements around a central motivation of preserving the collective and diffusing energy around disagreements, social justice can move us toward this ideal. Democracy has been unsuccessful, but social justice may offer potential transformation. Without abandoning democracy, social justice can become the commitment and path for maintaining diversity without requiring consensus and while shoring up the essential collective bargain.

In equally problematic examples, democracies have been the vehicle for social injustices. Whether because of colonialism and the injustices imposed by foreign territories, or whether it is through the more modern context of imposing democracy on other countries, these types of regime transitions have led to significant injustices. Dambisa Moyo's controversial argument that global aid is the fundamental source of these social injustices is supported by increasing disparities, chronic underdevelopment, and corruption.[18] Her agenda suggests that the end of aid can bring economic growth and leadership accountability. Whether the regime is authoritarian or democratic has not prevented corruption when aid funnels directly into the hands of leaders. Her argument is a bitter pill for many current social justice advocates who push for more aid to developing countries. Among entrenched but also newly emerging democracies, democracy as a regime-type does not necessarily correspond with engagement or effective participation. Across countries and democracies, there is disarming evidence of global, not just local, disengagement.

2. Deteriorating Community

Today's liberal democracy places far greater importance on tolerance as opposed to harmony. Especially in an increasingly diverse society, it is an important virtue that our liberal democracy protects individual rights. Minorities are shielded from the potential tyranny of the majority, and in principle, the institutions of liberal democracy preserve equality of opportunity. Preserving individual rights is an undeniable strength of a liberal democracy. However, institutionalizing the priority of the individual inevitably inflicts damage to the authority of communities. In *Identity in Democracy*,[19] Gutmann lays out how democracies vary across states, and over time, in terms of the balance between individual rights and community rights. Gutmann is sympathetic to the positive traditions and practices within communities. However, normatively, she appreciates liberal democratic principles that a priori protect the individual against community traditions and practices without individual consent.

If we agree, what is at stake in terms of the deteriorating authority of community? While addressing social order without the state, Michael Taylor introduces important virtues of communities.[20] Shared beliefs, reciprocity, and multisided relations nurture community relations, and they become the virtues of these communities as well. While some small groups exhibit these characteristics, it is unlikely, if not impossible, to observe all three characteristics as a pattern of human interaction today. Taylor's ideal communities are not a prevalent part of society. In fact, a critical source of tension between communitarians and statists may be that state evolution actually undermined the possibility of community and its concomitant characteristics. The process of bargaining to create the state dismantles allegiance of individuals to the community just as it reorients them into citizens within states. As defined in the sections above, there are clear benefits to the state, but the process of state-building may be the very cause that undermines community. While all states required individuals to surrender some of their community affiliation, liberal democracies entrenched the trend toward individual rights in unprecedented ways.

In addition to the virtues of community, Taylor's version of community has a lot to offer to the practical cultivation of social justice. In communitarian contexts, individuals can maintain social order without state oppression, and they maintain social order in a way that fosters human interdependences and cooperation. Social justice calls us to cultivate community solidarity independent of interests. However, there is an important distinction between Taylor's ideal communities and the ideal social justice. For social justice in our liberal democratic societies, individuals share commitment to a process of social justice with others who don't share those beliefs, and with others who share beliefs but belong to different communities. Small size and limited inequality are foundational prerequisites for Taylor's community. Obviously, we are a large-size society with profound inequality and a state. What are the possibilities for cultivating communities like those described by Taylor? What are the possibilities for these communities to coexist within a state? Today, the problem is much less how to surrender communities to the authority of the state but rather how to cultivate communities within the authority of the state. Social justice presents realistic possibilities.

3. Corruption

If we survey the current state of American democracy, we do not have the institutionalized violence and discriminatory laws that prevail in many emerging or new democracies. However, problems in established liberal democracies like the U.S. are just as systemic and institutionalized to the extent that it is difficult to determine responsibility for shortcomings and to determine the mechanisms for reform. Media and voters are comfortable blaming particular individuals or political parties rather than the institutional rules or organizational incentives. Yet we know that institutions matter; they constrain and define behavior.[21] The outcomes within institutional constraints may not be more laudable, but they are more certain. Through the institutionalist lens, American democracy *makes* "good" political representatives hard to find. Is it malevolent individuals, or is it the incentives and structured expectations that define, and then mold, the career of politicians? As much as media highlights the individual in terms of transgressions, American mainstream culture continually portrays the corrupting influence of political power. As a very popular and early example, the heroic Mr. Smith learns about institutionalized corruption in the film *Mr. Smith Goes to Washington* (1939), and we begin to anticipate the deleterious effects of the grooming process. But in *Mr. Smith goes to Washington*, we find a popularized solution as well, albeit a misguided one. The heroic Mr. Smith is the solution in the film. Unfortunately, it seems as though the American public also responds to systemic corruption with a cry that we need another Mr. Smith. Along these terms, Americans repeatedly seek out the visionary leader rather than a change in institutions.

From this perspective and without institutional change, visionaries start out very popular and with well-defined goals, but they inevitably become caught in constraints and requirements that seemingly transform their own expectations and behavior. However, rather than significant reform, the public often embraces another round of populist expectations.

4. Inefficiencies

While most states share these virtues of coordination, communication, and commitment, they vary widely in terms of ideology and the type of institutional regimes. Contrary to common associations that automatically connect democracy with social justice, there are many important historical and contemporary examples of the "progressive" possibilities under authoritarian regimes and also significant violations under many democratic regimes.

The connection between regime types and social justice is complicated by the empirical world. In a curious twist, many of the strategies and policy expectations of social justice sometimes fit comfortably with a benevolent authoritarian regime as well. Within the traditional perspective of social justice, there are many examples of authoritarian regimes implementing progressive policies and just as many examples of democracies implementing types of restrictive policies in terms of social justice. From the conflicting evidence, it is very difficult to conclude much about social justice in terms of policy outcomes and regime type. After summarizing this ambiguity, I approach the reconceptualized understanding of social justice in terms of regimes, and in spite of empirical complexity, I argue the ways that democracy can be considered more compatible with social justice.

A popularized version of social justice has been aligned with more welfare state policies. As an example, it is interesting to recognize the inconsistencies in terms of regime. Bismarck's authoritarian reign in 1870 Prussia marks the beginning of state welfare policies.[22] Turkey's Ataturk imposed women's rights.[23] Arguably, the only way these leaders were able to pass liberalizing reforms was through the nonparticipatory institutions of authoritarianism. Even more perplexing to many is the legacy of gender equality in Iran attributed to Pahlavi during 1941–1979. Not only did he abolish the veil, but he introduced progressive education rights that integrated women into public spaces and participation opportunities.[24] Clearly, authoritarian regimes are capable of introducing and implementing the currently popular social justice outcomes, and in fact, authoritarian regimes are much better equipped to do so efficiently.

In considering today's developed democracies, there is legitimacy to Winston Churchill's statement that "democracy is the worst form of government except for all others." Even further, Mancur Olson described the institutional sclerosis that insipidly has affected *The Rise and Decline of Nations*.[25] His description of social rigidities carries direct consequences in terms of the possibility of economic growth and human development. For the purposes of understanding this new framework of social justice, Olson's analysis makes sense of the current social justice impasse in the United States. Increasingly, social justice advocates and issues have become part of the political treadmill. They participate in the sclerosis of special-interest lobbies that undermine efficiency and increasingly polarize our political system. Waste, conflict, and rigidity have become the central characteristics of the U.S. political system generally, and social justice as it is today contributes to this corrupting system rather than ameliorating it. Rather than contributing something different, social justice practice today is part of these worst features of American democracy.

There are disturbing trends whereby social justice issues have become increasingly politicized, and political issues increasingly absorb the rhetoric of social justice. Yet according to Olson, our abilities to implement reform are increasingly limited. The central puzzle then is how to move from Olson's institutional sclerosis to more meaningful democratic practice and outcomes in terms of its possible virtues. New conceptual possibilities for thinking about social justice can contribute to reform. At a minimum, social justice practitioners might remove some of their agenda from the competitive and politicized dynamic in democracies today.

Communities and states offer virtues that can enhance the social justice process. At the same time, there is a tension between social order provided by well-formed communities and social order provided by well-defined states. On the negative side of communities, they are insular and self-reinforcing. On the negative side of states, they can be oppressive, relying on military capacity for legitimacy in lieu of providing services to society. While there are many virtues associated with the state, community can be undermined by an oppressive state, and the virtues associated with the state can also become increasingly pathological. In other words, our developed states are less capable of fulfilling the ideals beyond minimum functions of credible commitments, communication, and coordination. The puzzle is how to construct communities that coexist within the state. Then also, a puzzle remains how to construct communities that can become the catalyst for reform when a state becomes too powerful or fosters too much inequality. Social justice provides its own sphere, reinforcing the virtues of both community and state, and also functioning as a fluid vehicle for translating conflicting community values into structures of disagreement that can be more readily compromised and accommodated by the state. Some of the likely social justice benefits include easing existing polarization of issues as well as circumscribing fewer issues that translate into the realm of state interests.

SOCIAL JUSTICE AS THE FOUNDATION FOR DEMOCRACY

Today, developed democratic systems do not adequately reflect the ideals and possibilities of democracy. And given the terms of engagement, or disengagement, it is less likely that change can come from within these polluted political systems. I argue that the catalyst for transformative political change needs to come from a process initiated elsewhere. Social justice can become that catalyst and foundation for change. Rather than continuing within the tainted political system, social justice advocates should nurture the catalyst for change from outside the political system. This social justice map borrows extensively from recent theoretical discussions about pragmatism and deliberation. In fact, pragmatism and deliberation are concepts that help to define social justice. While recognizing that scholars focused on deliberative democracy firmly entrench their ideas in the tradition of political language and the political sphere, pragmatism and deliberation can be part of a phenomenon that is distinctly social.

The contemporary scholars who write about pragmatism and the scholars who write about deliberation readily admit the normative dimension of their claims. They argue that democracy would be better if it contained more of the virtues inherent in pragmatism and deliberative democracy. However, neither tradition really sorts out how to get there except by enlightened self-interest. If we admit that the political world has moved far away from the ideals of pragmatism and deliberative democracy, then it is especially difficult to imagine how the change will emerge from within the political world. My version of social justice brings these ideals into an agenda and practice that is distinct from the political sphere while aspiring for its longer run influence into a new type of democratic politics that reflects these social virtues. In this way, social justice is the foundation upon which a better type of democratic process can be built. And also in this way, social justice is the mechanism for change of the political system from outside of the political system. Not surprisingly, many political theorists may be too stuck on politics to realize that their ideals are more promising if they come from outside political institutions. Today, the social justice agenda has been swallowed by the political machine in a way that social justice issues cannot be discerned from political rights and economic outcomes. Dewey distinguishes between epistemic and deliberative democracy in a way that is helpful. Social justice here fits into Dewey's version of epistemic democracy, which is distinctly not political democracy. He emphasizes that "the best forms of inquiry and of decision-making in general, not just political inquiry and decision-making, are democratic in character."[26] Dewey's approach is further summarized below:

> Dewey's epistemic approach is "democratic" in the loose sense of emphasizing the community (the many) over the handful of exceptional individuals (the few). Knowledge is not produced mechanically by the repeated application of algorithmic procedures by expert investigators all trained the same way. It is produced by the tug of communal demands, the struggle between doubt and habit, the strivings of individuals of diverse background, aptitude, training, and experience, and the application of methods of inquiry, such as imagination and intuition, that owe little to expert training. No elite has a monopoly of truth. In

fact, truth is always just out of reach, is at most a regulatory, an orienting, ideal. If this is the case with scientific truth, it is all the more likely to be the case with moral and political truths as well.[27]

Carving a social space to cultivate the virtues put forward in this chapter holds the greatest possibilities for political change toward a healthier democracy. Subsequent chapters make sense of this space distinct from the political, economic, religious, and technological spheres. The final two chapters explain mechanisms for cultivating social justice and its implementation. From this foundation, meaningful change is possible.

As addressed in the introduction, the second justification for this shift from political theory to make sense of a unique theory of social justice attains credibility if we accept that some moral disagreements are best resolved outside of the political sphere. While these theorists maintain the importance of mechanisms to solve moral disagreements once they are political, I argue for a mechanism that resolves moral disagreements in a way that they may never enter the political arena. From talking with so many students on a college campus about their issues of injustice, it is increasingly apparent that for many of these students, resolution will never come in the form of rights or policies. For the young gay man in my social justice class, meaningful resolution won't be determined by more rights in terms of the state. For this young, gay, practicing Catholic, social justice means asserting, nurturing, and ultimately reclaiming human dignity in the eyes and actions of the Catholic Church. Through teaching social justice to young college students, I have come to realize that we need social justice now as much or more than ever. While students and activists speak in political language and in terms of political action, they often want social recognition and distinctly social justice. In their strongest form, political rights will never provide a comprehensive remedy for social injustices. In a more compatible version, political rights and justice need to be supplemented by something distinctly social and largely depleted in today's society.

HOW SOCIAL JUSTICE WORKS

Deliberation, fallibilism, transparency, and commitment to iterated play are requirements of the social justice process. The strength of these recent democratic theories is that diversity, with its potential conflict, is central to thinking about pragmatism and democratic possibility. Even further, those who disagree shouldn't be disavowed of their right to competing values and different self-interests.[28] At the same time, there should also be shared virtues of social justice that can be cultivated and that can frame and ultimately constrain those differences. According to Callan, "[V]irtue is no substitute for judicious institutional design. But neither is institutional design any substitute for virtue."[29] Social justice is a virtue that needs to be practiced and needs to be a part of civic life. From Dewey's observation that there needs to be a social as well as a formal democracy, this process of social justice is about interactions that affirm a collective virtue while providing a forum to express differences, engage opposition, and cultivate identity.

Just like my college classroom example in the introduction, social justice as a particular type of engagement does not anticipate any particular policy outcomes. This vision of social justice joins "proceduralists" in emphasizing the process as most critical. What is different here is that unlike "proceduralists" who focus on the political sphere, this is about social interactions independent of the formal political process and institutions. Important aspects of social justice include that participants are transparent about their beliefs and interests, and that they actively engage the beliefs and interests that seem contrary to their own, and that individuals are open in terms of outcomes, especially to changing their own beliefs.

SOCIAL JUSTICE REQUIREMENTS

From Rawls, I propose that social justice requires fair procedures and from Mill, I propose that social justice requires citizens to engage with others— especially others who hold views in opposition to their own. Both Rawls and Mill identify a shared goal of collective identity that is distinct and more relevant than any one individual's strategic preferences. Again, while drawing on the great political thinkers, the difference between these ideals presented by political theorists and this reconstructed social justice rests on the distinctly social, or nonpolitical, sphere of engagement. For political scientists, the conceptualization of social justice makes it distinct but highly relevant for current theoretical discussions of democracy. For practitioners, this version of social justice is meant to lay out a newly adopted agenda for social justice advocates. While it privileges procedure in a social sphere over particular outcomes in a political sphere, it affirms solidarity of humaneness at the same time that it can potentially transform the political and economic spheres.

Much of this chapter aligning social justice with democratic theory draws from the work of Jack Knight.[30] In addition to his seminal book, *Institutions and Social Conflict*, the co-authored book with Jim Johnson,[31] Knight puts forward claims about democracy, pragmatic democracy specifically, that echo in my description of procedures with social justice. Knight and Johnson's claims about pragmatic and deliberative democracy make sense in terms of realizing important values of diversity. Diversity, with some underlying harmony, is vital for democracy, and increasingly seems far removed from how democracies function today. Their perspective is attractive precisely because they set out the mechanism to effect coordination and most importantly, coordination precisely under conditions of disagreement. I share the value of diversity as an essential social value that is also tenuous. Unleashed diversity can be the seed for violent conflict as much as it is the source of creativity and development. My departure is wholly insignificant in terms of the integrity of their argument about pragmatism and democracy. Rather, my departure emphasizes social justice, distinct from the political sphere, as a possible vehicle of change towards their ideal democracy.

Knight and Johnson[32] and Gutmann[33] and Gutmann and Thompson[34] build theories of democracy that disavow the need for consensus and specifically the type of consensus often attributed to communitarians. Ideal community in the sense put forward by most communitarians is not a prerequisite for Knight and Johnson's ideal democracy. My version of social justice rests somewhere between a communitarian ideal and Knight and Johnson's ideal democracy, and it offers social justice as a potential mechanism to nurture both. Social justice is a pragmatic institutional arrangement that should shore up flexible but committed support for their ideal democracy.

Knight and Johnson conclude their book with a discussion of why those who participate in their form of democracy are less likely to engage in violence. Their argument rests on a group with positive beliefs toward the other and trust in institutions. Deliberation is an important quality of their pragmatic democracy and a source for nurturing these positive beliefs between citizens. Gutmann and Thompson also share an interest in deliberation as a central feature for the best institutions to resolve conflict. Deliberation is the core of their argument, but a particular type of deliberation that is central to my own argument. For them, reciprocity, publicity, and accountability regulate deliberation in a way that it can resolve the most fundamental and moral conflicts:

> the practice of deliberation should not be confined to the institutions of government. Unless citizens have the experience of reasoning together in other institutions in which they spend more of their time they are not likely to develop either the interest or the skill that would enable them to deliberate effectively in politics. That is why it is so important that the processes of decision making that citizens encounter at work and at leisure should seek to cultivate the virtues of deliberation. The discussion that takes place in these settings not only is a rehearsal for political actions, but also is itself a part of citizenship in deliberative democracy.[35]

So the critical contribution of social justice is that it becomes these "other institutions" and the foundation "to enable them to deliberate effectively in politics." Deliberation is one of the most important characteristics of social justice. Like Knight and Johnson, Gutmman and Thompson accept disagreement as an essential part of human interaction, and conflict emerges from competing self-interests,[36] incompatible values, and incomplete understanding. Nevertheless, they invoke Aristotle and Mill to argue that the better arguments become revealed through deliberation. And while there are risks of increasing polarization, the outcomes likely include clarifying the nature of the moral conflict and cultivating mutual respect as individuals continue to disagree.[37] First, I maintain that deliberation must be social or informal if it is to then become part of a healthier political democracy. Secondly, as suggested above, I maintain that some moral conflicts need not, and should not, inflict upon the formal political democratic process or institutions. Deliberation in a social justice context can be critical for both limiting and affecting the quality of deliberation in the political sphere. In *Identity in Democracy*, [38] Gutmann describes deliberative forums in a way that fits the ideal social justice. She poses the central question: "whether it is possible to oppose cultural practices that are foreign to your own while respecting (and not harming) people who are just as committed to engaging in those practices as you are to opposing them."[39] In the context of a cultural controversy around female circumcision, she addresses both informal deliberation and its important contribution to the democratic process:

> Such deliberation encourages individuals with different cultural perspectives to exchange their views, expand their understandings, and therefore arrive at a more broadly informed collective decision. Deliberation does not promise agreement; but even continuing disagreement is good for a democratic society to the extent that it reflects more mutual understanding than would otherwise exist and affords citizens a chance to demonstrate their mutual respect across cultural divides as they continue to disagree, as free people invariably will.[40]

Social justice offers the ideal social context to support democratic processes and outcomes. While it may be helpful to think of social justice preceding the formation of political institutions, it is both empirically not possible and theoretically unnecessary. In the section on mechanisms for introducing social justice, I offer potential ways that it can become relevant and much more prevalent in society.

MOTIVATION FOR SOCIAL JUSTICE

From the time of Plato, philosophers and political theorists have wrestled with the tension between individual and community. While social justice orients the individual toward values that make the community central, it is important to consider the status of the individual in this context. Does this reconceptualized social justice turn away from liberalism and individualism? And then, to borrow a religious concept, from my colleague Fr. Charlie Gordon (April 2, 2012) is social justice a version of "kenosis" where one "empties" oneself in order to find deep spiritual fulfillment in the surrender to others?

I emphatically disagree that social justice depends upon this type of altruistic surrender either in terms of its realization or in terms of its practice.

While a little more altruism would benefit the social justice process, it is an unrealistic starting point for its implementation. Instead, Charles Taylor's discussion of authenticity is a reasoned starting point for the motivation toward social justice and its expected realization.[41] His understanding of authenticity describes a bold ethic with the individual and individualism at its source. He begins with the twenty-first-century Western liberal democracy world as it is and argues for a social ethic that is entirely self-centered. After outlining the significant malaises that follow from this entirely self-centered orientation, he does not reinvent the world, but through the slight shift, he reasserts the relevance of considering the other as an integral part of one's self-fulfillment. It is only through consideration of the other that we know ourselves. The ego demands that we fill ourselves up, the antithesis of kenosis, and meaningful connections (ethics) with others form a central vehicle for this fulfillment. The quest for individual authenticity requires interconnectedness in ways that fit with my version of social justice. There may be rebellion and there needs to be openness to disagreement in order to achieve our authentic self. According to Taylor:

> Authenticity (A) involves (i) creation and construction as well as discovery, (ii) originality, and frequently (iii) opposition to the rules of society and even potentially to what we recognize as morality. But it is also true, as we saw that it (B) requires (i) openness to horizons of significance (for otherwise the creation loses the background that can save it from insignificance) and (ii) a self-definition of dialogue.[42]

My conception also fits for the world as it is in twenty-first-century liberal capitalist democracies. In accord with Taylor's description, individualism prevails. In order for social justice to be considered seriously, it needs to account for this core value that is central and pervasive today. If we expect to move beyond glassy-eyed responses by many whenever someone mentions social justice, and if social justice is more than a rhetorical device simply to add legitimacy to a cause, it needs to begin with people as they are. "Do-gooders," "idealists," "tree-huggers," and "granola-munchers" are the dominant images of social justice advocates today. From the caricature, you either fit the social justice mold or you don't. As a sharp contrast to this approach, this book puts forward an idea of social justice as a process of engagement.

The very motivation for creating social justice as a process of engagement needs to begin with the individual as he or she is today. In return, social justice provides the vehicle for discovering our authentic selves in a way that conjoins us to others. It reinforces harmony while allowing our individuality to flourish. If we appreciate that we discover our individual selves through others, then we become bound to each other in an inextricably necessary and self-conscious way. If it is about self-fulfillment rather than surrender, then it is a much easier shift from today's political and economic context. Social justice for individual self-fulfillment is very different from engaging individuals for instrumental purposes. Within this perspective, I need to know your identity as part of the process of figuring out my own identity; this motivation is different from altruism, but it is also different from a consumption orientation or from engaging relationships for their instrumental value.

THE MECHANISMS TO CREATE SOCIAL JUSTICE

While this chapter presents social justice as a valuable remedy for the weaknesses in many democracies today, it is clearly important to identify the ways in which social justice can be fostered. First, current participants in the social justice project can reorient their mobilization efforts and resources toward the goal of *social* justice rather than *political* justice. Hopefully, the arguments in this book are convincing enough for social justice advocates to realize that their rhetoric is increasingly hollow. Their goals are increasingly political in a way that most social justice advocates are not likely to see success. For them, there is "a tension between the inherently political nature of the institutionalization process and the social and institutional preconditions necessary for that very process to be considered normatively legitimate."[43] However, current social justice advocates have reasons to shift strategies away from the state, recognizing that a social foundation of engagement needs to be built independent of the political system in order to be truly effective.

Rather than changing policy, social justice needs to return to its roots of affecting society's values. These fostering values can't be particular policies but rather a way of being together that makes us more accountable to each other, more connected to each other, and more deeply tolerant of each other. If social justice advocates joined together to focus on these goals, even peripherally, there could be momentum around creating and sustaining groups that bring together members of society, even those who have damaged each other in a way that is collectively relevant. Like the TRCs, we can move forward better when we have responsibilities for shared understanding of the past injustices. As discussed in Chapter 6, one of my cases discovered the very real possibilities of individuals working against each other in a highly competitive market but coming together in community to share ideas, resources, and collective interests.[44] Competition does not supersede collective identity, but rather socially effective competition presupposes collective identity. Through informal engagement, often spontaneous, social justice does not anticipate consensus as an outcome nor does it refuse conflict as part of its process. However, it does require that individuals rid themselves of the competitive orientation, that is so often dominant in other spheres, like politics and the economy. While disagreements will exist and may prevail, the expectation to win some particular outcome in the social justice arena is absent.

A second mechanism for creating social justice and the focus of Chapter 7 is education. Especially because of the number of social justice programs being implemented across the country, it is possible for these programs to become the hub of something that is both academic and practice oriented. From my perspective, the classroom experience is potentially revolutionary. Students are captive, strategically tied to attendance, passionate, and diverse enough to make the experience a legitimate micro experiment. In many ways, nurturing a good citizenry has been the primary goal of liberal education. Just like democracy in the United States, however, something has changed in education. Students aren't as open as we think they should be, and educators are focused on content over process. Our education system replicates consumption and transaction more than enlightenment. In Chapter 7, I expand on education possibilities, especially in social justice programs. Here, it is sufficient to acknowledge and then begin to think about education as a vehicle for cultivating this new version of social justice.

A final mechanism for change can be the state. Of course, this raises a challenge. How does social justice reform the state if it is first and foremost emerging within a state and so to some extent a product of the state? There are two types of answers to this question. First, some of the most revolutionary outcomes have emerged from unintended consequences. Laws and organizations may be the outcomes of strategic bargaining, but the residual effects can lead to unintended streams of outcomes and subsequent power shifts. In the current climate of polarization and rising tensions around identity and disagreement, setting up TRCs throughout the country could be politically advantageous. Political representatives have moved one step in this direction already with town hall meetings. With their immense popularity, social justice is both strategically valuable and creative in terms of potential possibilities. The biggest difference between town hall meetings and these social justice meetings is that people agree to meet again. Reiteration of the process is critical to social justice success. In line with thinking about unintended consequences, while political representatives may not buy into the final outcomes of social justice for reform of the political system, they might be convinced to set up the initial conditions. While its problems are explored in Chapter 5, there is definitely momentum around consensus-building possibilities through social media.

Another implementation mechanism through the state returns to those current participants of the social justice project. I often invite my students to think much more creatively about politics in terms of unintended consequences. How did a conservative measure to pacify labor lead to revolutionary labor reform? How did a condition of depleted state resources from depression give birth to Keynesian commitments that began a welfare state? How did conservative reform of the Soviet State lead to the capitalist democratic wave? Theoretically, Knight explored rigorously how institutions change often as a result of the unintended consequences of distributional conflict.[45] Imagine if much of the money and resources directed at particular policies by social justice advocates shifted focus to lobby for state supported (financed) town hall meetings. Currently, the state pays for parks for people to play in, it pays for food banks, and it pays for schools, so why can't it pay for meetings? Judges can be paid to adjudicate without punishment, clerics can be paid to record the testimonials, and identified leaders of current organizations as well as the public can be invited to participate. TV programs put together panels like this all the time. Like the town hall meetings, the only difference between the TV programs and the social justice intention is the requirement of repeated interaction.

It is important to reiterate that social justice is not intended to replace the state or existing political institutions. An excellent example of state sponsorship of social justice in the form of TRCs has been set already. Social justice is a space where we remove blame and judgment from the individual and instead accept collective responsibility for the causes. Communities don't concede to the perpetrator, but they commit to go forward. There is a tendency for Americans to look at the world, especially the developing world, as recipients of models of our political and economic institutions rather than these countries providing models for the United States. In this instance of social coordination, those countries recovering from far worse injustices and plagued by challenges of development offer a rich model for social engagement that is exactly the type of model that can and should be transported to the U.S. context.

In the introduction, I outlined that social justice needs to emphasize its *social* qualities, conceptually distinct from political and economic institutions and outcomes. If theorists and advocates intend to assert something other than political or politicized preferences, then social justice needs to reclaim territory as a uniquely social phenomenon. Because those who practice social justice dominate its articulation, the social justice concept has become entirely bogged down in the language of political rights and economic outcomes. Certainly forging an intellectual and academic agenda for social justice is relatively uncharted territory at the same time that the need for social justice has never been greater.

Not surprisingly, political theorists focus attention on the political world, and the interpretation of the political world is through the widest lens. However, just because an academic lens is pushed far enough to consider issues does not make it appropriate or completely relevant. Politics cannot be the focus for social justice issues and for practicing social justice. On the one hand, social justice activists seem to be keen participants in its politicization. On the other hand, and perhaps because of its politicization, social justice has not had much intellectual muscle. This book develops the conceptual space and analytical framework for social scientists to take social justice seriously while admitting its distinctive place in relation to other disciplines. At the same time, the separate conceptual space defines a new agenda for social justice advocates. Social justice becomes social.

Community and the state are often posed as alternative sources of social order. The communitarian perspective focuses on the virtues of community in a way that contrasts with those who appreciate the virtues of state. Rather than one or the other, we need to find ways to cultivate the strengths of both but also their correspondence and compatibilities. My version of social justice cultivates a reflexive relationship with both communities and the state, and social justice is a process to deliberate and consolidate community values into interests before the state. Similarly, it is a vehicle for digesting the outcomes of the state into community systems. Through its process, social justice reinforces communities in a way that more naturally minimizes demands on the state. The more narrowly prescribed state then focuses more specifically on interests that funnel through social justice spheres.

NOTES

1. Letter to John Taylor, 1814. The Patriot Post. http://patriotpost.us/quotes. Accessed July 26, 2013.
2. My comment is an adaptation of the observation by Keynes that the market was not self-correcting. John Maynard Keynes, *The General Theory of Employment, Interest, and Money* (New York: Harcourt Brace, 1936).
3. Jack Knight and James Johnson, *The Priority of Democracy: Political Consequences of Pragmatism* (New York: Russell Sage Foundation, 2011).
4. Steve York, *Truth Commissions and Societies in Transition: Confronting the Truth* (Washington, DC: York Zimmerman, 2007), Documentary.
5. Douglass North, *Institutions, Institutional Change, and Economic Development* (Cambridge: Cambridge University Press, 1990). See also Douglass North and Barry R. Weingast, "Constitutions and Commitment: The Evolution of Institutional Governing Public Choice in Seventeenth-Century England," *Journal of Economic History* 49 (1989): 803–32.
6. Thomas Schelling, *Micromotives and Macrobehavior* (New York: W. W. Norton & Company, 1978).
7. Timur Kuran, *Private Truths, Public Lies. The Social Consequences of Preference Falsification* (Boston: Harvard University Press, 1997).
8. Gutmann, Amy, and Dennis Thompson, *Democracy and Disagreement* (Boston: Harvard University Press, 1998), 43.
9. Knight and Johnson, *The Priority of Democracy*.
10. Gutmann and Thompson, *Why Deliberative Democracy*.
11. Knight and Johnson, *The Priority of Democracy*, 26.
12. Knight and Johnson, *The Priority of Democracy*.
13. Knight and Johnson, *The Priority of Democracy*, 34.
14. Friedrich A. von Hayek, *The Constitution of Liberty* (Chicago: University of Chicago Press, 1960), 6.
15. Anthony Downs, *An Economic Theory of Democracy* (New York: Harper Collins, 1957), 288.
16. David Levy, "Interview with Milton Friedman," *Region*, June 1, 1992, http://www.minneapolisfed.org/publications_papers/pub_display.cfm?id=3748.
17. Yuxing Zheng, "Public Officials Struggle to Reverse Tide of Political Incivility in Government," *Oregonian*, Sunday, August 20, 2012, 1.
18. Dambisa Moyo, *Dead Aid: Why Aid is not Working and How There is a Better Way for Africa* (New York: Farrar, Straus and Giroux, 2009).

19. Amy Gutmann, *Identity in Democracy* (Princeton: Princeton University Press, 2003).
20. Michael Taylor, *Community, Anarchy and Liberty* (Cambridge: Cambridge University Press, 1982).
21. Kenneth A. Shepsle, "Institutional Arrangements and Equilibrium in Multi-dimensional Voting Models," *American Journal of Political Science* 23, no.1 (1979): 27–59.
22. Knoke et al., *Comparing Policy Networks: Labor Politics in the U.S., Germany, and Japan* (Cambridge: Cambridge University Press, 1996).
23. Jenny B White, "State Feminism, Modernization, and the Turkish Republican Woman," in "Gender and Modernism between the Wars, 1918–1939," *National Women's Studies Association Journal* 15, no. 3 (2003): 145–59.
24. Shahrzad Mojab, "Theorizing the Politics of 'Islamic Feminism'," in "The Realm of the Possible: Middle Eastern Women in Political and Social Spaces," *Feminist Review* 69 (2001): 124–46.
25. Mancur Olson, *The Rise and Decline of Nations: Economic Growth, Stagflation and Social Rigidities* (New Haven: Yale University Press, 1984).
26. Richard A. Posner, *Law, Pragmatism, and Democracy* (Cambridge: Harvard University Press, 2005), 99.
27. Posner, *Law, Pragmatism, and Democracy*, 103.
28. Hume in Gutmann and Thompson, *Why Deliberative Democracy*, 23.
29. Eamonn Callan, *Creating Citizens: Political Education and Liberal Democracy* (Oxford: Clarendon Press, 1997), 7.
30. Jack Knight, *Institutions and Social Conflict* (Cambridge: Cambridge University Press, 1992).
31. Knight and Johnson, *The Priority of Democracy*.
32. Knight and Johnson, *The Priority of Democracy*.
33. Gutmann, *Identity in Democracy*.
34. Gutmann and Thompson, *Why Deliberative Democracy*.
35. Gutmann and Thompson, *Why Deliberative Democracy*.
36. Hume in Gutmann and Thompson, *Why Deliberative Democracy*, 23.
37. Gutmann and Thompson, *Why Deliberative Democracy*, 43.
38. Gutmann, *Identity in Democracy*.
39. Gutmann, *Identity in Democracy*, 69.
40. Gutmann, *Identity in Democracy*, 79.
41. Charles Taylor, *The Ethics of Authenticity* (Cambridge: Harvard University Press, 1991).
42. Taylor, *The Ethics of Authenticity*, 66.
43. Knight and Johnson, *The Priority of Democracy*, 255.
44. Lauretta Conklin Frederking, "Getting to Green: Niche-driven or Government-led Entrepreneurship and Sustainability in the Wine Industry," *New England Journal of Entrepreneurship* 14, no. 1 (2011): 47–61.
45. Knight, *Institutions and Social Conflict*.

3   Capitalism and Social Justice

If ye love wealth greater than liberty, the tranquility of servitude greater than the animating contest for freedom, go home from us in peace. We seek not your counsel, nor your arms. Crouch down and lick the hand that feeds you; and may posterity forget that ye were country men.

—Samuel Adams[1]

INTRODUCTION

In the early 1990s, the collapse of communism announced the end of an economic system. The command economy was abandoned widely, and countries became much more integrated into the world capitalist system. Communism seemed politically, economically, and ideologically defeated. However, the opponents of capitalism pushed forward with criticisms, and in many ways, the ideal of capitalism was also collapsing.[2] Some of the scholarly criticism emphasizes that market economies are increasingly characterized by political access and corruption. Other criticisms emphasize insipid individualism and deteriorating traditional values. Among citizens, it is common to hear a lament around the capitalist system because of yawning inequality, but it is less common to hear their criticism directed at the system of capitalism. Anticapitalist activists rarely propose an alternative, and as the rhetoric around the recent Occupy Movements suggests, opponents are often not clearly critical of capitalism[3] as much as they are opposed to their position within the capitalism system.[4] These popularized criticisms blame particular institutions and the unexpected bad behavior of corrupt leaders and wayward elites but they maintain overwhelming support for the system of capitalism.

This chapter identifies some of capitalism's undeniable successes as well as its prevalent problems. Together, these trends capture the complexity around capitalism in terms of social justice. In spite of its many virtuous outcomes, capitalism cloaks its fundamental problems, and it has become the fertile ground for growing these problems exponentially. Articulating the sources of this vicious cycle is an important step in separating the best possibilities for capitalism from its wrenching problems. Scholars who study the history of capitalism address how power relations drove capitalism forward. They emphasize how capitalism became a set of institutions with power embedded within them and cultural and economic consequences to justify them. The transition in public perceptions to institutions that individuals so deeply and widely embrace, regardless of their winning or losing status within them, is an enduring puzzle. From my social justice perspective, a solution to this puzzle isn't revolution or retribution by criminal courts, nor is it a command economy. In line with the theme of this book, the solution is distinctly *social*. The capitalist system can be held responsible for these negative consequences without destroying it. While the legion of current social justice advocates shares a legitimate foundation in criticizing these negative consequences, it is neither helpful nor necessary to annihilate the entire system of capitalism. Nor is it helpful to expect the political or economic system to be able to repair itself from within. In accord with path dependency, the set of institutions that define capitalism have lock-in mechanisms through culture and political institutions that reinforce these institutions and the existing distribution of power.

Social justice as a process and space distinct from the political and economic sphere is the central point for recovery and reconceptualization of the market. I argue that there is not so much "wrong" with the market system except that it has become the primary place for cultivating values as much as manufacturing goods and providing services. For the market to work for most people, not just the privileged few, it needs the fundamental values to come from alternative spheres. At least there needs to be a reliable and enduring foundation for alternative values outside of those cultivated and perpetuated by the capitalism machine. It requires carving out space and a procedure where we cultivate our values independent of the market, our identities within it, our attractions to it, and its central focus in our lives. We need to shift from our ubiquitous participation in a closed capitalist system to carve out participation in a foundational context that cultivates values independent of the market. The goal is not to oppose capitalism but to reaffirm its potential limited relevance without succumbing to the market as a philosophy or the map for our preferences or normative projections. Social justice needs to emerge apart from the market and remain distinct from market transactions.

There is a pithy familiar phrase that "Europeans work to live," whereas in the United States, we "live to work." Within this comparison, there is praise, but more likely nostalgia, for a different way to approach work. Today the distinction is less certain; recent austerity packages throughout Europe include delayed retirement, a longer working week, and fewer social services. With looming debt and policy reform, European countries look more like the United States and less like an alternative. Even if regional comparisons across the globalized world are becoming more antiquated compared to the past, the contrast defines a civilized version of work in Europe where one puts in time at a job in order to provide the necessary means to enjoy a good life outside of one's job. Somewhat curiously, neither the U.S. nor European model convey the potential for labor to be both meaningful and more circumscribed as an essential part, but not all, of one's good life. This chapter proposes that labor can be much more than the means of remuneration to the end of whatever we pleasure. Capitalism will work more effectively if labor can be conveyed as absolutely essential and valuable to our identity formation and articulation. We need to take our potential labor much more seriously, no longer seeing it as merely a way to earn money but rather as an effective way to figure out and develop our authentic selves.

A central part of Marx's criticism of capitalism emphasized the division and commodification of labor. The working class was exploited. Workers in factories lost their identity independent of production. For his model of economic determinism, this identification with exploitative forces could mobilize a revolution. Clearly Marx's model failed to predict economic and political change. Rather than mobilization and revolution, economic development has expanded and entrenched our livelihood to our productive potential. However, perhaps even worse, within our more developed economy, we are much further removed from our production. So often we don't identify with our work value except as a means to an end, an income. Except for those directly on the factory line, most of us are unable to identify our concrete role in what is produced. Economic progress means that many more of us work in the service industry or support labor. We have ancillary and often important roles; however, the higher we get in a corporate system, the less connected we are likely to be with the final output. From this disconnected place, it is difficult to feel emotional or responsible, let alone to feel ethical constraints or relevance. Today's corporate culture reflects this disconnect and reinforces the alienation of the worker from his or her labor. Simultaneously, we put in more hours and work harder at our segmented, disconnected jobs to make more money and to climb a seemingly infinite ladder of success. We work harder but feel distant from the productive *social* value of our labor. We buy more things but feel less relevant. We have many more transactions with people but feel less connected. Ultimately, as a society, we increasingly define our personal value by the wealth potential of our jobs, but we feel less emotionally and spiritually engaged by these jobs and by what our employers produce. These two trends put ethical considerations into the far recesses of our daily corporatized lives.

Through supply and demand, the market system enables transactions and the production process efficiently. However, the primary criticism of capitalism in this chapter is that the market increasingly moves beyond its role as a system of allocation to become more of a holistic and determinative role. In other words, the market tells us what to value, not just whether we can afford to make it or buy it, or how to make it or buy it most effectively. Historically, certain core values came from places other than the market—the family, the community, religion, and even the state. These other value-producing founts generated ideas about what we needed, and then the market served to materialize these needs most effectively. The market used to be an effective instrument for making products that corresponded with our values—values generated elsewhere. Today, the system has evolved in a way that we have become much more like instruments of the market working to perpetuate and justify the market and its value-producing role. Today, the primary actors in the market are businesses, and businesses increasingly tell us who we are, who we want to be, what is important, how to feel good, and how much we need. Not surprisingly, needs are veritably endless in this system that is more and more closed to other sources of value determination.

The arguments against capitalism from a social justice perspective are compelling. From the summary above, it seems appropriate to connect any path forward in terms of social justice issues with opposition to capitalism. Given glaring inequalities, insidious corruption, and omnipresent commodification, capitalism needs to be reevaluated, at the very least, and perhaps more widely renegotiated in terms of priorities and function. However, this section provides a cautionary tale. Through a glimpse at the potential and significant benefits of capitalism and concrete ways that capitalism furthers the social justice project, it is unclear whether capitalism is the problem or the way forward. Before taking up this very important question with the answer of my social justice framework, it is important to address a few of the ways in which markets and market motivation have led to success in terms of redistribution, innovation, and human development. After articulating the positive outcomes of a market economy, as well as the criticisms, I present the reform potential through social justice.

CAPITALISM AND ITS VIRTUES

1. Microfinancing

Muhammad Yunus redefined aid and loans in a way that is more, not less, compatible with capitalism. Through very small loans offered directly to individuals, he challenged traditional frameworks for distributing aid to the poor. The poor are natural entrepreneurs; each day is a significant and creative struggle to find shelter and food. The key for development is to unleash the entrepreneurial energy that is currently caught in a vicious cycle of poverty, and he argued that a small direct loan could do this. One of his inspiring examples came from the realization that women making baskets in his local area were constrained by a system that denied them the opportunity to do better than survival. Without savings, they were obliged to purchase materials for their baskets each morning by borrowing through the local "money." Each day, the money lender would lend them just enough money to buy the daily materials. So rather than buying the materials directly, and likely earning a profit each day, they were paying high interest each day, never making enough money to pay back the money lender and then to buy materials directly the next day. Instead, they would return to the money lender each morning and fulfill the cycle of poverty dilemma. Without capital, they could not improve their economic position. Dismissing banks and other intermediaries, Yunus showed that those in poverty are entrepreneurial and more than willing to repay loans. The example of the woman who makes baskets crystallizes how the cycle of poverty has very little to do with ingenuity, hard work, or potential. Prior to Yunus's microfinance loan, local artisans had to borrow money or supplies to make exquisite baskets for sale. No matter how hard they worked or how beautiful their baskets, the women could never get ahead of the supplier-money-lender. If only they could accumulate sufficient funds to buy supplies directly, they could cut out the usurer, but without the capital, however small it needed to be, they were stuck in a poverty cycle.[5]

By his own version of the story, Yunus stepped out of his ivory tower and realized that he could eradicate a cycle of poverty by eliminating the middleman usurer. Without contracts, without excessive checks and procedures, individuals capitalized on the smallest sums and turned them into exponential profits. His Bangladesh model has now become institutionalized and globalized through the Grameen Bank, and he introduced an entirely new way to assist the poor within the capitalist system. Rather than charity as the vehicle for giving, Yunus unleashed vast undervalued entrepreneurial potential. Current versions of microfinance include websites that invite global participation with interpersonal connection. Organizations like Kiva (www.kiva.org) allow people anywhere in the world to learn the profile and plans of dozens of potential entrepreneurs like the basket-making woman. Through one click, you offer a small loan directly to that individual. With many sites boasting close to a 100 percent return rate, microfinance is a promising opportunity for development that shouldn't be dismissed. As a vehicle for improving human development and reinforcing dignity for those in poverty, microfinance is an ideal solution firmly embedded in capitalism.

2. Multinational Corporations

Criticism against multinational corporations for abuse and labor exploitation is common—especially within the United States, where one travels less than a mile from the border to realize that multinationals perpetuate gender inequality, economic disparities, environmental devastation, and community instability. The free flow of capital between states often leads to a seeming "race to the bottom" in terms of corporations seeking the cheapest labor with the least regulation. During the World Trade Organization (WTO) meetings in Seattle in 1999, protestors targeted Starbucks as an emblem of everything wrong with globalization and free market capitalism. In 2002, Starbucks had 5,700 stores in twenty-eight countries, made more than $215 million profit and $3.29 billion in sales.[6] It bought out local competition, established its supply chain throughout impoverished nations, and exploited local farmers in underdeveloped nations. The Starbucks brand was so global and so successful that it seemed unlikely to be a frontrunner of social issues.

However, Starbucks is part of a growing trend among multinational corporations to adopt corporate social responsibilities (CSR) that emphasize attention to fair wages, transparency, and sustainability.[7] Whether in terms or procurement, supply chain, financing, or human resources, Starbucks demonstrates levels of transparency, consciousness, and improvement that are impressive. Porter and Kramer describe the necessary shift in corporate strategy as "shared value":

> The concept of shared value can be defined as policies and operating practices that enhance the competitiveness of a company while simultaneously advancing the economic and social conditions in the communities in which it operates. Shared value creation focuses on identifying and expanding the connections between societal and economic progress.[8]

Multinational corporations have created departments devoted to social development issues, and collaboration between government, multinationals, and nongovernmental organizations (NGOs), are more common. Social responsibilities have emerged even within oil production companies; Memoranda of Responsibility (MOUs) have become a familiar part of negotiations for oil exploration and production.[9] Through pressure from international organizations, corporations disclose their investments and thereby hold potentially corrupt governments accountable. MOUs include provisions for oil companies to participate in community improvement through investment in healthcare, education, transportation, and infrastructure.

Beyond the traditional multinational corporations adopting socially conscious practices, there are newly emerging social enterprises oriented around profit but focusing on products and services that benefit the poor in particular. Partly in response to a changing demographic with many more women attending and demanding socially conscious business practices, top Ivy league business schools are teaching students how to make a profit and benefit the most impoverished communities simultaneously.[10] There is a burgeoning industry around environmentally sustainable goods, for example. It is no longer just a matter of adding costs in the supply chain in order to comply with governments' environmental regulations. Companies have discovered that environmental sustainability is a brand that brings new consumers, protects loyalty, and provides great growth and competitiveness potential. It is profitable to be green today in a way that breaks the profit model expectations of lowering costs of production in order to generate higher profits.

3. Innovation

Whether one draws from the historical references of Mao Tse Tsung's China or Khruschev's Soviet Union, a sharp criticism of communism was its inefficiency. And while Soviet Russia was able to launch Sputnik, it was not able to introduce the stream of innovation necessary to sustain economic growth. By 1989, the Soviet Union collapsed under the pressure of these inefficiencies, and China continued its shifting paradigm toward the state-owned enterprise model, which relied on state investment, but much more critically, responded to market forces.

U.S. multinationals today bear a striking resemblance with a mix of state support and private finance. Innovation is one of the most beneficial outcomes from competition rooted in unfettered capitalism. Profit drives investment in new products and new technologies that push the frontier possibilities for everything. Even along the path of rewarding individual self-interest, innovation brings vast collective benefits. Perhaps it is inevitable at the same time that it is unfortunate, but as much as innovation is a product of competition, it is also very much aligned with oligopoly structures of industry and therefore inequality.[11] Innovation requires profit and so conditions of imperfect competition present better conditions for heavy return and reinvestment in new long-run innovation. While the excessive profits from oligopoly systems sit uncomfortably with social justice advocates, excessive profits are the precondition for long-run innovation. According to Kuttner: "The large company, with significant economies of 'scale,' 'scope,' and 'speed' as well as steep 'learning curves,' is often the natural habitat of both technological and organizational innovations."[12] Numerous examples, from lower airfare, telephone service, and the internet, come from innovation that has served the public well and emerged from monopoly-like conditions. While monopoly conditions don't guarantee innovation, corporations able to capture rents are in a unique position to innovate in socially productive ways.

The United States has been a model country of entrepreneurship, characterized by its innovation as much as its skyrocketing profits. However, the United States is a clear example of a country where government plays an important role in fostering the entrepreneurial environment in ways to maximize its collective benefits as well as its individual profits. In *Good Capitalism, Bad Capitalism*, Baumol, Litan, and Schramm emphasize the growth potential in the United States, and they argue that it is not a zero-sum game. Through spillover benefits and diffusion of new technologies, the innovations provided by profit-making corporations contribute collective gain. However, at the same time that monopoly-like conditions are capable of generating innovation, they are also capable of its reverse effect. Without competition, corporations can become exploitative, and too much monopoly can have the reverse effect and actually reduce innovation. Government can create laws like antitrust legislation to prevent monopoly but also to preserve the value and outcome of competition, which arguably is the foundation for the benefits of capitalism. The key to socially just outcomes is not to deny the capitalist model or profit but to educate individuals and to create institutions that reward socially useful entrepreneurial activities in particular. Government can play a role in nurturing competition through institutions that make it easy to start a business, easy to hire and fire employees, and easy to obtain patents for new innovations.[13]

For these authors, government is an integral part of the synergy surrounding capitalism and social justice. Indeed, government best serves its citizens by recognizing that capitalism is not the enemy of social justice and that its efficiency mechanisms outweigh inequality outcomes. Capitalism can provide social justice outcomes, and innovation within capitalism also depends upon government's role in fostering institutions likely to promote entrepreneurship. At the same time, through social services and provision of goods, like education, government also provides more fair and equitable opportunities. According to Stiglitz, "while there is a vigorous debate in the United States and elsewhere about what the *precise* role of government should be, there is broad agreement that government has a role in making any society, any economy, function efficiently—and humanely."[14] Through education and "good" institutions, capitalism brings profit to individual entrepreneurs as well as collective benefits. For example, in my studies about entrepreneurship and immigrant communities, social capital, like the values of trust, solidarity, and even hierarchy, emerge as qualities that contribute to economic success. Values typically espoused in terms of social justice matter—not just as benefits to workers—but as key ingredients for development.

Most multinational corporations recognize the increasing prevalence and relevance of new stakeholders for their bottom-line profit. Media, culture, and public opinion generate a new sensitivity to social justice issues, such as diversity, fairness, and transparency. Corporate Social Responsibilities (CSRs) are now mainstream aspects of multinational corporations and reorient the rationale of social justice from one of charity or privilege to one of necessity. In terms of the environment, for example, "such efforts are seen less as part of building a reputation as a responsible business and more as part of risk management strategies and the development of more robust supply chains."[15] Social justice may be helpful for competitiveness, especially for competitiveness in the long run. Porter and Kramer describe corporate activism on issues like hunger, literacy, education, and environmentalism:

> Each company can identify the particular set of social problems that it is best equipped to help resolve and from which it can gain the greatest competitive benefit. When a well-run business applies its vast resources, expertise, and management talent to problems that it understands and in which it has a stake, it can have a greater impact than any other institution or philanthropic organization.[16]

Critical to their analysis is the essential role of social activism in acquiring corporate strategic advantage. According to a 2011 McKinsey survey, one-third of executives cite operational efficiency and lowering costs as the top reasons for sustainability strategies.[17] Here, social justice as strategy may be much more compelling, especially to those coming out of the neoclassical economics tradition, and increasingly it is not just rhetoric but sound corporate strategy and structure. Michel Albert articulates the position originally presented by Joseph Schumpeter: "The Austrian economist Joseph Schumpeter summed it up in a famous metaphor: it is only because they have brakes that cars can go faster. And so it is with capitalism. Because the authorities and the citizenry set certain limits and intervene to correct certain faults in the machinery of market forces, capitalism can be made to perform more efficiently. . . . no reason to believe the new orthodoxy when it proclaims that economic progress must be accompanied by increasing social injustice."[18] Albert's focus is a comparison of the neo-American model, which has allowed the foundation of social justice to wither away, and the Rhine model, which exemplifies his ideal capitalism. The Rhine model is characterized by more security for workers, the reduction of inequalities, and conscientious efforts to preserve open and fair opportunities.[19] Here, the company is as much a social institution cultivating loyalty at the same time as it is generating profits.[20] While historically the model brought economic success, it has drifted to become more, not less, like the American model. Both politically and ideologically, the Rhine model, with social priorities integrated into the profit motive, has been deteriorating.

Even if we accept the possibility of these twin outcomes, social justice and economic success, we need to address the current problem in the United States and most other shared developed economies today. Even within the countries that make up the Rhine model, social justice paired with economic success is simply not the prevailing trend. What went wrong? How did we move from the collective benefits of capitalism to its more vicious cycle of poverty, even within the most developed economies?

WHAT WENT WRONG: POWER, INSTITUTIONS, AND PATH DEPENDENCY

Nobel Prize winner Douglass North crystallized the importance of path dependency in terms of long-run economic development.[21] Path dependency captures the ways in which institutions create incentives to reinforce their own existence and perpetuation. Behavior much more often adapts to current institutions rather than reconstructing new ones. Patterns of behaviors and decisions that reinforce institutions over time can be challenged through the unintended consequences of institutional outcomes, or exogenous shocks that affect the extant distribution of power. However, trajectories of economic development and underdevelopment follow predictable paths precisely because asymmetries in power are reinforced through institutions.

A perspective made popular from economics and a misappropriation of Adam Smith states that the market emerged spontaneously in order to maximize efficiencies from barter, but prominent anthropologists suggest a very different history. Instead, currency and the accompanying institutions of a market economy were created in order to reinforce power relations. While neoclassical economics insists that the market replaced barter economies, anthropologists find no evidence to support this a priori assumption. As quoted by David Graeber in his extensive survey of the history of currency and debt, "No example of a barter economy, pure and simple, has ever been described, let alone the emergence from it of money; all available ethnography suggests that there never has been such a thing."[22] Adam Smith's legacy and foundation for neoliberal economics is mythical, and quite contrary to the idea that markets are opposed to states, the historical record reinforces that markets were created in the interests of states, and in particular, the interests of leaders of the states.[23]

In contrast, if we trace the history of state development, it is a long robust tale of institutions that cultivate the power of the state. What emerged from power relations becomes reinforced historically through the seemingly benign process of bureaucratization and rationalization. While Max Weber heralded bureaucracy and the bureaucratization of the state as the height of rationalization, he also signified the dominance of process over outcome, division of labor over cohesion, and rationality over humanity. Eventually, over time, Western capitalism brought virtues of industrialization, but simultaneously, it brought forward the vices of segmentation and deteriorating empathy. Such vices are present in all modern industrial societies and are common in modern corporate America. Through path dependency and institutional incentives, behavior responds in ways that become patterned and ingrained. Rather than simply attributing responsibility for the problems of capitalism to specific institutions, today we have to accept the insipid values and behaviors as more deeply entrenched than institutions. Today, these behaviors are our values and define our Western culture. Current culture reinforces the prevailing institutions in a much more compelling and comprehensive way than the power asymmetries that created them. What had been institutionalized through power, and then institutionalized through the division of labor and bureaucratization, has now become reinforced through voluntary behavior.

In *Moral Mazes*, Robert Jackall presents an anthropological study of corporate America. One of Jackall's CEOs describes the sharp disconnect between morality and business practices today. About his corporate environment, the CEO states: "why is it in life today that we have to deny any morality at all? But this is exactly the situation here. I was just too honest for that company. What is right in the corporation is not what is right in a man's home or in his church. *What is right in the corporation is what the guy*

above you wants from you. That's what morality is in the corporation."[24]
In his compelling account, the author cites three primary forces driving the
moral vacuum. First, corporate America has become absorbed by a type of
rationality that privileges practical rather than moral reasoning. Within this
paradigm, problems are puzzles to be solved with strategy rather than with
ethical considerations. Secondly, workers have become abstract categories
that allow high-level decision making that is fundamentally "devoid of the
feel of the texture of workers' lives and of the gut-level empathy that such
knowledge can bring."[25] Quoting another CEO:

> Well, actually, I don't worry about the workers. From my perspective, I
> don't intend to divest our total overall productive capacity because that
> would lead to other problems. I presume that those workers who lose
> their jobs because you close a particular plant will be able to find a job
> somewhere.[26]

Rather than considering the long-term implications of decisions in terms
of the well-being and sustainability of human capital, labor has become part
of transaction analysis built upon a short-run decision-making process. The
final force driving the deterioration of morality within corporate America is
the tendency to bureaucratize rather than humanize risk. One high-ranking
manager described the type of brutal decision making that dehumanizes as
it rationalizes decisions:

> Suppose that you had a candy bar factory and you were touring the
> plant and you saw with your own eyes a worker slip a razor blade into
> a bar. And before you could stop the machine, there were a thousand
> bars more made and the one with the razor blade was mixed up. Well,
> there's no question that you would get rid of the thousand candy bars.
> But what if it were a million bars? Well, I don't know what I'd do.[27]

So over time, these institutions of power have cultivated a set of values
that reinforce them. These values of consumerism, commodification, and the
unrelenting transaction forces of the market are shared by those who benefit
from the institutions as well as those who don't.

CRITICISMS OF CAPITALISM

In 1970, Milton Friedman wrote his declarative piece "The Social Responsibility of Business is to Increase its Profit."[28] In its justification to ignore
ethical perspectives and social forces in reaching business decisions, the
line seems clearly drawn for social justice advocates to oppose capitalism.
And for those on the social forces side of the line, criticisms of the market
are widespread. The recent Occupy Movements reveal the extent to which

the wealthiest countries in the world are not immune to market backlash. Certainly, for the developed as well as the developing countries, the consequences of our current system of capitalism are grave in terms of the social justice project. However, these consequences are not necessarily about capitalism but rather how it is currently manifest in developed countries, the United States in particular. Before addressing social justice as a meaningful remedy to the current economic trends of capitalism, it is important to outline mainstream accusations against the current state of the global market system.

1. Inequality

Whenever I play a game with my son, he reminds me about the power of agenda setting. He wants to play fairly, and he wants to win or lose by agreed upon rules. At the same time, he intuitively understands that rules control outcomes. Not surprisingly, he wants to invent and control the rules that we would follow. Is it any surprise that his rules repeatedly capitalize on his strengths? My seven-year-old son is a strategic player. While I can't confirm that we are all hard-wired this way, his age and the context of a "game for pleasure" suggests that there is something deeply rooted in all of us to think ahead, weigh possible outcomes, make decisions based upon probabilities, and whenever possible, control the agenda to minimize risk and maximize the possibilities of winning. Equally frank and indicative of broader trends, his rather unsurprising victory was perceived by himself to be both fair and legitimate. Within the discussions of the global economy, we often and similarly acknowledge rules that dictate trade and interstate economic relations. However, is it any surprise that the rules favor those who made the rules?

Academic terms often carry propagandistic suggestions, and like fair trade, free trade is one of the many misnomers to describe economic principles addressed by academics and practitioners. Free trade is not "free" in terms of the ideal image of a market liberated from government and power. Rather, free trade is organized by a set of rules and commitments that require decision making and consensus precisely by those in positions of economic and political power. In order to implement free trade, there are rules that need to be established around currency, distribution, marketing, and supply chain standards as widely ranging, from the environment to health, to weights, and transportation security. So it can't be surprising that leading countries set up the particular rules of free trade to support their strategic interests. International organizations like the WTO coordinate free trade, but their timing as well as the particular rules that regulate free trade are not satisfying fair trade any better than my son satisfies fair play when he defines the rules to his advantage.

After World War II, countries that aligned with the United States and other World War II victors embraced a system to promote the flow of goods and services between countries. Economic growth provided by comparative advantage depended upon exporting goods to other countries, and the countries that emerged victorious after the war were ready to maximize production and profit opportunities. Not surprisingly, the rules of the General Agreement on Tariffs and Trade, and then the WTO, were set up by the war victors, who also had economic power and economic incentives to expand their influence. And not surprisingly, "Third World debtor nations are almost exclusively countries that have at one time been attacked and conquered by European countries—often, the very countries to whom they now owe money."[29] As the Cold War set in, underdeveloped countries were pushed into political pawns of the emerging bipolar distribution of power between the United States and the Soviet Union.

Countries accepted aid from the United States and the World Bank, but they also accepted the rules of free trade defined by the United States and World Bank. Instead of protecting domestic industries during the early stages of economic development, these countries accepted the newly defined and globalized rules of free trade, which restricted tariffs and government subsidies to domestic industries. The wealthy developed countries today enjoyed the protectionism that nurtured domestic industries in the past. However, late developers who want the benefits of trade have to play by the rules of WTO. *Conditionality* determined the availability of aid and loans in return for policies that ostensibly contributed to positive economic reform but simultaneously increased the stream of benefits to the developed countries. According to Stiglitz, for the developing countries "*conditionality*—the imposition of a myriad of conditions, some often political in nature—as a precondition for assistance did not work; it did not lead to better policies, to faster growth, to better outcomes."[30] It is within this historical context that developing economies accepted the opportunity to sell their own goods, primarily agricultural, and so also accepted the particular rules of free trade, which were constructed to promote the strategic interests of established economies. At the same time that free trade offered a potential mechanism for growth for all countries, inequality became institutionalized.

The debate on the political economy of development was articulated early on between modernization theorists and dependency theorists. In retrospect, the academic debate presented intellectual concepts and reasoning that cloud a much more clearly defined battle between the countries who benefitted from the institutionalization of free trade as supported by the United States and those who didn't. According to modernization theory, the rules of free trade set up the potential comparative advantage, and then competitive advantage,[31] of each nation, thereby promising economic growth for each nation. According to dependency theory, the rules of free trade institutionalize a historical moment characterized by unequal terms of trade between countries in a way that bound developing economies to dependency without equality. The history of poverty and sustained underdevelopment includes lending by international organizations, such as the International Monetary

Fund (IMF) and World Bank, with accompanying structural adjustment policies (SAPs). Reducing foreign investment restrictions and government subsidies as well as tariffs were all part of the rules, the conditionalities, set up by international organizations in the interest of the developed world. The Washington Consensus within the World Bank and IMF imposed policies around fiscal and monetary reform but implied prescriptive governance and social policies as well. Not only did the developing world accept free trade, but they also accepted the policy reforms imposed on them as part of aid and loans.

The current WTO stalemate revolves around the unwillingness of developed countries to give up agricultural subsidies while they impose the reduction of trade barriers in areas crucial for countries to catch up economically. The Doha round of trade negotiations in 2001 addressed historical and institutional imbalances. Late developing countries are increasingly confronting the developed countries with the unfairness of the trade agreements issued under WTO. Just as my son may get away with this sort of strategic gain with a board game, this hypothetical construction of free and fair seems equally preposterous in its conceptualization of free and fair trade between states and in terms of economic development. Nevertheless, a proverbial question among development scholars and about terms of trade between the developed and developing countries is "how many bushels of wheat does it cost to buy a car or a computer?" This standard frame of development economics confirms a version of strategic play that may be free, according to the rules, and free, in that countries' leaders offered consent, but it is fair only to the extent that the running race described above is fair.

Advanced countries agreed to discussions and even some concessions through the Doha rounds of WTO economic negotiations and in response to the subsequent impasse around subsequent negotiations.[32] However, recent movements away from the WTO and toward more bilateral trade agreements are an ominous response to pressure by developing countries to reform WTO standards and shift institutionalized power inequalities.

Despite exponential economic growth and overwhelming prosperity, poverty is far from eradicated, and the gap between the "haves" and the "have nots" is growing. Both within countries and between countries increasing inequality is a problem with far-reaching negative social and political consequences. Migration flows, environmental issues, and political stability respond to this economic trend of inequality in ways that hurt the prospects for human development. The pressures of migration flows to wealthier countries make immigration a much more salient issue in democratic elections. Across Europe, the anti-immigrant backlash can be seen by the rise of right wing parties and even in the rhetoric of mainstream leaders.[33] Globalization propaganda is everywhere, cultivating the perception that it is an inexorable movement and it includes free movement of goods, services, and people. And yet, the free movement of people associated with globalization seems to be bifurcating sharply between the elite beneficiaries of capital flows and those who are most desperate to migrate precisely because they are most hurt by globalization.

However, just as it is difficult to call fair trade, free trade, it should also be difficult to lay infinite blame on the developed world. Like the example of my son, if we have an opportunity to set up rules to favor our strengths, shouldn't we? Certainly, this is the type of question that must be asked in order to critique our institutionalized version of capitalism, but it is also the type of question that can't be answered with the concepts, tools, and measurements of capitalism. If we want to take this question and its potential outcomes seriously, it must be addressed outside of the sphere of capitalism.

2. Aid

At the national level, redistribution can happen formally through taxes and government programs, with government as the primary mechanism for redistribution. Alternatively, redistribution can happen informally, privately, and often more directly through giving to nongovernmental charities. Americans present a puzzle. While historically supporting one of the lowest tax rates in the developed world,[34] Americans also give more per capita in terms of charity. The recent fiscal cliff debate would suggest that a significant portion of the population is opposed to higher taxes, but together with the charity data, it appears that the opposition may be more around government as the vehicle for redistribution rather than the redistributive process itself. Americans' charity giving offers a bold emblem of generosity and willingness to offer assistance to those in need, but it leads to the question of whether or not the social justice lens should prioritize one over the other. Whereas government responsibility for redistribution connotes collective responsibility, gift giving allows the economically privileged to select who is worthy of gifts and who is not. In this context of interpersonal redistribution, those who are on the receiving end may be more grateful rather than mobilized to expect more from their government.

At the national level, and in spite of impressive levels of charity contributions, statistics about the United States reveal an alarming rate of poverty. A recent Frontline documentary cited that one in five Americans under the age of ten is in poverty.[35] While it is hard to imagine that one of the wealthiest countries in the world is so vulnerable to inequality and the myriad of social problems that accompany poverty, it is important to spend some time thinking about our international obligations in the context of these high levels of domestic poverty. Especially in terms of the competition over scarce resources, it is worthwhile to ask whether our global outreach to assist development in other countries is in competition with our nation's commitment to alleviate poverty here within the nation-state. Should we prioritize our commitments with national poverty over global poverty in terms of targeting our resources? Or is it more appropriate to conceptualize and realize solutions to global and national poverty together as part of the same package? These are tough questions that need to be addressed by social justice advocates. At the end of the chapter, I argue that the conceptualization of social justice put forward in this book demands a more local, less global, perspective on aid. To the extent that social justice is about interpersonal engagement and accountability, it is about opening ourselves up to those around us in meaningful, noninstrumental ways. It is not so much that social justice should privilege local over global interests, but rather that the process of social justice laid out here will likely lead to this prioritization. For many social justice advocates, this could represent an uncomfortable turning away from global need. Before launching into full support for local over global, we need to consider the success of aid abroad. American universities are propagating service opportunities abroad, and the best and the brightest join international nonprofits as a way to fulfill professional and spiritual aspirations. However, we need to be more discerning as to whether the difference of aid and international interference contributes to the reduction of global poverty and political instability.

From seminal work as early as Cardoso and Faletto, dependency theorists have criticized the globalized market economy because it perpetuated economic dependence and underdevelopment of the "South."[36] Inequality, but also political instability, characterizes late development for many countries. Civil war and underdevelopment have become the twin problems that reinforce a vicious cycle of violence, poverty, and civil war. Simultaneous with the initial conditions problem of globalization, we also see significant efforts to remedy problems through the support of NGOs. Aid has been a driving focus for social justice advocates with few critics from within the ranks of NGOs. However, *Dead Aid* by Moyo and *War Games* by Polman challenge this expectation that aid contributed to economic, political, and social development. Practitioners and academics suggest that international aid is not fulfilling its expectations or the intentions of those offering it. Often much worse than a Band-Aid, international aid exacerbates individual and collective characteristics that contribute to the vicious cycle of poverty. From this critical perspective, aid contributes to a culture of humiliation within the group receiving aid and a righteous culture among those who are winning the economic, political, and social game.

Dambisa Moyo argues that aid simply hasn't worked to elevate countries, and significant populations within these countries, out of debt. She presents a compelling argument against Western donor aid. Her argument is historically located and unpacks how aid was primarily motivated by security interests and the Cold War. By supporting military development, aid propped up dictators and did little to introduce development policies. Secondly, she argues that aid was administered through weak institutions within the countries receiving aid. Within the context of weak institutions, it is not surprising that aid fed corruption and made the necessary reforms to nurture stronger institutions even less likely. According to Moyo, "A World Bank study found that as much as 85 per cent of aid flows were used for purposes other than that for which they were initially intended, very often diverted to unproductive, if not grotesque ventures."[37] Even to the extent that aid has contributed to democratization in Africa, she contests that this institutional outcome is not stable nor has it pushed economic growth.[38] More typically, aid does not just stall development, but it reverses stages of economic and political growth. For example, Moyo highlights the Western donation of a million dollars used to purchase 100,000 mosquito nets to fight malaria. Rather than contributing to economic growth through a healthcare provision, aid perversely put the local mosquito maker out of business. With this example, Moyo highlights how aid was primarily directed by strategic interests, but even when more benevolent interests prevailed, the best intentions were not realized. Rather than an outlier case here and there of misdirected aid, Moyo argues that the mixed motives and missing grassroots foundation of strong domestic institutions meant that Western aid propped up weak leaders. Aid delayed mobilization around effective participation and institutions. Historical factors that led to the current institutional context make Western aid extremely limited in its potential to assist growth and development.

While tied aid makes sense through the strategic lens of world politics, a more devastating critique comes from Linda Polman's insider revelation about the NGO/IGO industry. Among her tragic examples, she writes about the strategic manipulation of fundraising efforts around poverty and war-torn society. With emotional cache surrounding civil wars in several African countries, the funds fostered a "humanitarian mega-happening" that seemed to represent the height of global cooperation and contribution. However, in an increasingly typical path, the heights of global giving became funneled into an erupting industry of unregulated nonprofits. Like profit industries, nonprofits succumb to the market logic of growth. Polman quotes a staff member of a prominent U.S. aid association:

> It's perhaps embarrassing to admit, but much of the discussion between headquarters and the field focused on contracts [to implement donor projects]: securing them, maintaining them, and increasing them. The pressure was on: Get more contracts! How many contracts did we have? When were they up? What were the chances that they would be renewed? Were there any competitors?[39]

What appears to be an international community of giving and salvation for those victimized by war, violence, and environmental disaster masks a reality that "the most powerful link between humanitarian aid agencies is that of commercial competition."[40] Polman describes how organizations compete as much as they give, and they often inadvertently sponsor military villains, as much as innocent victims. Rather than contributing to healthy growth and development, they often reinforce underdevelopment: "Wherever aid workers go, prostitution instantly soars. I've often seen bar stools occupied by white agronomists, millennium-objective experts or gender-studies consultants with local teenage girls in their laps. I've known aid workers who cared for child soldiers and war orphans by day and relaxed by night in the arms of child prostitutes."[41]

What Clinton praised as the "unprecedented democratization of charity"[42] has become the wild west of a market free from standardization, government regulation, and accountability. Humanitarian buzzwords market the giving organization and guarantee its own institutional sustainability. Popular aid concepts, such as capacity building and citizen participation,[43] entrench the aid organization for perpetuity in a disaster setting, and in this way, the arsenal of workers within aid organizations becomes the primary source of government revenue rather than the aid itself. There is a mutually reinforcing relationship between the government that offers formal permission with corrupt but official permits to carry out the business of aid on the one hand, and the revenue provided by the workers, their rent, and consumption on the other. It is often a very small slippery step to the aid organizations becoming sub-state actors,[44] propping up corrupt, often violent, inefficient, and ineffective governments. According to Polman: "If you use enough violence, aid will arrive, and if you use even more violence even more aid will arrive."[45] The cycle has been given a name: WAR. In the developing world, WAR has new meaning—"Waste All Resources," so that aid organizations can come to repair the damage. The problem is that aid organizations have become more a part of the problems of violence and poverty, participating in a vicious cycle of global underdevelopment, rather than leading populations away from them.

3. Access Capitalism

Without the civil war and extreme poverty experienced in the "South," the United States has its own version of aid that contributes to systemic corruption and institutionalized inequality. Dan Briody addresses how monetary interests became entrenched in Washington politics. Their comingling of business and politics began with a tax loophole created in order to assist native-owned companies in Alaska. The consequence of government aid led to exaggerated losses, investment funds funneled into unproductive activities, and a boon in corporate malfeasance.[46] From this modest beginning, the Carlyle Group exemplified a pattern of money making built much more on access to political representatives able and willing to pass legislation in the interest of profits rather than a "collective good."

Increasingly, there is a disturbing trend in which production gives way to a focus on legislation. Increasingly, profit from competitive advantage gives way to profit from privileged access. Examples like The Carlyle Group drive a new approach to capitalism that is not grounded in making products better and at a lower cost; rather, profit and competitive advantage come through political access and influence. Without changes in production or new technologies, a single piece of legislation can make millionaires over-night. Corporate strategy is tied to generating access and political influence in a way that diverts resources from productive activities but also under-mines the potential strength of different noncorporate voices acting and influencing within the political sphere. There is a line that has become intol-erably blurry between economic interests and political influence. Carlyle has a growing number of international political representatives and leaders on its corporate roster in a way that pushes political influence even further into economic profit. Our global leaders have institutionalized economic inter-ests into the political system, and now the political system benefits their own individual economic interests in unprecedented ways. We have an increas-ingly closed system with few interests relevant enough to provide the will or capacity as the potential drivers for change.

Access capitalism is nurtured throughout the entire electoral cycle. Politi-cal Action Committee (PAC) and Super PAC influence is unprecedented in the United States. Since the 2010 Supreme Court decision,[47] interest group money dominates electoral outcomes in ways that threaten the democratic ideal of one person, one vote. At the same time, monetary influence is cloaked in virtue as free speech, and winning a seat has become a market-able good for sale to the highest bidder. As an example, the cost of winning a seat in the Senate rose from $3,067,559 in 1986 to $8,993,945 in 2010, while the cost of winning a seat in the House of Representatives increased from $359,577 in 1986 to $1,434,760 in 2010.[48]

As a process of social engagement that brings meaningful discourse and exchange between citizens, clearly social justice does not benefit from cor-rupt economic interests embedded into our political system. Neither the political nor economic system seems available for reconsideration let alone reconstruction. How is it that there is less space for alternative visions or interests when both systems abide by the rhetoric of participation, libera-tion, and competition? Why don't those who are relatively but perpetually ineffective oppose these modern rules of capitalism and democracy? At least historically, the world offers different state and market models. Why are we unable to effect change in our current U.S. system in ways that might renegotiate the patterns of inequality? Part of the answer to our apathy or acceptances has to center on the seductiveness of these systems and the false securities and interests that perpetuate them.

4. Consumerism

Years ago, I used to pass by Adidas headquarters in North Portland, Oregon on my way to work. I compulsively checked the building for the draped cloth with the latest statement about how to live well. The messages like "Impossible is Nothing" always remind me of my childhood drive past a church. Each week brought a different message that drew you in with humor, poignancy, and a pithy life message. The church wasn't my church and it wasn't my religion, and switching to this church or this religion never crossed my mind. They were messages that were like public offerings; a reminder that we are in this together. So why do these Adidas messages that offer the same generous humanitarian messages both captivate me and simultaneously make me feel squeamish? After the first blush of a public offering, the residual impact seems to remind me that I can be that statement not by deep reflection but by my next purchase. In contrast, and because the membership option to the church was so unlikely, its messages seemed like thoughtful gifts to digest or dismiss. From the Adidas billboards, there is a seemingly instinctual response to buy the product, perhaps quite simply because I can. Since I can purchase Adidas products in a way that I cannot purchase the church, this modern market message is much more appealing, just as it is unsettling. Perhaps owning it can move me toward realizing the values of the message. Perhaps I can become an emblem of this goodness simply through the products that I buy.

In the 1960s, Herbert Marcuse wrote about an emerging one-dimensional man. His book claims that capitalism removed the autonomy and creativity of individuals. In line with the perspective of a closed system, capitalism generates exactly the values that can be satisfied by the market system.[49] We want whatever is available for purchase, and what we can purchase defines our future wants. Michael Sandel describes this transition as a systemic shift from *having* a market economy to *being* a market economy.[50] The system isolates us from each other but also from ourselves, and in particular, from imagining a future self that is independent of the market. Our autonomy is lost not to other people but to the treadmill of capitalism. The equation for a good life becomes simplified and uncontestable: we want more in order to be more, rather than simply being *well* regardless of the commodities in our possession and regardless of our market transactions.

In many ways, this commentary is even more relevant today. We have become pacified by goods in a way that we don't demand change, nor do we even realize what changes might be necessary. Rather than a systemic change, which may take the form of political revolution or a social revolution along the lines of the social justice proposed in this book, we push for more within the existing system. Since we have so completely surrendered ourselves to capitalism and what we can purchase, it is the yardstick by which we increasingly measure our own value. Whereas in the early stages of market formation, we had values that we brought to the marketplace, and we had self-worth independent of what we purchased in the marketplace, the market now defines values for us and the self-worth of each one of us. The market is a social construction as much as a material one, and in this way, we have been willing participants in our own constraints. Rather than slowing down the pace and reach of market values, scholars admit that social spaces independent of the market are increasingly rare. In *Everything for Sale: The Virtues and Limits of Markets*, Robert Kuttner argues that "As the market vogue has gained force, realms that used to be tempered by extra-market norms and institutions are being marketized with accelerating force."[51] Similarly, Michael Sandel's book outlines example after example of previously public spaces now captured by market forces. His sports example conveys a particularly compelling tragedy in which a university sports stadium had been "a place where autoworkers and millionaires can come together to cheer on their team."[52] Today's skyboxes ensure that these public places reinforce division, while they also reinforce the importance of market power in order to enjoy previously free pleasures. More regularly, rather than triggering a desire for less market, these vast areas swallowed by the market system serve to whet our appetites to want more relevance within the existing market.

We have privatized so many services previously reserved or elsewhere reserved for government. A heavily privatized prison industry has now earned a seat of effective participation at the table of immigration reform debate. Our social issues are increasingly economic issues with the incentive of profit driving decisions. Not only do we willingly participate in the commercialization, and therefore our commodification, within the market, but the seduction of the market crowds out alternative values. Lafeber describes the global effects of contemporary U.S. imperialism, which is much less about the dominance of a nation-state and much more about the dominance of its accompanying capitalism and capitalist values. While the invasion of hegemonic values is not a new phenomenon, U.S. market values have been less contested than other examples of hegemonic influence in history. Why? For many neoclassical economists, the market is neutral, and many of us seem to accept this interpretation precisely because it offers choice. But however much choice suggests liberation and freedom, choice also cloaks the systemic nonneutral consequences of our choices. LaFeber says, "When South African officials warned that in such post-colonial societies as theirs the people could both admire—but also deeply resent-colonial power, an American replied that it was the British who had colonized South Africa. The United States had not done so. 'Oh, yes you did,' came the answer. 'Culturally you did.'"[53] More recently, in 1982, a French official warned against this version of "American cultural imperialism." A cartoon appeared in 1986 showing the noble European continent defended by the great literary figures of d'Artagnan, Don Quixote, and Shakespeare against a U.S. attack—from the skies—led by Mickey Mouse, E.T., Marilyn Monroe, and a hamburger.[54] But again, it may seem neutral and a celebration of freedom for the individual who chooses a hamburger over Don Quixote. Why and how should my proposed system of social justice deal with this type of freedom and choice?

Certainly, if markets are neutral, it is difficult to argue against the freedom of individual choice, but markets aren't really "neutral" at all. Economic systems were built by individuals with interests. While Sandel does not write about social justice, he very effectively captures the need for limits to the market, and he aptly describes the types of motivation for my proposed system of social justice: "imprinting things with corporate logos changes their meaning. Markets leave their mark."[55] In the concluding remarks of *What Money Can't Buy*, Sandel acknowledges that the precise meaning and influence of markets is contestable, but it is precisely this type of discussion and debate that is missing. A society that is captured by the market no longer asks:

> where markets belong—and where they don't. . . . Such deliberations touch, unavoidably, on competing conceptions of the good life. This is terrain on which we sometimes fear to tread. For fear of disagreement, we hesitate to bring our moral and spiritual convictions into the public square. But shrinking from these questions does not leave them undecided. It simply means that markets will decide them for us. . . . And so, in the end, the question of markets is really a question about how we want to live together. Do we want a society where everything is up for sale? Or are there certain moral and civic goods that markets do not honor and money cannot buy?[56]

Markets can become more neutral only if we circumscribe their limits. Precisely because market systems are not neutral, society must decide the limits of the market and its subsequent market value determination (or value deterioration), rather than the market deciding what we should value.

SOCIAL JUSTICE AS THE FOUNDATION FOR CAPITALISM

It should be clear that the market is a transmission process that can be as positive as economic growth and collective gain just as effectively as it can be negative with growing inequality and vicious cycles of underdevelopment. The key is not whether we accept capitalism or not but rather if we have a parallel system in place to generate values independent of transactions and the market place. It requires a distinct space and a procedure where we cultivate our values independent of the market, our identities within it, our attractions to it, and its central focus in our lives.

Typical social justice responses to global inequality and commodification have argued in favor of changing the rules of economic exchange or tearing down the institutions of capitalism. However, while this chapter presented some of those familiar accusations, it also demonstrated the possibilities born from the capitalist system. Here, a new conceptualization of social justice is offered as a solution to the crises of capitalism as well as the vehicle for a new type of capitalism to emerge. Ultimately, just like the argument in the chapter on political democracy, it is not that we need to tear down our current institutions. Rather, we need to carve out a meaningful space of social engagement to construct values independent of the market. The market has become our values rather than our values becoming the foundation for our market. As Sandel points out, we have become a market society rather than having one.

In order to return our market to its proper place as the setting for transactions that complement our lives rather than becoming our lives, we need to find a way to generate values and ideas apart from our transactions. In the present crises of capitalism, this is not just a matter of finding a remedy for a valueless society, but it is quite fundamentally a matter of preserving the market itself. In *Capitalism vs. Capitalism*, Michel Albert describes the relationship between the market and norms: "the ultimate paradox: morality—or at least ethical behavior—is not just a luxury, a decorative afterthought. It is a structural necessity for the proper functioning of a capitalist system."[57] Unbridled capitalism can self-destruct: contracts become tenuous, labor becomes unreliable, and the entire system becomes extremely unstable.

Whereas traditional neoclassical economics assumed that preferences came from outside the market, we have to realize that more and more the market is creating our preferences through identity formation. To the average consumer, this may feel exhilarating to realize that I become a strong, morally courageous woman by purchasing a pair of running shoes, but this example highlights how the market becomes my source of values rather than merely a forum within which I can conduct matters of daily survival more efficiently. On the one hand, there is nothing wrong with wealth, and there is nothing wrong with adopting an economic growth model at the level of the individual, corporation, or state. What matters is that economic decisions need to be made from values that are at least somewhat independent of the economic growth model. It was stated well by Desmond Tutu and Bettina Gronblom in a recent article: "It is fine to make a living; we are meant to enjoy abundant lives. The conflict comes when we separate ethics and economic progress and when we equate the latter with happiness."[58] I would chisel the argument a little further to suggest that the problem is that there is little conflict today because ethics, quite problematically, have become increasingly empty. Rather than ethics defining the market, ethics have become circumscribed by the rules of engagement in the market. The problem is not that we don't include ethics in our business decisions but rather that we have let the market become our guiding place for defining ethics.

From Adam Smith's *The Theory of Moral Sentiments*,[59] we understand the critical role of morality before the construction of markets and as a guiding force informing market decisions and behavior. Essentially, we have lost this moral foundation that is independent of the market. Rather than determining our values from outside of the market, we allow our values to be defined by the market. Rather than thinking about the correspondence of our identities with our purchases, we let our purchases provide our identities. The new path of social justice needs to prioritize a space for constructing values that is independent of economic transactions and interactions. Just like the argument presented in terms of democracy and political activism, there needs to be a distinctly social space that informs citizenry and nurtures values that impact political and economic action. As one considers how much the political space has been swallowed by economic interests, it becomes even more important to conceptualize and realize social justice independent of these spheres.

A second comment about values centers on how social justice advocates have splintered society into those who need help because of the economy and those who don't because they win in the economy. Today, advocates for reducing inequality, increasing opportunities, and protections for the collective enter an economic arena that is fully rigged against them. However, tearing down the perpetual winning team doesn't change the game. Protests like these can prolong disputes and elevate the controversies, but everyone remains tied to a system that reinforces a winning team. There is a better way for change that is meaningful. Certainly, increasing inequality highlights that there is a power dynamic in current capitalism such that political power, social power, and money are increasingly concentrated. However, the agenda of identifying winners and losers through the lens of social justice misallocates central problems as relevant for some but not all. It politicizes the market problems and divides society by who is winning and who is losing within the rules of the game rather than uncovering a systemic problem that hurts all of us. As part of the process of carving out a distinct space that is particularly social, the new version of social justice must bow out of this politicized and polarized game. Social justice can best move forward on economic issues if it locates its goals outside of the existing economic system. Rather than denouncing the 1 percent, and rather than tearing down the vehicles for economic growth, social justice can nurture distinctly social values that limit the potential strangulation of market values for all.

Apart from values generated outside of the market and therefore agenda setting through the social sphere, there is one distinct policy prescription that emerges. I will take up the argument further in the two last chapters of the book, but it is worth addressing here. It seems to me that globalization, as we are living it today, is not compatible with this new path of social justice. If values nurtured in the social sphere are going to be relevant in the economic and political realms, we need to narrow our lens from the global to a more local orientation. One of the benefits of living in Portland, Oregon for the last ten years has been my immersion in a gastronomical haven of local food and local wine that ranks among the best in the nation. Perhaps from this privileged location, it is easy to argue in favor of a local social movement over a global movement. However, my advocacy for a capitalist system that is rooted in local sourcing and local transactions centers around the emphasis on social engagement. Through the social justice process, values will emerge that are distinct from economic and political spheres but arguably influence these other spheres in the most promising ways. For the value outcomes from the social justice process to have transformative meaning, individuals need to become closer to the products that they consume. Jonathan Sacks describes the crisis of disconnect in the current economy:

> In the past there was a living connection between the owners of wealth and its producers. The feudal lord and the industrialist, however exploitative, had at least some interest in the welfare of those they employed. Today's global elites have little connection with the people their decisions affect. They do not live in the same country as those who produce their goods. They may have little if any contact with those who buy them, especially when purchasing is done through the Internet. This is important because moral responsibility is no mere abstraction. It grows out of face-to-face relationships. We see how what we do affects others. That is how we learn what to do and what not to do. The distance and depersonalization of contemporary life have robbed us of the immediate connection between act and consequences and this too has weakened our moral sense.[60]

The local movement promises a return to the potential for social meaning to determine economic relations. Transactions become informed by values created outside of the market place. Portland's branding centers around the importance of knowing the farmers who produce your food, being able to enjoy the craftsmen who make your furniture, and accepting economic transactions built upon the solid and distinct foundation of social relations. A Jesuit economist, Heinrich Pesch, S. J., proposed a doctrine of "solidarism." Invoking earlier teachings of Thomas Aquinas, he proposed that we need to return to a principle of community responsibility and accountability. Pesch called it "solidarism" to treat the economy not as a set of individual transactions but as an organic whole. The individual is primordially connected to a community, and his or her identity and values need to reflect concern for community precisely as part of his or her individual self-fulfillment.[61] Politics and capitalism are bereft in providing the civility, trust, and accountability that are necessary as the foundation for better, more equitable development. A space independent of political and economic decisions can become instrumental in creating new values and new decisions in both these spheres. However, the critical question remains how to create this conceptual and practical social space. The mechanisms for social justice are addressed in the final chapter.

NOTES

1. Samuel Adams, August 1, 1776. http://patriotpost.us/alexander/2857. Accessed July 26, 2013.
2. For an excellent seminal analysis of the problems of capitalism, see Arthur M. Okun, *Equality and Efficiency: The Big Tradeoff* (Washington, DC: The Brookings Institution, 1975).
3. In 2010, 59 percent of Americans agreed "strongly" or "somewhat" that the free market was the best system for the world's future. This is a decline from 80 percent in 2002. "Market Troubles: Which Countries are Most in Favour

of the Free Market," *Economist* (blog), April 6, 2011, Accessed July 26, 2013. http://www.economist.com/blogs/dailychart/2011/04/public_opinion _capitalism.

4. In 2009, more than 50 percent of the American workforce was not engaged in the workplace (State of the American Workplace: 2008–2010 Gallup Consulting). Further, since 2008, Americans have been more likely to perceive the economy as getting worse than getting better in each weekly average since Gallup began daily tracking. "U.S. Economic Confidence Retreats from Five-Year High," GALLUP Economy, May 14, 2013, http://www.gallup.com/ poll/162413/economic-confidence-retreats-five-year-high.aspx.

5. See http://www.youtube.com/watch?v=TPk2gRuIdj0 http://www.youtube.com/ watch?v=0C3XQ3BTd4o http://www.youtube.com/watch?v=LZ1P3W8ABiU for interviews with Yunus.

6. David Conklin, *Cases in the Environment of Business International Perspectives* (Thousand Oaks: Sage Publications, 2006), 438.

7. One of the most exciting initiatives around corporate responsibility centers on Michael Porter's "Shared Value Initiative" emerging from the conceptual analysis by Michael Porter and Mark Kramer, "Creating Shared Value," *Harvard Business Review*, January/February 2011, 62–77.

8. Porter and Kramer, "Creating Shared Value", 65.

9. Macartan Humphreys, Jeffrey Sachs, and Joseph Stiglitz, eds., *Escaping the Resource Curse* (New York: Columbia University Press, 2007).

10. Emmanuelle Smith, "Won Over my Social Enterprise; Women at B-School; Increasing Numbers of Women are Being Drawn to MBAs that Offer a Strong Emphasis on Sustainability," *Financial Times*, March 26, 2012.

11. Robert Kuttner, *Everything for Sale* (Chicago: University of Chicago Press, 1996), 203.

12. Kuttner, *Everything for Sale*, 202.

13. William Baumol, Robert Litan, and Carl Schramm, *Good Capitalism Bad Capitalism and the Economics of Growth and Prosperity* (New Haven: Yale University Press, 2007).

14. Joseph Stiglitz, *Globalization and Its Discontents* (New York: W.W. Norton & Company, 2002), 218.

15. Sarah Murray, "Companies to Reduce Humanity's Footprint," *Financial Times*, Tuesday April 24, 2012, Special Report, 1.

16. Michael Porter and Mark Kramer, *Strategy and Society: The Link between Competitive Advantage and Corporate Social Responsibility* (Boston: Harvard Business Review, 2006), 14.

17. Murray, "Companies to Reduce Humanity's Footprint."

18. Michel Albert, *Capitalism vs. Capitalism* (New York: Four Wall Eight Windows, 1993), 167.

19. Albert, *Capitalism vs. Capitalism*, 147.

20. Albert, *Capitalism vs. Capitalism*, 146.

21. Douglass North, *Institutions, Institutional Change, and Economic Development* (Cambridge: Cambridge University Press, 1990).

22. David Graeber, *Debt* (Brooklyn: Melville House, 2011), 29.

23. Graeber, *Debt*, 50.

24. Robert Jackall, *Moral Mazes: The World of Corporate Managers* (Oxford: Oxford University Press, 1988), 115.

25. Jackall, *Moral Mazes*, 133.

26. Jackall, *Moral Mazes*, 133.

27. Jackall, *Moral Mazes*, 134.

28. Milton Friedman, "The Social Responsibility of Business is to Increase its Profits," *New York Times Magazine*, September 13, 1970.

29. Graeber, *Debt*, 5.

30. Joseph Stiglitz, *Globalization and Its Discontents*, 242.
31. Conklin makes an important distinction between comparative and competitive advantage. While neoclassical economics often refers to comparative advantage in terms of natural resources, Conklin broadens the understanding. Competitive advantage refers to the wide range of resources in a country that allows a firm to adjust, to respond, and to innovate in order to maximize global competitiveness. See David Conklin, *Reengineering to Compete* (Scarborough: Prentice-Hall, 1994).
32. Stiglitz, *Globalization and Its Discontents*, 245.
33. For a summary of anti-immigrant popularity around 2010 elections, see Tony Barber, "Tensions Unveiled," *Financial Times*, November 16, 2010, 11.
34. See "The Numbers: How do U.S. Taxes Compare Internationally," Tax Policy Center, http://www.taxpolicycenter.org/briefing-book/background/numbers/international.cfm.
35. *Poor Kids: An Intimate Portrait of America's Economic Crisis*, Frontline (PBS, Posted November 20, 2012), Accessed July 26, 2013. Documentary, http://www.pbs.org/wgbh/pages/frontline/poor-kids/.
36. Fernando Enrique Cardoso and Faletto Enzo, *Dependency and Development in Latin America* (Berkeley: University of California Press, 1979).
37. Dambisa Moyo, *Dead Aid: Why Aid is Not Working and How There is a Better Way for Africa* (New York: Farrar, Straus and Giroux, 2009), 39.
38. Moyo, *Dead Aid*, 43.
39. Linda Polman, *The Story of Aid and War in Modern Times* (New York: Penguin, 2010), 34.
40. Polman, *The Story of Aid and War in Modern Times*, 37.
41. Polman, *The Story of Aid and War in Modern Times*, 47.
42. Polman, *The Story of Aid and War in Modern Times*, 49.
43. Polman, *The Story of Aid and War in Modern Times*, 180–81.
44. Polman, *The Story of Aid and War in Modern Times*, 126.
45. Polman, *The Story of Aid and War in Modern Times*, 157.
46. Dan Briody, *The Iron Triangle: Inside the Secret World of the Carlyle Group* (Hoboken: Wiley, 2008), 7.
47. See *Citizens United vs. Federal Election Committee*. Appeal from the United States District Court for the District of Columbia No. 08–205. Argued March 24, 2009—Reargued September 9, 2009—Decided January 21, 2010.
48. The Campaign Finance Institute. "The Cost of Winning an Election." Accessed July 26, 2013. http://www.cfinst.org/data/pdf/VitalStats_t1.pdf.
49. Herbert Marcuse, *One-Dimensional Man* (Boston: Beacon Press, 1964).
50. Michael Sandel, *What Money Can't Buy* (New York: W.W. Norton & Company, 2012).
51. Robert Kuttner, *Everything for Sale*, 54.
52. Sandel, *What Money Can't Buy*, 175.
53. Walter LaFeber, *Michael Jordan and the New Global Capitalism* (New York: W.W. & Norton Company, 2002), 139.
54. LaFeber, *Michael Jordan and the New Global Capitalism*, 82.
55. Sandel, *What Money Can't Buy*, 201.
56. Sandel, *What Money Can't Buy*, 202–3.
57. Albert, *Capitalism vs. Capitalism*, 82.
58. Desmund Tutu and Bettina Gronblom, "Camels Can Pass through the Eye of a Needle," *Financial Times*, Thursday, April 5, 2012, 9.
59. Adam Smith, *Theory of Moral Sentiments* (London: A. Millar, 1759).
60. Jonathan Sacks, *The Dignity of Difference: How to Avoid the Clash of Civilizations* (New York: Continuum, 2003), 35.
61. Robert Kuttner, *Everything for Sale*, 54.

4   Technology and Social Justice

It should be your care, therefore, and mine, to elevate the minds of our children and exalt their courage; to accelerate and animate their industry and activity; to excite in them an habitual contempt of meanness, abhorrence of injustice and inhumanity, and an ambition to excel in every capacity, faculty, and virtue. If we suffer their minds to grovel and creep in infancy, they will grovel all their lives.

—John Adams[1]

INTRODUCTION

This semester, the administration at my daughter's middle school is introducing a new grading system so that parents can log in to find out their child's weekly grades. I have learned that many schools already have this type of system in place. Presumably, this keeps parents up-to-date and prevents any sort of deception or withholding of poor grades. On the one hand, this type of surveillance may be an effective and efficient way that parents can monitor their kids. On the other hand, it certainly dismisses the possibility of deepening, or learning trust, and it potentially undermines communication between parents and children. Through this monitoring process, a parent maintains power in the parent-child dynamic rather than releasing some significant responsibility to an emerging adult. With full access, the parent determines when to monitor and how to evaluate what is there. A child has very little control, for example, to wait a few days to tell her parents about a bad grade. (I doubt I am the only one to have learned just around middle school the skillful art of timing disclosures in order to minimize potential hostility and punishment. I distinctly recall waiting until *after* the Friday night episodes of *Love Boat* and *Fantasy Island* before revealing a rather horrible test score.) We have to practice in order to figure out ways to build trust, relying on a parent or friends for support, and building confidence. Instead, the monitoring mechanism reduces the grades to a transaction between the teacher and parent and alienates everyone from the emotional connection that could be forged within the teaching-learning set of experiences.

This suggestive anecdote highlights the broader trend that technology can turn education into a transaction that actually undercuts some of the most important values about learning from the education experience. Curiosity, responsibility, and mistakes are some of the early building blocks essential for learning, but we have stunted their possibility in a relatively sanitized environment for the sake of surveillance. Studies by a Stanford psychologist affirm that students, especially the academically talented ones, increasingly see mistakes as failure. In the most curious and frustrating ways, students lie and cheat in order to protect their identities around the transaction of an "A" grade. In many ways, this is another example of market orientation encroaching upon our education system, and it is also a strong statement about the use, and potential misuse, of technology. Surveillance is extremely appealing (especially for the person with power to conduct the surveillance); it satisfies our desire for control and certainty. However, especially between parent/teacher/student relationships, or employer/employee relationships, technology cultivates a higher value around certainty where we used to rely upon human connections and deeper bonds. While the sense of certainty around human connections may be more tenuous and ambiguous than surveillance, these human bonds satisfy other positive externalities as well. Emotional connections are both flexible and enduring as they build foundations of reliability and trust. To the extent that our relationships function like market transactions, we become more dependent upon rules rather than emotional linkages and reliance. To the extent that we rely on rules and formal transactions, we limit the potential development and deepening of emotional connections.

Daniel Goleman broke through the traditional paradigm of IQ intelligence and introduced the idea of emotional intelligence. He highlights a new educational standard that emphasizes a deep understanding of "social politics" and social perceptiveness that qualifies as an important intelligence for success throughout life.[2] Importantly, emotional intelligence is a talent "that an education can nurture rather than ignore or even frustrate."[3] Like all talents, emotional intelligence needs to be practiced. To the extent that technology deprives us of this practice, technology then may be part of stunting or even sacrificing our emotional intelligence in ways that make it irretrievable.

The middle school experience brought yet another alert to the benefits and risks of technology. Amelia came home from school one day and told me about some atrocious behavior on her bus. The incidents went way beyond foul language and silly behavior. Students were demeaned and threatened, and a familiar practice of "daring" was escalated into more sexual, more bazaar behavior. It seemed like my child's fifteen minute bus ride was turning into a 20/20 news magazine story, and the increasing intensity made me uncertain whether there was an end point without some tragedy. Within hours of an email sent to the principal, I was confronting the best and worst of technology. Every bus had been equipped with cameras, and so my daughter's testimony could be corroborated very quickly. Each guilty child was paraded into the office to watch his or her own behavior on video camera, and much to the horror of the parents and kids, there was no denying the capacity for seemingly "good" kids to engage in very, very bad behavior. Furthermore, by the afternoon, the school had installed three more cameras on the bus to capture more angles and to ensure complete recording of all future behavior. It may not be surprising that there has not been another incident on the bus. In this story, technology both saved my daughter (perhaps from nothing more than reckless words and empty threats—luckily we will never know) and denied engagement along the lines of social justice. Through the surveillance provided by technology, she was affirmed, and perpetrators were punished. They were caught, and we were protected.

However, as soon as I was absolutely delighted with the outcome, I also began to feel uneasy. Like the more national debates on big brother technologies, I was caught between gratitude for the surveillance and security, but discomfort about both the process and subsequent muzzling of the others. In particular, I was haunted by the question as to whether or not anyone learned anything really meaningful amid the transaction of surveillance and punishment. The badly behaved students learned that they can get caught. I guess that is something. But did they learn why and what impact their behavior had? Did technology interfere in a potentially more meaningful, relationship-driven solution? There aren't clean answers to these questions, but they should be bothersome enough to be considered by society. Furthermore, the uses of technology need to be considered outside the realm of practicing technology and pushing technological breakthroughs. Should we use technology just because it is available? And precisely because it is so easily and readily available, perhaps we need to amplify the ways in which we are accountable for its use.

Technology is irresistible. For the Western world, technology has brought a steady stream of innovation with greater economic efficiencies and lower costs. The undeniable impacts extend beyond the economy to permeate aspects of our social relationships as well. Like the previous chapters, I describe ways in which technology has benefitted society with a focus on the opportunities for developing countries to catch up economically. Technology may ease inequality, but fertile conditions for technological breakthroughs often include conditions of inequality. An increasing flow of new technology requires high levels of investment, which depend upon the wealthiest to forgo consumption and profit for long-term investment. The Austrian economist Joseph Schumpeter argued that imperfect competition and monopoly conditions may be an essential part of innovation and technical progress.[4] According to Kuttner, "Large, oligopolistic firms often turn out to have the deepest pockets. They keep on innovating, to defend their privileged market position and to fend off encroachment. Innovation within a structure of stable oligopoly may be more reliable than innovation in a context of fierce and mutually ruinous price competition."[5] The juxtaposition of technology as an instrument for distributing growth more equitably, while it depends upon conditions of inequality, poses challenges. After all, do we want the collective benefits of technology even if the primary conditions are significant inequality? It is an enduring puzzle to figure out how technology facilitates communication and funding opportunities at cheaper costs in ways that potentially ease inequality, but at the same time, how the pursuit of technology thrives most especially under conditions of inequality.

How should we embrace technology, especially social media, with its complexity in terms of sources and consequences? Not surprisingly, many scholars begin their studies of the internet by recalling Socrates and his fear of books. He worried that the increasing prevalence of books would undermine our memory capabilities. Scholars offer Socrates's cynicism as a cautionary tale for modern critics of new technologies. Similarly, when I began talking to my colleagues about this book, one of them felt strongly that I should really call it *Social Justice in the era of Social Media*. I responded that my conceptualization of social justice didn't really fit with an unadulterated celebration of technology. In fact, immersing myself in the scholarship on technology convinced me that many aspects of technology significantly challenge my conceptualization of social justice. The dramatic guffaw of my colleague was followed by the warning that technology, especially social media technology, was not on the table for debate. It is a widely shared sentiment that "No one wants it to go away or to be curtailed or criticized, especially by an 'elder' like myself." I really did appreciate what he was saying. These days, students don't even hide the roll of their eyes when I ask them to put away their electronic gadgets and when I invite them to come to my office rather than email me.

According to Nicholas Carr, between 2005 and 2009, adults in North America have doubled the number of hours they spend online each week. The trends are global, with one international survey reporting that people are spending 30 percent of their "leisure time" online, with younger adults typically spending more time than older adults.[6] Marc Prensky begins his volume with the following statistics describing the socialization of today's "Digital Native": "over 10,000 hours playing video games, over 200,000 emails and instant messages sent and received, over 10,000 hours talking on digital cell phones, over 20,000 hours watching TV (a high percentage fast-speed MTV), over 500,000 commercials seen—all before the kids leave college."[7] Even the harshest critics of the internet seem to accept its inevitability. Prensky identifies the "Digital Immigrant," who is usually "older" (my forty-something age bracket fits comfortably here) but obviously new to and often overwhelmed by the tools of the internet.[8]

Furthermore, technology exacerbates some of the problems outlined in Chapter 3 on capitalism. As much as technology offers economic efficiencies, technology also contributes to trends of globalization and international labor exploitation with an unequal distribution of wealth. Humans are more alienated from their output and work because of technology. Technology increases the polarization of beliefs between individuals and contributes to the fragmentation of beliefs into pockets of often contradictory beliefs. The evidence is clearly mixed, and it is difficult to settle in favor of technology or against technology from a social justice perspective. Ultimately, technology and our attitudes toward technology need to follow a pattern similar to the approach explored for democracy, capitalism, and in the next chapter, religion. Criticisms are legitimate, and the inevitable weaknesses within each of these spheres—political, economic, technology, and religion—are evident. However, rather than engaging in a battle to combat the existence and persistence of these spheres, we simply need to develop the foundation that allows these spheres to be tools or spaces that we use rather than tools that define us.

Technology is not going away, and I don't want my ideas to be dismissed as the rant of a modern Luddite. The argument I present around technology and the need for circumscribed limits fits into the claims about social justice in terms of democracy, capitalism, and religion as well. Rather than dismissing or criticizing technology entirely, the main criticism is that we are increasingly "consumed with that which we were nourished by."[9] None of these spheres is problematic except in excess and except insofar as they encroach upon the possibility of a separate distinct foundation for meaningful interaction and connection—social justice.

TECHNOLOGY AND ITS VIRTUES

1. Economic Development

Chapter 3 explored the role of capitalism in terms of social justice, and economic development was a central focus in this analysis. This section focuses on technology more specifically and its particular role in terms of economic and political development. Thomas Malthus and the population threat in the mid eighteenth century is an excellent historical example of technology outpacing social problems. Malthus predicted that food production could not keep up with population growth, and his dire predictions included mass starvation, disease, and war as likely consequences. At the time, he advocated moral restraints and conservative government policies to limit aid, which he argued served as an incentive to the poor. Contrary to Malthus's predictions, technological advances in agriculture expanded production possibilities and eliminated this version of the population problem. More generally, the Malthus challenge demonstrated the strength of technology to lower costs, increase production, and to solve society's most intractable problems.

In the twentieth century, Alexander Gerschenkron continued the optimism for technology to improve economically underdeveloped countries. While there were stages of economic growth, Gerschenkron's book argues that developing countries could skip stages by adopting technology from advanced economies.[10] Technology provides a unique opportunity to level the development playing field for countries. If international aid and investment orient around technology transfers, developing countries could leap into globally competitive agricultural and industrial production. The Asian miracle of economic development around rapid industrialization in the 1980s was built upon catching up with Western technology, and it became a model of Gerschenkron's concepts.[11] Direct technology transfers became part of aid programs; the expectation of benefits from technology transfer also created legitimacy for multinational corporations to expand into new areas, particularly into developing countries. However, while the catching-up model oriented around technology had worked effectively in parts of Asia, it was not always so successful in other regions. The "green revolution" was another example of technology transfer to advance economic growth. Multinational corporations and nongovernment organizations introduced high-yielding varieties, irrigation expansion, and fertilizers into developing countries. However, the types of emerging problems emphasized the complexity of technology transfers. In spite of increasing agricultural yields in many instances, problems surfaced from the misappropriation of technology in areas with conditions that were not similar to the original source of the development. Soil degradation and crop failure undermined the uniform appeal of transferring technologies across countries and climates. A second common problem was the introduction of new technologies without the infrastructural support, the technical support, or the social contextual support for them to perform similarly. Cases of underdeveloped countries nationalizing industries in order to obtain ownership over the materials and production potential present many examples of this type of problem.[12] Resources without the accompanying supports, both human and capital, were limited in their potential to launch development.

Despite political problems associated with the international transfers in some countries, and despite criticisms by those advocating more biodiversity and less trade, technology clearly offered opportunities for economic growth and international competitiveness. Another important aspect of technology and economic development centers around the fact that the most challenging problems today are global, and it becomes increasingly evident that solutions require cooperation among countries. Fighting poverty, terrorism, and corruption demands sharing technology for communication, surveillance, and counterterrorism equipment, for example. Technologies around basic needs such as clean water, recycled houses, sanitation systems, and food production facilitate basic development as the foundation for economic development. Communication technologies are an important part of progress, as engineers, scientists, doctors, and policy-makers work together to solve the most troubling problems. When technology is borrowed or imposed from abroad, it can bring significant spillover benefits into other areas of development. Militaries are often the leading source of technological breakthroughs, carrying positive impacts, such as cost efficiencies in a range of consumer relevant industries, like airlines and electronics. As a positive political spillover at the international level, technological transfer agreements between states can foster greater economic and political cooperation. In spite of the complexity in adapting new technologies to unfamiliar environments, the same procedures or programs applied in different locations serve as an experimental springboard. Technology applied in diverse settings provides a natural experiment to test and refine innovation.

2. Technology and Political Development

From a political and social perspective, technological innovations like the printing press introduced the population to newspapers and encouraged literacy. Through generalized access to information, technology contributed to the democratization of early European populations by encouraging participation.[13] More recently, one of the precipitating factors for the democratizing revolution throughout the Middle East was social network communication. In China, it has become a cat and mouse game for the Communist Party to monitor and censor activists. Clearly, these cases support the idea that technology democratizes access to information, and through increasing transparency, it can become an important vehicle for change.

In earlier chapters, I referred to *Private Preferences and Public Lies*.[14] Timur Kuran presents a framework to understand revolutionary social, economic, and political change as part of the collapse of communism. Especially under oppressive regimes, citizens offer a set of public preferences that are often very different from their private ones. Sweeping change happens when there are sufficient incentives for sufficient numbers of people to behave in accordance with the more genuine private preferences. The frontrunners of change, like the heroic "tank man" in Tiananmen Square or democratic activist Aung San Suu Kyi, are types with very low thresholds for the disconnection between their public and private preferences. Often these frontrunners oppose the oppressive regimes earlier, more transparently, and more actively than others. Then there are tipping points and thresholds when greater numbers of potential activists shed their public "lies" in order to realize their private preferences.

In December 2010, a Tunisian street vendor named Mohammed Bouazizi was frustrated with government corruption and poverty. After an altercation with a city inspector, he responded in a spontaneous act of protest and set himself on fire. The act captured the private preferences for regime change, and it became a symbol of widespread anger. How does the suicidal act of an impoverished man in Tunisia foment a revolution? With Kuran's framework, we can understand how one act drives many to follow, not because one incident changes their minds but precisely because the act reinforces their own *authentic* preferences. While most revolutions can be explained in this way, we witnessed a unique aspect of this type of revolutionary change in terms of its speed and widespread effects. The impact of this individual's self-immolation was immediate and profound, largely because of social media. It was his image posted across countries in the Middle East that sparked the Arab revolution. Without today's social media, most events of protest like Bouazizi's were more likely suppressed before they expanded. Global dissidents continue to utilize these technologies to document repression, to motivate potential dissidents, and to cultivate solidarity.

With global attention through communication technologies, the net of solidarity is much wider and potentially influential as well. Victims of oppressive regimes find that they don't need to rely solely on the domestic pool of support. The all-female rock band Pussy Riot was jailed after they performed their controversial song "Putin Wet His Pants" and stripped down for a protest against the Orthodox Church because of its support of Putin (in January 2012). Described in a recent *Financial Times* article as "a gift for Russia's sputtering opposition movement,"[15] the group is a catalyst for mobilizing and organizing potential opponents to Putin's regime. Russia has become Europe's biggest internet audience with a trifecta of "low-cost, high-speed internet access, LiveJournal, and social networks," which are driving new civic movements. According to one motivated blogger: "For many years, there was no means for people living here to do anything that relates to the organization of society in any way."[16] Likened to the Arab Spring, the recent postelection protests, which dispute the presidential election in Russia, acknowledge an awakening civil society and "the new politics" of the internet. Obviously, technology removes many of the costs of organizing and eases mobilization efforts around social movements. Through today's communication technologies, single events are capable of reviving and focusing global attention on the consequences of oppression.

3. Technology and Global Education Opportunities

Last semester, each of our university departments met with the Information Technology (IT) department to learn about the new technologies available to improve our teaching. I balked when the expert technician casually suggested that there was no need for faculty to miss a class because of a conference or illness. Quite comfortably, the IT staff could record all of our lectures and keep them on file for any unforeseen or anticipated absence. My colleagues and I laughed smugly all the way back to our offices. But once inside the quiet of my office, it didn't take long to realize that while I pat myself on the back for finally learning how to upload my lecture outlines on "Moodle," it is clear that the wave of change is fully affecting education and my job as an educator.

Distance learning is fundamentally transforming pedagogy and the education industry in the United States. With the era of encyclopedias long gone, information is much more readily available. Individuals can find answers to questions faster than ever. Youtube and now Moocs have made it possible for highly motivated individuals to study a curriculum from the most prestigious professors at Ivy League universities. Khan Academy makes elementary and high school math and science curriculum available to anyone without fees. It is startling and impressive to think about the pace and vast extent of democratizing education that has taken place through the computer and internet communications.

Without fees, without timetables, and without accountability, individuals are free to learn more than ever. From a credential perspective, technology makes formalized and accredited distance learning increasingly possible as well. These technological advances introduce new tools, but much more importantly, new opportunities for democratizing education. The *Financial Times* calls it a veritable tsunami that threatens to topple ivory towers of higher education. Coursera and EdX are online education sites that bring together a consortium of schools, including such top universities as the prestigious Princeton, Stanford, University of Pennsylvania, Michigan, MIT, Harvard, and Berkeley. One of the innovations in education came from a few Stanford professors who offered a course on artificial intelligence for free. Not surprisingly, perhaps, 160,000 students enrolled. Through standardized testing, available without cost, the professors were able to offer each student a letter of accomplishment as well as their ranking in the course. In the most provocative way, Christopher Caldwell of the *Financial Times* asks, "If you were a Silicon Valley chief executive hiring artificial intelligence engineers, would you prefer the top student in the privilege minority who took CS221 in the 'old' days? Or the best of the 160,000 self-motivators in the online class?"[17] Technology successfully tears down some of the most daunting and discriminatory barriers. Limited language skills, limited access to transportation, limited resources to attend school, and physical handicaps, are irrelevant within this new model of education. In this new environment, it is difficult to predict the direction for schools that hold onto the value of their traditional experiences. It is a curious possibility that the pedigree of Ivy League universities in terms of proffering the best faculty for student learning may be less sustainable than the small liberal arts colleges that offer the best learning experiences in terms of contact and connection. Undoubtedly, the former will have to reform most significantly. The latter might be pushed to adapt to the new system of education with additional distance course offerings. Some universities have introduced late night courses, which meet the twin demands of professor contact with maximum flexibility. How elite universities find new ways to brand high education learning amid the sea of anonymous, transactional alternatives is a significant challenge upon us.

4. Social Media and Social Enterprise

Technology can even turn small-scale ideas, like microfinancing, into globalized phenomena. Beyond democracy, ideas can be conveyed across countries at faster speeds, and they can be implemented more widely. Muhammad

Yunus revolutionized economic development with his microfinance initiatives. Recognizing the problems associated with giving aid and loans to corrupt governments and ineffective institutions within developing countries, Yunus focused on the local level. By emphasizing small sums of money for individual entrepreneurs who had good ideas but who didn't have the collateral to access traditional funding, Yunus cut out middle-level corruption and put money directly into small-scale development. Not only were the effects felt more immediately and more locally, but the example transferred globally. Combining both local and global, the idea became popularized and transferred across cultures, political systems, and levels of economic development. Because of technology, the possibilities of microfinancing have changed the way people offer aid and consider development. In *The World if Flat*, Friedman summarized the social entrepreneurship potential provided by new technologies:

> What they all have in common, though, is burning desire to make an impact and a firm belief that the flattening of the world makes being an activist-entrepreneur easier and cheaper than ever before. In fact, this kind of activism is now so easy, so cheap, so readily available . . . You want to raise money for African poverty relief, for Darfur refugees, or to save the elephants of Sri Lanka? The Web provides you a global platform and a global audience. You want to highlight environmental degradation in the Amazon or potholes in your own neighborhood? You can post the pictures on www.flickr.com or upload your own documentary on youTube or record your own podcast. You can blog about injustice and you can blog to raise money for your favorite candidate. If your arguments or video or photos or voice are compelling, you'll eventually find an audience or it will find you.[18]

Technology ensures that individuals in the United States can select their causes, and through websites like Kiva.com, they can instantly provide a small loan to any individual or project that he or she feels is worthy. Without the costs of transportation, and without the accompanying bureaucratic inefficiencies of trying to make a difference on location, it is now possible to turn aid into a more direct contact and individualized effort. Recipient and donor connect in a cyberworld in new and meaningful ways.

But at the same time that technology has revolutionized giving and fostered intimacies and ingenuities across countries, there are compelling challenges that need to be addressed. These are challenges that cannot be resolved within the sphere of technology, precisely because the challenges approach the social implications, or morality, of its vast potential uses. The challenges remind us about the many ways that we have relinquished control of our authority over our instruments and tools of development. In the current unleashed world of technology, we may be increasingly defined by our technologies, and in not so flattering ways, as much as it is being used by us.

CRITICISMS OF TECHNOLOGY

1. Information is not Neutral

Around a year ago, a neighbor decided that he and his partner would create a neighborhood blog. We received the flyer in the mail announcing that this neighborhood site would be an ideal place to connect about pets, recommendations, babysitters, security, and essentially any concerns about the neighborhood. Access was limited to the postcard recipients, and it promised to bring us closer together. I didn't sign up for the blog. Fundamentally, it bothered me that I would be connecting through social media with people who don't smile or wave to me any of the many times I walk through the neighborhood. Then quite recently, I was walking my dopey, very soft-hearted boxer when a woman approached me because a few hours earlier her daughter was bitten by a boxer. We were both alarmed and shared information about what she knew, and I assured her that Mugsy had never been off of his leash, never shown any aggressiveness. I encouraged her to bring the daughter to my house to meet Mugsy and to feel assured that he was not the perpetrator of the dog bite. I thought that was the end of it.

A few days later, I found myself approached by countless people in the neighborhood—coming out of their houses, crossing the street. Each person wanted to know if Mugsy was the dog that bit the young woman. Beyond the people who approached me for the first time in our five years living in the neighborhood, there are the many others who just started to glare at me. It didn't take long to learn that the neighbor who started the blog responded to the dog bite announcement on the website and posted his "information" that a boxer lived two doors away. Now, I know this neighbor very well, and he knows Mugsy very well. What I couldn't understand is why he didn't pick up the phone and ask me. Why did he post Mugsy's home location when he knew that Mugsy was very likely not guilty? In our ensuing argument, it became clear that he was absolutely righteous in defending his decision to post the information. How did he do anything wrong when it was information only? From his perspective, information without an accusation is neutral. I think I eventually made an impact when I assured him that the next time the news announced the search for a criminal with a beard, I looked forward to posting his name and address on the website. After all, people in our neighborhood deserve to know where all bearded men live.

Others might share my concern that this is one critical dilemma around information and social media technologies. Information wears a cloak of neutrality and then disguises our responsibility for the information we convey. Posting information online should be considered in much the same way as one makes a phone call to one's neighbors, or even better, walks door to door to warn them of potential dangers. However, easy access and information addiction has suspended our willingness to hold ourselves accountable by these standards. It is likely that most postings never get "called out" for their inhumanity, which is another difference. If someone knocked on your door and suggested you should be aware of a particular person in the neighborhood, it would lead to questions and discussion to figure out the legitimacy. If the information is somewhat dodgy and unfounded, biases become quickly apparent, and many town "callers" might be cowed somewhat. And most would agree that restraint, in this case, is a good outcome. However, in the cyberworld, the very best possibility is that we digest the unfounded rude and crude comments as white noise. We pick up on the information that might affect us or directly hurt us, but we too often digest it too quietly and individually rather than in dialogue and socially.

As another general example, Dove's parent company, Unilever, enjoyed consumer success by a wave of popular support and then just as quickly received the critical thrust by another wave of public opinion. The popularity came with a seventy-four second video ad called "Evolution," highlighting the profound transformation of a rather ordinary girl into a billboard supermodel. By showing the fakeness of beauty typically portrayed in ads, Dove's video scored 18.5 million viewers and likely a large pocket of new consumers. However, with popularity and access comes greater scrutiny. One of Dove's new fans noted that Unilever also makes Axe, with its advertising tag focusing on women who would strip for any man wearing Axe cologne. As described by Tapscott, "Mockumentary" videos followed with scathing comments about Unilever's contradictory messages: "A message from Unilever, the makers of Axe and Dove. . . . Tell your daughters before Unilever gets to them."[19] These waves of popularity made possible through internet access are unprecedented, but so too are the levels of scrutiny and potential "gotcha" criticisms. The extreme waves of support, as well as the rapid shifts toward criticism, take place largely independent of the efforts of the company itself.

2. Technology and Globalization

One of my colleagues in the sociology department studies the effects of technology on transnationalism. Her research of Filipino migrants in the United States presents one of the most compelling arguments in favor of technology as a vehicle for maintaining traditional role relationships and patterns of communication within a family. Through interviews with both families in the Philippines and with migrants in the United States, she explores the impact of computer communication technologies, such as Skype and Facebook, in terms of gender roles, types of communication, and bonds across these vast geographical spaces.

Francisco's research emphasizes the ways in which migrants remain "present" in family routines, such as cleaning the house, preparing the kids for school, and sharing a meal. Especially because of the time difference, a Filipino migrant can return from work at the end of the day New York time and tune in to the morning preparations for school and work in the Philippines.

During one interview in New York City, Francisco recalled how she heard dishes being washed in the kitchen but knew that no one else was in the apartment. When the interviewee realized that Francisco was hearing the clanking of dishes, she pointed out that they were being washed in the Philippines. The interviewee keeps the family "turned on" the computer, even when they are not communicating directly. This keeps the migrant connected and provides mutual support to the disconnected family.

Francisco quotes from one of her interviews:

> You know when we're always online, you find out what's going on, you start to know what's happening everyday. It makes me feel better when I know everyday they are doing homework and taking care of each other. It's like I see they're maturing. You believe in yourself that you didn't fail as a Mom.[20]

Francisco is particularly interested in gender roles and how migration disrupts traditional gender roles especially when the women are mostly migrating and becoming the family breadwinners. She traces the transformative effects of these shifting identities through computer communication. Rather than simply departed, absent, and transactional, the migrant's transnational relationships become extremely relevant and transformative. Women teach the men how to cook the family meals, and women share work experiences while simultaneously fulfilling their traditional caregiving roles.

In assessing the merits of technology, this case is quite a bit more complicated than it appears. On the one hand, there are clear benefits to bringing families closer together, especially when a woman may be working abroad for most of the child-rearing years. However, another more critical perspective suggests that this type of technological benefit may prolong migration, with its accompanying material benefits, in lieu of return migration, with physical and emotional benefits. Even more critically, technology is merely a Band-Aid for the troubling sources of inequality between the global North and South. As long as technology mediates the pain and challenge of migration flows, it can be seen as a mechanism that passively contributes to the perpetuation of broader problems of globalization—and global inequality, in particular. As Francisco ends her paper, she says, the "exploration of families' technological dexterity in maintaining a family is both impressive and depressing. Instead of solely celebrating the innovations in transnational family life arrangements, I am also reminded that these families *have* to think outside of the box to keep up with one another because they are apart."[21]

Ultimately, technology is incapable of offering its own critique of the tools and services it provides. Migration leads to physical and emotional distances within families. Technology can ameliorate the disruption, but it does so in ways that ultimately preoccupy attention away from a proper critique and reconstruction. Therefore, one of the most fundamental problems with technology is that it potentially distracts us from the *real* problems, the sources of problems, and it reduces our individual and collective will to find solutions.

3. Technology as a Tool for Justice

Recalling the story at the beginning of the chapter, through the surveillance provided by technology, perpetrators were punished. I expressed uneasiness at muzzling others through threats of surveillance. Education, and administering justice more generally, becomes much more like another type of transaction rather than a mechanism for healing society. These questions become even more challenging in the context of security and liberty debates. How much freedom are we willing to surrender in the process of increasing our surveillance potential in the name of security? In the aftermath of the Boston bombings, citizens were amazed by the pace and effectiveness of neighborhood cameras in tracking down the terrorists. In the instance of successfully finding the terrorists, it seems easy to weigh in favor of surveillance. However, what about a parallel situation when we consider the possibility of being put on the "no-fly" list? The impossibility of ever knowing why we were put on it, who to appeal to, and how to appeal, makes our society verge into Kafkaesque territory. The question of whether or not we access all the potential uses of technology is the type of issue that needs to be debated prior to our own involvement either as a victim of terrorism or a victim of the engines protecting against terrorism. As put forward by Rawls, if we hypothetically place ourselves in the worst-case scenario, then we are much more likely to implement fair laws for the collective. We need to debate its use, consider the potential worst-case miscarriages of justice, and then make these decisions as much as possible behind the "Rawlsian veil," or at least removed from direct and immediate interests.

Kony 2012 is another challenging instance of global justice via the internet. In a matter of days, Jason Russell on behalf of his organization Invisible Children turned Joseph Kony into a household name, and the call for his arrest became a global movement for justice of the Ugandan convicted war criminal. Kony 2012 became a popular cause for celebrities who used Twitter and Facebook to motivate many millions more to join. Hits for the video explained a version of the political story and appealed to the world to join a global wave demanding justice; presumably, although not entirely clear, justice meant Kony's incarceration. The video received over 100 million hits. Through social media, an unknown criminal became the number one enemy primarily among young high school and college age people with support torrentially moving across countries. People who knew very little about Uganda and its domestic politics became immersed in Russell's version about Kony's role in recruiting children soldiers, fomenting violence, and perpetuating poverty. Many joined the condemnation of this one warlord leading the Lord's Resistance Army. The cascade of awareness was stunning and reached from individual computers to entire college campuses all the way to Congress. As much as Kony 2012 highlights the strength of internet communication to stimulate, motivate, and mobilize, it also addresses many of the problems. To reiterate from one of my earlier examples, information is not neutral.

As Teju Kole wrote in his piece "The White-Savior Industrial Complex,"[22] the songwriter may be innocent but the song never is. Amid the emotional draw for attention and donations there was much less effort, especially early on, to scrutinize the implications or "constellation" of causes. Information is neither neutral nor objective, especially when it is the instrument for raising money. Public opinion in support of Russell's project turned just as quickly and almost as effectively to oppose his project. For some, this affirms the internet as a public square of accountability. However, the speed and polarization of the extreme cascades chisel away at our own sense of our abilities to discern the authentic causes and to sift through the complexity of issues. Some were critical of the use of funds to produce the film, while others opposed the emotional grab effect of the film without reasoned analysis of the political conflict, or the consequences of supporting the existing regime. Too many avalanches of unregulated and suspicious appeals and all songwriters begin to seem suspicious. Too many appeals for public action and many activists slip into entertainment at best, and more white noise at worst.

4. Crowding Out and Cognition

In addition to the "political" effects of immersing ourselves, indeed becoming ourselves, in the sphere of the internet, many psychologists and neuroscientists are studying the cognitive effects of our technology obsessed pastime. "Crowding out" in terms of cognition is one of the problems addressed by scholars who study the psychological and sociological effects of excessive internet use. In particular, the time we spend googling, 'facebooking, twittering, and surfing is time spent away from reading. Most significantly, books have lost out to new technologies. While many regale the end of pressures to read books like *Don Quixote* and *War and Peace*, our brains are changed by the process of reading fewer literary texts. Carr cites a literary professor's insight that reading a book is "multisensory." We have made a shift from processing content through both tactile and visual stimulation (books) to a much heavier reliance on visual stimulation only. We don't actually read anymore, at least not from left to right and from top to bottom.[23] Scanning, or "power browsing,"[24] for relevant information has become the new form of absorbing content. There is a great deal of debate about whether our brains are better or worse by a series of measurements, but there is clear convergence within the scholarship that our brains have changed. Apart from particular attitudes and beliefs, our brains just don't think the way they once did.

Carr quotes Cory Doctorow in describing an "ecosystem of interruption technologies."[25] How we think has changed, but what we think about has changed as well. In many ways, the answer is that we think about "what is next" far more than what we are doing now. We surrender to an ongoing emotional anticipation of the next stimulation, and our brains have responded to these expectations accordingly. Sherry Turkle describes the loneliness of many of her subjects after internet connections. Technology allows people to stay connected, such as "Ellen" and her grandmother, who now Skype twice a week. While Ellen's conversation is seemingly rich, she confessed that while she "talks" to her grandmother, often for an hour, she is busy multitasking: "I do my email during the calls. I'm not really paying attention to our conversation."[26] The technology world becomes far more stimulating and appealing than the real world "unplugged."

Whether walking in the halls of the university, waiting in an airport, or sitting in a coffee shop, my own observations reinforce Ellen's story. One of the more absurd images emerged when my brother and I took a trip to New York City a couple of years ago, and we ended up at a very posh bar in Soho. I insisted my brother spend some time unplugged, focused on our conversation as we walked through the streets of my favorite city. But perched at the bar, I realized how quiet it was except for some melodic crooning coming out of the speakers. I looked around to see at least a dozen exquisitely beautiful people, collected in groups of two or three, and not one of them was talking. Each person had a drink in one hand, a companion across the table, and very little interest beyond their little hand-held stimulants. Life in the world is so much less stimulating than the hypertexting and instant messaging of our technology world. It triggers our primitive "seeking" instincts and easily evolves into a craving very much like any other addiction.

Turkle traces the distraction and addiction qualities of the internet among scholars, the supposed experts of books, writing, and deep thinking:

> "I'm trying to write," says a professor of economics. "My article is due. But I'm checking my e-mail every two minutes. And then, the worst is when I change the setting so that I don't have to check the e-mail. It just comes in with a 'ping.' So now I'm like Pavlov's dog. I'm sitting around, waiting for that ping. I should ignore it. But I go right to it." An art critic with a book deadline took drastic measures: "I went away to a cabin. And I left my cell phone in the car. In the trunk. My idea was that maybe I would check it once a day. I kept walking out of the house to open the trunk and check the phone. I felt like an addict, like the people at work who huddle around the outdoor smoking places they keep on campus, the outdoor ashtray places. I kept going to that trunk." It is not unusual for people to estimate that when at work, but taken up by search, surfing, e-mail, photos, and Facebook, they put in double the amount of hours to accommodate the siren of the Web.[27]

Turkle's research describes a profound emotional alienation as "easy connection becomes redefined as intimacy" and "cyberintimacies slide into cybersolitudes."[28] Although the hyper stimulation of a computer is instantaneously gratifying, we are losing out on relationship, with its complexities, mysteries, deep emotions and understandings, and on the potential to learn about ourselves in society.

Websites and blogs have become important aspects of today's school experience. Parents expect to be able to log on and see what was accomplished within a class each week. Teachers who attach new photos most regularly are praised. From work or from home, and at any time of day, parents can see what happened in the class. Teachers are not just educators these days. They are news correspondents, they are photo journalists, and they are "on call" with parents as long as they log onto email accounts. Is it surprising that these trends correspond with an increasing rate of burnout among teachers? Other factors, like salary and budget pressures, must be contributing as well, but imagine what could or should our teachers do instead of taking care of parents and their insatiable appetite for information about their kids? What if teachers focused on kids during the day, not worrying about taking pictures to convey the glimpses of activity to document that the kids learn? Just the other day, my son's teacher emailed midday because Nathanael was anxious about whether or not a particular book was actually in his room or if he had lost it? For a few minutes, I was completely dumbfounded. Why did she write an email? And why did she write an email about this menial issue of a book that seemed temporarily lost? I guess because she could, and in some sense, it was very efficient because then my son knew and presumably settled back into the school routine. The *problem* was solved by an answer to the question. Imagine the amount of time it takes away from her work as a teacher to solve these types of particular problems rather than nurture other lessons like patience. Then it was also frustrating to realize that my son's impatience and uncertainty was so instantly satisfied. We expect so little from each other when technology appears to be able to provide answers, immediately satisfying answers. The title of Sherry Turkle's book conveys this ubiquitous dilemma: *Alone Together: Why We Expect More from Technology and Less from Each Other*.

Ultimately, one of the generalized points from the classroom example is the opportunity cost of emailing and utilizing technology instead of building relationships. Rather than understanding people and connecting with them, we solve their problems as efficiently and as effectively as we can—which is much more efficient and much more effective because of technology. Another aspect of opportunity cost is the time we could spend doing other things. Instead of surfing the net, answering every email question as urgent, and following the minutiae of friends' lives via facebook, we could be talking and touching and living life together rather than "alone together" as described by Sherry Turkle.

5. Emotional Distance from Labor

Whereas nineteenth-century early industrialization focused on natural resources and industrial goods, late twentieth-century success focused on technology and knowledge exchange around design, management, and organizational innovations. This new stage brought exponential growth, and with the changing economy, technology sped up and facilitated many of the effects of capitalism described in Chapter 3. As long as there was economic growth, the success of some parts of the production process with deleterious effects on other parts seemed to go unnoticed. According to one executive, "Impersonality provides the psychological distance necessary to make what managers call 'hard choices'."[29] By transferring parts of the production process to facilities overseas, there is an increasing gap between management and the goods produced. Whereas, in the 1890s, Americans hired locally, by 1980, 80 percent of U.S. corporate revenues came from overseas production.[30]

For managers, the geographical distance translates into psychological distance. It is much easier for managers to lay off labor in other countries and also to feel removed from the final product. According to Robert Jackall in *Moral Mazes*:

> Social insulation permits and encourages a lofty viewpoint that, on its face, "respects the dignity of workers," but seems devoid of the feel of the texture of workers' lives and of the gut-level empathy that such knowledge can bring.
>
> At the highest levels of Weft, as in most big corporations, workers become wholly abstract categories. A divisional president in the same company, from the vantage point of his northern office 800 miles away, talks about closing some plants to maximize the productive utilization of capital under the spur of regulations . . . : "Well, actually, I don't worry about the workers. From my perspective, I don't intend to divest our total overall productive capacity because that would lead to other problems. I presume that those workers who lose their jobs because you close a particular plant will be able to find a job somewhere."[31]

Rather than work as an extension of emotional relations, technology breaks the tie between individuals making decisions about labor and the labor workforce. With emotional barriers removed, it is easier to engage in instrumental rationality, solely weighing financial costs and benefits of business decisions.

As a society, we are confronting one of the most significant ethical issues of our modern warfare program. Drone technology echoes the challenges of a disconnection between our job responsibilities and our identities. Studies of our Air National Guardsmen suggest that the remote killing of targets brings psychological consequences on par with posttraumatic stress disorder.

However, the remote aspect of combat brings particular stresses unique to this type of high-tech warfare. In this instance, remote pilots linger before and after the attack:

> "You do stick around and see the aftermath of what you did, and that does personalize the fight," said Col. Chris Chambliss, commander of the active-duty 432nd Wing at Creech Air Force Base, Nev. "You have a pretty good optical picture of the individuals on the ground. The images can be pretty graphic, pretty vivid, and those are the things we try to offset. We know that some folks have, in some cases, problems."[32]

Another challenging aspect is the absence of camaraderie associated with this type of combat. As described by Air Force Lt. Col. Robert P. Herz, pilots put missiles in chimneys to destroy "bad guys," and within an hour, they are picking up their kids from school. This regularized disconnect leaves pilots vulnerable to posttraumatic stress disorder, especially because they are experiencing the war in an isolated and especially fragmented way.

6. Technology and Polarization

Sunstein addresses problems associated with internet communication technology. In a phenomenon he describes as the "daily me," Sunstein points out that most people associate freedom with the right to tailor websites and surf independently of imposed sites and propaganda. This type of thinking suggests that as long as there is no censorship or an imposed agenda, then the individual can experience the height of freedom. Access to so much information promises new frontiers in terms of diversity and understanding differences in our society. This seems very promising from the perspective of democracy. However, Sunstein cautions that:

> it is a view that underlies much current thinking about free speech. But it is badly misconceived. Freedom consists not simply in preference satisfaction but also in the chance to have preferences and beliefs formed under decent conditions—in the ability to have preferences formed after exposure to a sufficient amount of information, and also to an appropriately wide and diverse range of options.[33]

Sunstein conveys the extent to which people online tailor their news, social circles, and general exposure to the seemingly infinite possibilities. This tailoring process reinforces existing views and often contributes to entrenching polarization between views. While we imagine the cultivation of a more liberal society through exposure to diverse views, just as likely, the internet deepens existing divisions. Contrary to an ideal vision of increasing exposure and, therefore, tolerance, web-based interactions just as likely, and perhaps more likely, divide us.

Sunstein identifies some solutions to the problems associated with the "daily me" phenomenon. These solutions are a good introduction to my reconceptualized and renewed social justice as a foundation for technology.

SOCIAL JUSTICE AS THE FOUNDATION FOR TECHNOLOGY

With the increasing exposure and vulnerabilities of people on the internet, most especially young people, it is likely that we will see more informal as well as formal regulation. At the same time as authoritarian regimes face scrutiny for political censorship of the internet, more liberal societies are sorting out a new balance between unregulated freedom of speech and protection of others from defamation. Apart from the most extreme crises of social media impropriety, Sunstein proposes some valuable remedies to the "daily me" phenomenon:

1. Deliberative domains;
2. Disclosure of relevant conduct by producers of communication;
3. Voluntary self-regulation;
4. Economic subsidies, including publicly subsidized programming and Websites;
5. "must-carry" rules, in the form of links, imposed on the most popular Websites, designed to produce exposure to substantive questions; and
6. "must-carry" rules, also in the form of links, imposed on highly partisan Websites, designed to ensure that viewers learn about sites with opposing views, perhaps through linked sites and perhaps through hyperlinks.[34]

These recommendations are promising. The idea of deliberative domains has been made manifest in chat rooms and even more elaborate sites, but if it were tied to membership and commitment to engage regularly, openly, and for an extended period of time, then it could be closer to an ideal public square than an anonymous chat room. If signing on to a website included acknowledgement and acceptance of oversight, then additional transparency could include disclosure around conduct. Voluntary self-regulation is ideal, but it requires magnanimous individual decision making that is not realistic without incentives or binding enforcement. Public websites could definitely provide platforms for these healthy exchanges with accompanying guarantees of oversight and protections. Like the lock sign that guarantees some sort of protection of your credit card information, these websites could offer a visible sign of particular standards, and thereby set the trend and be a welcome refuge for people looking for credible information and exchange. The "must-carry" rules that complete Sunstein's list extend standards of fair play into the internet world. While ideal in terms of imposing alternative views and bigger questions, it is far too gargantuan a task to expect government to enforce and far too unlikely to meet compliance without effective enforcement.

The challenging aspects of technology have been covered throughout this chapter, and they emphasize the extent to which technology has encroached upon our time, our brains, and our relationships. At its worst, we have become "pancake people" skirting along the surfaces of each other's lives preferring to spread ourselves widely with many "friends" regardless of the quality of our online friendships. We flit through content online that seems to make us smarter while it more evidently reinforces how scattered we have become. Patricia Greenfield is a developmental psychologist, who describes the effects of this type of engagement: "new strengths in visual-spatial intelligence" go hand in hand with a weakening of our capacities for the kind of "deep processing" that underpins "mindful knowledge acquisition, inductive analysis, critical thinking, imagination, and reflection."[35] And while it is possible to be a conventional reader with a fleeting, flitting mind, just as it is possible to be a deep thinker online, the habit of online activities "encourages and rewards"[36] and thereby elicits a generalizable shift in our cognitive and emotional capabilities.

Finally, in terms of our relationships, Turkle had imagined that the internet and social media could be an ideal setting to "practice" and to "learn" our identities, a veritable "identity workshop."[37] However, she imagined a very different and broader context within which technology might be the first step, or certainly a small part, and where these tentative identities developed in chat rooms and on blogs would then be practiced and learned through interpersonal, physical relationships. Social media has cultivated a deep loneliness that can be repaired by social justice. Technology has disaggregated our lives, and morality has changed significantly as a result. Tapscott argues that today's "Net" generation is at least as, if not more, moral than previous ones. From his research, he generalizes that Net Geners "expect other people to have integrity, too. They do not want to work for, or buy a product from, an organization that is dishonest. They also expect companies to be considerate of their customers, employees, and the communities in which they operate . . . young people look for companies they can trust. They have a low tolerance for companies that lie."[38] However, instead of morality defined comprehensively and by mechanisms of social accountability, morality is confined to closed systems that are self-selected. Not buying a product because a company lies may be evidence of one's integrity, but it is fairly thin integrity that feels more transactional and self-serving than relational. Tapscott acknowledges that the integrity frame for a Net-gener is more about telling the truth than it is about doing good and holding people or companies accountable in terms of social responsibility.[39] Clearly another problem with online virtues is that most often the exchanges remain anonymous. Ultimately, technology needs to remain as a tool for people, and social engagement deserves priority in terms of its collective accountability over individualized surfing and the practice of calling out companies.

The synergy of human interaction is the foundation necessary for successful human interaction. The less we interact with each other the less likely we are to be good at it. Without eliminating technology, we need to recognize that ultimately people are attached to the words and identities created online. If we want healthier online interactions, then we need to humanize them. Rather than letting the instruments dehumanize us, we need ways of engagement that bring our people selves into the technological sphere, not some fragmented, polarized, undefined, and unaccountable self. Sunstein offers different measures to create new behaviors online, but they focus on different versions of regulation and censorship.

We need social justice as a space to consider our human selves, distinct from our virtual selves, and to practice and engage in a sphere that nurtures values to carry into our technology space. We need a space to hold each other accountable for the hurts and sorrows conveyed in cyberspace. The wave of confessional websites online is an interesting consideration. On the one hand, they achieve a version of social accountability and post confession reintegration. However, without the certainty of human face-to-face connection, there is significant doubt that lingers. Like Ellen with her grandmother, the medium and its uncertainty means we question the depth and commitment and therefore the credibility of our interactions online. Especially when we are considering emotional relationships and social commitments, this becomes particularly uncomfortable to settle for the cyberworld. Information needs a social context to make it meaningful and relevant. Social justice can be a foundation for technology to be meaningful and relevant in important ways. And without social justice, technology risks deterioration into some of the worst patterns described above. The pace of technology, and the practice of interacting through communication technologies, denies the essential role of relationships to enhance the human condition. Technology offers more communication but not necessarily healthy, meaningful communication. Certainly, communication is part of relationships, but we need much more face-to-face communication as the foundation for better relationships. Only from a social justice foundation can social networking and technology become highly successful tools of engagement.

NOTES

1. John Adams, Dissertation on the Canon and Feudal Law, 1756. Patriot Post. http://patriotpost.us/quotes. Accessed July 26, 2013.
2. Daniel Goleman, *Emotional Intelligence* (New York: Bantam Books, 1994), 36.
3. Goleman, *Emotional Intelligence*, 37.
4. Robert Kuttner, *Everything for Sale* (Chicago: University of Chicago Press, 1996), 25.
5. Kuttner, *Everything for Sale*, 26.
6. Nicholas Carr, *What the Internet is Doing to our Brains* (New York: W.W. Norton & Company, 2011), 86.

7. Marc Prensky, "Do They Really *Think* Differently?" in *The Digital Divide*, ed. Mark Bauerlein (London: Penguin Books, 2011), 12.
8. Marc Prensky, "Digital Natives, Digital Immigrants," in Bauerlein, *The Digital Divide*, 3–11.
9. Sherry Turkle, Shakespeare quoted in *Alone Together:Why we expect more from technology and less from each other* (New York: Basic Books, 2011), 227.
10. Alexander Gerschenkron, *Economic Backwardness in Historical Perspective* (Boston: Belknap Press of Harvard University Press, 1962).
11. Steven, K. Vogel, *Japan Remodeled: How Government and Industry are Reforming Japanese Capitalism* (Ithaca: Cornell University Press, 2006), 33.
12. For good examples, see Terry Lynn Karl, *The Paradox of Plenty Oil Booms and Petro-States* (Berkeley: University of California Press, 1997).
13. Ernest Gellner, *Nations and Nationalism* (London: Blackwell, 1983).
14. Timur Kuran, *Private Truths, Public Lies. The Social Consequences of Preference Falsification* (Boston: Harvard University Press, 1997).
15. Courtney Weaver, "The Philosophical Punks on Trial for Blaspheming Putin," *Financial Times*, August 19, 2012, 9.
16. Julia Ioffe, "The Blog Society," *Financial Times*, December 17/18, 2011, 9.
17. Christopher Caldwell, "Ivory Towers will be Toppled by an Online 'Tsunami,'" *Financial Times*, August 11/12, 2012, 9.
18. Thomas Friedman, *The World is Flat* (New York: Farrar, Straus and Girous, 2005), 492.
19. Don Tapscott, "The Eight Net Gen Norms," in Bauerlein, *The Digital Divide*, 140.
20. Valerie Francisco, "'The Internet is Magic': Technology, Intimacy and Transnational Families," *Critical Sociology*. Forthcoming.
21. Valerie Francisco, "'The Internet is Magic.'"
22. Teju Cole, "The White Savior Industrial Complex," *Atlantic*, March 21, 2012.
23. Carr, *What the Internet is Doing to our Brains*, 9.
24. Nicholas Carr, "Is Google Making Us Stupid," in Bauerlein, *The Digital Divide*, 66.
25. Carr, *What the Internet is Doing to our Brains*, 91.
26. Turkle, *Alone Together*, 14.
27. Turkle, *Alone Together*, 227.
28. Turkle, *Alone Together*, 16.
29. Robert Jackall, *Moral Mazes: The World of Corporate Managers* (Oxford: Oxford University Press, 1988), 134.
30. Walter LaFeber, *Michael Jordan and the New Global Capitalism* (New York: W.W. & Norton Company, 2002).
31. Jackall, *Moral Mazes*, 133.
32. Scott Lindlaw, "UAV Operators Suffer War Stress," *Associated Press*, August 7, 2008.
33. Cass Sunstein, *Republic* (Princeton: Princeton University Press, 2001), 50.
34. Sunstein, *Republic*, 169.
35. Carr, *What the Internet is Doing to our Brains*, 141.
36. Carr, *What the Internet is Doing to our Brains*, 116.
37. Turkle, *Alone Together*, 12.
38. Tapscott, "The Eight Net Gen Norms," 144.
39. Tapscott, "The Eight Net Gen Norms," 144.

5 Religion and Social Justice

> We have no government armed with power capable of contending with human passions unbridled by morality and religion. Avarice, ambition, revenge, or gallantry, would break the strongest cards of our Constitution as a whale goes through a net. Our Constitution was made only for a moral and religious people. It is wholly inadequate to the government of any other.
>
> —John Adams[1]

INTRODUCTION

Up to this point, the chapters analyze social justice in terms of the prevalent systems that characterize the United States. Democracy, capitalism, and technology dominate our social relationships, and this book argues for carving out a sphere of social engagement independent of these activities and interest areas. At the same time, with its capacity for institutionalizing transparency, deliberation, and compromise, democracy is most compatible with social justice as a *social* process. Capitalism also brings opportunities as well as challenges, but in spite of its complex outcomes, capitalism is neither the enemy of social justice nor a healthy foundation for it. In the cases of democracy and capitalism, social justice can be the remedy for the weaknesses in each of these areas. Similarly, technology offers at least as many potentially beneficial outcomes as risks. Here again, social justice cultivates a sphere independent of these activities. In this way, social justice can become a key to reform and maintenance of social relationships, and it can become the foundation for decisions and activities in the political, economic, and technological realms.

Rather than the current trends in which advocates of social justice approach democracy and capitalism as the focus for the solutions to their causes, social justice renews community and becomes a better long-run solution for the prevailing weaknesses of both democracy and capitalism. Religion is another sphere of our society that needs to be considered in relation to social justice. Like the other spheres, religion has been a vehicle for the support and opposition of social justice advocates. Like the other spheres, social justice can serve and strengthen religion, particularly if it remains independent of religion.

This chapter follows the pattern of the previous chapters, in this case, outlining the ways in which religion can be associated with social justice outcomes. Most religions have a rich tradition for advocating issues that fit into the social justice camp, as well as principles of faith that support the reconceptualized understanding of social justice. Ultimately, the best characteristics that carry through most religions make it an ideal fount for the social justice project. However, in the pattern of the previous chapters, I also address the ways in which religion has been the source of injustice. Most significantly, religion has become too politicized. By focusing its resources on political outcomes, it loses credibility. Religious leaders and organizations participate too readily in the political game, pursuing policy outcomes that reflect their interests as much as their spiritual values. After laying out the contradictory empirical evidence, in the final section, I explore the ways in which my reconceptualized social justice can assuage weaknesses of religion in America today. Analysis here unpacks the way in which religion can comfortably become more aligned with social justice and less aligned with political positions. As I have described it, social justice is also a place where religions can come together and must come together to sort out agreements and disagreements. Social justice is an arena for healthy dialogue and bonding in a way that removes the political focus of religious disagreements, too often escalating rather than defusing potential conflicts.

RELIGION AND ITS VIRTUES

1. Action

The argument in this book emphasizes that far too many positions, often contradictory, are crammed under the umbrella of social justice today. However, there has been a comfortable consensus around some of its historical heroes, and many of these heroes found inspiration and guidance from religion. From their biographies, we learn that some sort of religious conversion, often toward deepening faith rather than switching faith practices, preceded the conviction to serve the marginalized. DeYoung describes the lives of prominent social justice activists, such as Dietrich Bonhoeffer, Malcolm X, and Aung San Suu Kyi. Each of these leaders framed his or her efforts by the spiritual direction of faith traditions,[2] and DeYoung calls them mystic activists. Each of these activists experienced a religious conversion that grounded his or her efforts to fight for change within their respective societies. Bonhoeffer was born into an academic family that was religious but did not participate in organized religion. He became a theologian in his early twenties, which led to his religious conversion into a practicing

Christian. Similarly, Malcolm X was born and raised in a religious family but a family that did not formally tie their religious beliefs or practice to religious institutions. He describes his own conversion in a way that carries through the experiences of other mystic activists as well: "I still marvel at how swiftly my previous life's thinking pattern slid away from me, like snow off a roof. It is as though someone else I knew of had lived by hustling and crime. I would be startled to catch myself thinking in a remote way of my earlier self as another person."[3] Aung San Suu Kyi practiced Buddhism throughout her life but experienced a deepening conversion toward a "living faith" with daily practice and commitment.

Each of these individuals connected their religious conversion with a mystical experience and simultaneously a focused commitment to worldly issues. For Bonhoeffer, it was a commitment to "the view from below," and he wrote about this comprehensive worldview: "We have for once learnt to see the great events of world history from below, from the perspective of the outcast, the suspects, the maltreated, the powerless, the oppressed, the reviled—in short, from the perspective of those who suffer."[4] His living faith led to persecution and death in defense of the Jews suffering under Hitler's Germany. For Malcolm X, conversion to Islam led him to deny racial hierarchies and the contemporary debates around integration or separation. As part of his life work as an activist, he embraced the fundamental and all-relevant equality of individuals as human beings. Aung San Suu Kyi described an inner strength that defied challenge and yet also brought forward a heightened sensitivity to the most subtle dynamics in struggle.

Each found inspiration from scripture and religious doctrine, fought for the marginalized in society, and rebelled against existing hierarchies of social, economic, and political exploitation. As examples of activism, spiritual inspiration defined their commitment to societal change. Each of these heroes was deeply immersed in the problems of their society, and often a particular social problem was the catalyst for spiritual growth, which in turn inspired action. None of the leaders considered a reclusive life as part of their spiritual fulfillment. While religions offer a monastic path for spiritual growth, these individuals tied their faith to an urgent demand for action.

In the U.S. context, religion plays a special role in terms of mobilizing around social problems. This special role has been recognized throughout history from the Founding Fathers to contemporary political, economic, and social life. When dealing with our most unsettling social problems, political leaders rely on religious institutions as partners. When acknowledging the most daunting social problems, our political leaders readily call upon citizens to rely on faith. Bush's faith-based initiative institutionalized a partnership of federal funds for religious organizations to contribute their solutions of social problems. Introduced in 2001, the faith-based initiative acknowledged the many ways that religious organizations are particularly well situated to combat issues of poverty, homelessness, and drug addiction. It opened up access for churches, synagogues, mosques, and temples to obtain federal funding for programs to solve these social problems. The government sought to capitalize on the strength and presence and impact of religious organizations. At the same time, it carefully maintained boundaries between the charity functions and evangelizing functions. An individual couldn't be compelled to attend a church service or listen to religious doctrine as part of obtaining a meal or staying in a shelter, for example. The balance was critical and controversial, but the overwhelming impression of the executive order was affirmation of the obvious and unique role of religious institutions. There is a drive and call to action in terms of society's most pressing problems that is evident across religions and amenable to engagement with those who suffer.

The legacy of giving, sharing, and assisting those who are marginalized has deep roots in most religious organizations. While social justice does not require religious affiliation, religious groups offer organizational strength in terms of resources, mobilization, and commitment. And as discussed above, religions place collective concerns for humanity at the core of their identities. To be spiritual in most contexts means a movement in one's thinking toward the undefined "other." Regardless of faith, to practice one's faith includes giving to others, to consider your own identity and interests in relation to others' circumstances, and to measure life by standards other than politics or the market. For the reconceptualized social justice, this empathetic and open engagement is critical. Therefore, spiritual identity has a special affinity to social justice at the same time that I assert the possibility for social justice to repair religion as it is experienced by many in the United States today.

2. Conscience

The market forces of globalization maximize choice. Individuals have unlimited opportunities to consume products, buy services, and participate in online social networks built upon a very narrow band, or single interest. The market does not define moral limits for our choices, pushing a culture of consumption while maintaining neutrality about the content of what we consume. We can be entirely disaggregated, disconnected, and unfulfilled but continuously affirmed by market principles. Typically, religions present a cerebral and spiritual space to evaluate the conditions of our choices, our impact on the lives of others, and the possibilities for different choices in the future. Religion is neither the sole space nor the necessary one for this type of conscience calling, but religious spaces do regularly accord attention to individual consciences—a deeper part of the self that reflects and affects decision-making. A conscience pushes individuals to weigh decisions by a yardstick that moves beyond immediate gratification, beyond transaction, and beyond current comforts. Jonathan Sacks describes the dilemma for individuals who not only act in spite of their consciences but no longer have places to cultivate their consciences. According to Sacks:

> We have delegated away much of what matters in our lives, partly to governments, police forces, judges, courts, social workers, managers and teachers, in part to therapists, counselors, advisers, coaches and gurus, each of whom we pay, through taxation or fees, to manage our affirms, relationships, conflicts or emotions better than we can or have time to do. This constitutes a massive loss of sovereignty over our lives, and it means that when things go wrong, as at times they must, we are liable to despair, because our destiny now rests in other hands, not our own. That is the weakness of contracting out large aspects of our lives, as against assuming personal and moral responsibility.[5]

Most religions include conscience as a core motivation for human behavior. Conscience, as the spiritual muscle guiding morality, is a meaningful individual mechanism used to address the social impact of decisions. What becomes critical is that past, present, and future decisions are evaluated on principles other than those defined by the market or government. The terms of the market present conscience, or any constraint on consumption, as an arbitrary hindrance to pleasure through consumption. From the market yardstick, conscience is a leash on freedom to consume. However, for those who attach themselves to some faith, conscience not only connects us to one another more meaningfully, but it actually provides the ultimate check to preserve our individual autonomy as well. Through conscience, we can free ourselves from the Promethean experience of the market place, and we explore a different source of freedom from unbridled consumption. A conscience cultivates meaning to our day-to-day lives, and it cultivates a comprehension of seemingly disconnected aspects of daily life. The religious source of individual autonomy brings us closer together in terms of feeling our interconnectedness and engagement—the foundation shared by my version of a reconceptualized social justice. Religion is neither unique nor necessary, as explored at the end of the chapter, but its affinity in terms of the social justice project is undeniable.

3. Equality

Religions convey a fundamental equality of individuals, whether it is in terms of creation and first beginnings, in terms of a God or gods, in terms of the afterlife, or typically some combination of all of these. It is the human world that structures people into more or less capable, competent, and deserving. A religious context reminds and reinforces the arbitrariness of these divisions and inequalities. In ancient times, Jewish society acknowledged this inevitable social grading, and as a remedy, it also introduced measures to reassert fundamental equality. The Jubilee was enacted every fifty years and removed all debts incurred by individuals in relation to others, and it redistributed all accumulated property and profits. Borrowing from the ideal concept of the Jubilee (which my colleague in theology assures me was more idealized in scripture than realized in society) there is an international movement to introduce debt forgiveness to developing countries. Clearly, debt and its forgiveness are not new realities, and religions continue to offer criticism of the social tendency to ratchet inequality and to equate that inequality with anything other than historical contingency or happenstance.

The resistance to debt forgiveness emphasizes the extent to which we have become tied to our privileged positions, but most likely tied to the identities we associate with our privileged position. Students fall easily into a script of underdevelopment that emphasizes corruption within society, violent conflict, and rampant borrowing. From a young person's perspective, these popularly attributed *causes* then carry legitimacy as explanation for the outcomes of poverty, famine, and disease. Through this lens, countries have been sorted by objective criteria over which any group could have or should have success. It is easy for students in the Western world to attribute individuals in indebted countries with equality of opportunity, which then slips into a righteous justification for inequality of outcomes. Both at a domestic and international level, then, helping individuals becomes much more about charity and kindness to those who are "disadvantaged" by their own choices and their own actions. Within this framework, aid becomes an extension of "our" goodness rather than a responsibility tied to "our" collective decisions historically and currently. Today's society empowers individuals in ways that justify the hierarchy upon which we order ourselves. Rather than good luck, bad luck, good decisions, bad decisions, we carry social, economic, and political status as *value* and identity signifiers.

Similar to the reckoning and leveling of resources through the Jubilee, in Caesar's time, a "Triumph" was both a march of exaltation for a military general and a persistent reminder of his shared humanity. As part of the march of a victorious general throughout Rome, a slave was appointed to walk closely behind the victorious general. In the historical fiction account, the slave's responsibility was to raise a gilded laurel wreath above the general's head and also to whisper continually in the General's ear "Remember thou are mortal."[6] The practice in Caesar's time was meant to caution against arrogance and misinterpreting worldly success with some innate sense of being better and above the rest of humanity. In more recent times, a similar reminder was expressed by the visionary peacemaker Mohandas Gandhi: "We are all, first and foremost, human beings and we must relate to one another on that naked basis."[7] And in today's society, religion is one of the few places left where we self-consciously and explicitly remind ourselves of an essential equality that is not predicated upon our good luck, our families, our decisions, nor our institutionalized trajectory of good outcomes.

Apart from religious doctrine that emphasizes equality, there are also very few places in the world today where one is anonymous in terms of economic status. For example, even shopping at Whole Foods as opposed to the local grocery chain immediately sets one apart in terms of socioeconomic standing. While economic efficiencies in the travel industry have brought a great "flattening" trend, the act of hopping on a plane with everything from luggage to seat assignments, offers strong cues about economic status. Even further, for those in the working world, we all live fairly isolated lives in terms of limited exposure to those outside of our similar economic position. The consumption choices we make strongly reinforce those income differentiations and segmentations rather than exposing us to different economic levels and livelihoods. Certainly the particular neighborhood one lives in is an obvious reflection of economic standing, but I used to praise public education as the one mechanism for bringing together people of different socioeconomic statuses. However, I am now more aware that in spite of sending my kids to school in the public education system, their school receives tens of thousands of dollars more in support through parental donations than the public school down the street. Clearly, even public education is no longer "the great equalizer" in terms of society.

Perhaps public transportation might be considered one setting where individuals from dramatically different backgrounds, experiences, and positions economically, socially, and politically comingle, but clearly there are fewer places for this type of exchange. Sandel describes the decline in public spaces with a particular lament about the shift in sports from civic role to its insipid marketization:

> Like few other institutions in American life, baseball, football, basketball, and hockey are a source of social glue and civic pride. From Yankee Stadium in New York to Candlestick Park in San Francisco, sports stadiums are the cathedrals of our civil religion, public spaces that gather people from different walks of life in rituals of loss and hope, profanity and prayer . . . the public character of the setting imparts a civic teaching— that we are all in this together, that for a few hours at least, we share a sense of place and civic pride. As stadiums become less like landmarks and more like billboards, their public character fades. So, perhaps, do the social bonds and civic sentiments they inspire.[8]

When I look around our church, I realize that it may be one of the few remaining places where members of different classes actually "mix." Parks and public transportation may be places of interaction, but it is much more sporadic and unintentional than the celebration or shared experience around a sporting event, or a sermon, for example. Obviously, with regards to religious institutions, a neighborhood effect remains, but it is likely much looser around a church than a school. Whereas schools have strict property constraints, you can join any church regardless of your residence location.

At the beginning of service, there is a meet and greet with those around you, and I always appreciate that after shaking hands with someone it is an easy slip into conversation after the service. These types of interactions include different languages, different generations, and I suspect different socioeconomic statuses. Likely, individuals' radar detections for these types of social divisions don't disappear, but the church and interpersonal exchange within the church mutes them significantly. This type of equalizing condition is an important part of social justice. While my version of social justice doesn't mandate any redistribution of wealth or other resources, it is critical to carve out spaces where people of very different economic statuses interact and listen to each other. Rather than reinforcing difference through isolation, social justice promises to cultivate the ideal of human equality through engagement.

4. Values

Any religion offers a set of values at least somewhat independent of the economy and independent of the political system. Even though religious groups today actively engage in economic activities and care about economic viability, the spiritual focus pushes away from the hyper-market fetishism. Similarly, even though religious groups participate in lobbying for particular policies that reflect interests, the spiritual focus turns away from competitiveness. Increasingly, the pushing away from consumerism and political competition is more ideal than reality, but the religious sphere is one place where one can anticipate alternative values defining human identity and meaning. For example, the Dalai Lama stresses the importance of shared values, such as compassion. Compassion can be conveyed as empathy, respect, dignity, or generosity, but in spite of any conceptual variants, "all the great religions stress compassion as a fundamental spiritual value. Whether it is in scriptural prescriptions for leading a good life, in the ideal of life that is admired and propagated, or in the exemplary lives of many of the remarkable individuals of different faiths, past and present (some of whom I have been privileged to meet), I have no doubt that compassion lies at the heart of all of these religions."[9] Similarly, there is a profound convergence around a fundamental ethical principle to treat people fairly and to practice restraint along the lines of The Golden Rule.

> Hinduism: "*This is the sum of duty; do naught onto others what you would not have them do unto you*" (Mahabharata 5:1517)
>
> Judaism: "*What is hateful to you, do not do to your fellowman. This is the entire Law; all the rest is commentary*" (Hillel, in the Talmud for the Sabbath 31a)
>
> Zoroastrianism: "*That nature alone is good which refrains from doing to another whatsoever is not good for itself*" (Dadisten—I-dinik 94:5)

Buddhism: "*Since others too care for their own selves, those who care for themselves should not hurt others*" (Udanavarga 5:20)

Jainism: "*A man should wander about treating all creatures as he him self would be treated*" (Sutrakritanga 1.11:33)

Daoism: "*Regard your neighbor's gain as your gain, and your neighbor's loss as your own loss*" (Tai-shang Kan-ying P'ien).

Confucianism: "*Do not do to others what you would not like yourself. Then there will be no resentment against you, either in the family or in the state*"(Analects 12:2).

Christianity: "*So in everything, do to others what you would have them do to you, for this sums up the Law and the Prophets*" (Matt. 7:12)

Islam: "*No one of you is a believer until he desires for his brother that which he desires for himself*" (Hadith of al-Nawawi 13).[10]

These fundamentals cross particular religious doctrine and traditions and provide a foundation of values relevant for the practice of social justice as a type of social engagement. Certainly, the spiritual dimension of religion invites individuals to measure themselves from a yardstick for living that is distinct from market consumerism and the political process, and not oriented around competition.

Compared to previous civilizations, today's society is much gentler, even to those who are harmful to society: executions are rare, slavery is outlawed, and prison conditions are reasonably good. In this sense, we acknowledge Western civilization as socially advanced compared to other civilizations in history. However, as much as there are signs of progress, we are also a very punitive society. It seems to be a part of every parenting manual to teach our children that there are consequences to bad behavior or decisions. One of the greatest virtues we attach to mistakes is that they won't be repeated. Perhaps, then, it is not surprising that our society has become masterful at avoiding the public acknowledgment of mistakes. Great cover-ups can follow, and often with disastrous consequences, but we don't address the potential root of the problem, which is a collective unwillingness to let people admit mistakes. Religion is a sphere that offers this space to acknowledge that part of being human is to make mistakes. And then almost simultaneously, it offers forgiveness to each other for these mistakes. Whether through moments of silent prayer or collective prayer, through offering peace to one another, or breaking spiritual bread with one another, we admit our frailties in rituals that carry us through honesty to public accountability to forgiveness. Beyond sin and forgiveness as part of the ritualized service, usually once a week, there are places for more extreme admissions of guilt and victimization.

Most religious communities offer many vehicles for spiritual healing and confession, like the truth and reconciliation commissions, which represent an ideal example of my reconceptualized social justice in the chapter on implementing social justice. What is different about these religious confessions is that they are often private with individual accountability to clergy, rather than public, with the potential for collective accountability and responsibility. For Catholics, the responsibilities of the clergy include serving as the intermediary and representative of the community. Social justice demands more in terms of public accountability, but the fact that religious practices invite acknowledgement of human frailties and injustices facilitates social justice.

Below is a summary of the conceptualization of compassion across religions. It emphasizes our shared values in ways that highlight the possibility for coexistence, but even greater, the possibility of collective harmony.

a. Hinduism

Within Hinduism, there is the understanding that humans seek pleasures and worldly successes, like wealth and power, but these outcomes limit our full potential. Beyond kama (desire) and worldly success (artha), there are two other principles that guide Hindu faith. Truth (dharma) and spiritual freedom (moksha) also form the fully human life, and "of these, the first two constitute the path of desire, the second two constitute the path of renunciation." This renunciation brings us to the totality of reality, "a state where the individual becomes one with the reality itself."[11] The process of desire and renunciation depends upon openness as a characteristic feature of the practice of Hinduism throughout its history. Through openness, we deepen our compassion, which is also a central characteristic of Hinduism. Found in the Dharmastra of Gautama, compassion is listed as the first of the eight virtues of the self (8:22–3).[12] The Bhagavad Gita (5:25) states that those "whose doubts have been dispelled, who have restrained themselves, who delight in the welfare of all beings, reach the nirvana of Brahman."[13] Egoistic concerns are oppressive, whereas freedom comes from transcending self-concern.

For Hindus, compassion is a goal and quality of an "enlightened" being. The social/ethical is not tangential to individual self-fulfillment but clearly fundamental to individual self-fulfillment.

b. Buddhism

For Buddhists, the individual and society are completely interdependent. According to Payutto, "The Buddhadhamma sees the internal life of the individual as intimately related to the external life of society and holds that values in the two realms are inseparably connected, compatible, and are, in fact, one and the same thing."[14]

Along with devotional symbols and meditations, rituals with water are particularly important as blessings for New Year celebrations, for weddings, and for healing. After the fall of the Khmer Rouge in Cambodia, walks for peace included spontaneous water cleansing. Rituals heal, but fundamental to Buddhism is an abnegation of justice as conceptualized by Westerners. Buddhist emphasis on collective identity, empathy, and fulfillment in response to our version of injustice is powerfully conveyed by Nhat Hanh's poem, "Please Call Me by My True Names":

> I am the mayfly metamorphosing on the surface of the river, and I am the bird which, when spring comes, arrives in time to eat the mayfly.
>
> I am the frog swimming happily in the clear water of a pond, and I am also the grass-snake who approaching in silence, feeds itself on the frog.
>
> I am the child in Uganda, all skin and bones, my legs as thin as bamboo sticks, and I am the arms merchant, selling deadly weapons to Uganda.
>
> I am the 12-year old girl, refugee on a small boat, who throws herself into the ocean after being raped by a sea pirate, and I am the pirate, my heart not yet capable of seeing and loving.[15]

The poet's own commentary is further revealing: "In my meditation I saw that if I had been born in the village of the pirate and raised in the same conditions as he was, I am now the pirate. There is a great likelihood that I would become a pirate. I cannot condemn myself as easily."[16] Nhat Hanh is describing a perspective and a place where we remove blame and judgment from the individual and accept collective responsibility.

When Aung San Suu Kyi was asked to define Buddhism, she identified enlightenment to be used in the service of others. Greed, hatred, delusion, ignorance, clinging, selfishness, and heedlessness are all challenges to social connection, of course, but they are also barriers to individual self-fulfillment.[17] For Buddhists, empathy is part of human nature, and so when we disconnect from others we become uneasy precisely because we have strayed from the natural condition. As a natural condition, my good life depends upon the goodness of your life, and in this vital connection, there is no "I" independent of "we."

c. Islam

Islam emphasizes a way of life that should not be separated from the individual's spiritual beliefs or from his or her commitments to society. Work is also inextricably connected to spiritual fulfillment and must be approached as part of one's religious devotion. Ritual fasting (sawm), prayers (salah), ceremonial profession of faith (Shahadah), and pilgrimage (haj) ceremony are central pillars of Islam. Zakat or almsgiving is also central and formalizes charity as an essential act of living faith and joins other religions in this emphasis on compassion. Living faith in all aspects of life is emphasized. Qutb articulates that religious life cannot be separated from social life, including politics and economy.[18] He says: "Such is the position of Islam in regard to works and faith; and hence it is clear that there can be no separation between the faith and the world, or between theology and social practice."[19]

d. Judaism

These simple statements from the Old Testament elegantly summarize a way to live the good life:

1. You shall have no other gods before me.
2. You shall not make for yourself an idol, whether in the form of anything that is in heaven above, or that is on the earth beneath, or that is in the water under the earth.
3. You shall not make wrongful use of the name of the Lord your God.
4. Remember the Sabbath day and keep it holy. Six days you shall labor and so all your work. But the seventh day is a Sabbath to the Lord your God; you shall not do any work.
5. Honor your father and your mother.
6. You shall not murder.
7. You shall not commit adultery.
8. You shall not steal.
9. You shall not bear false witness against your neighbor.
10. You shall not covet your neighbor's house; you shall not covet your neighbor's wife, or male or female slave, or ox, or donkey, or anything that belongs to your neighbor.[20]

The rules for living explicitly acknowledge each individual's essential roles within community. "Love the Lord your God with all your heart and with all your soul and with all your strength" (Deut. 6:5).[21] This directed proclamation to individuals invokes a great tradition of collective responsibility and emphasizes the practices that then cultivate values for a good life. Rather than a very defined and singular relationship between the individual and God, it is a call for compassion between individuals. Compassion not only protects, but it reveals truth. Most importantly, it opens and deepens the relationship with God. The Hebrew word for compassion comes from "womb" and conjures the intimacy of mother with child in the broader terms of interpersonal relationships.

Time and memory are central aspects of Judaism, and with time and memory, there is a deep collective responsibility that resonates as part of living faith. The label of "chosen people" has been misinterpreted as arrogance and instigating inequality among groups. In fact, scholars reinforce that the understanding of the Jews as "chosen people" implies the overarching responsibility to carry human suffering in order to redeem all humanity.

e. Catholicism

Since 1891 and Pope Leo XIII, social teaching has been a central part of Catholicism. In Leo's encyclical letter, *On the Condition of Labor*, he addressed the poor working conditions of laborers. He emphasized the importance of a meaningful and just relationship between workers, property, and the state. By this letter, Pope Leo announced the relevance and the importance of the Church in order to tend to all aspects of injustice in society. In 1971, the world's bishops wrote *Justice in the World*. It demanded action and expanded the sphere of relevant action to include liberation of the human race from every oppressive situation. With more specific focus, the U.S. Catholics Bishops addressed the issues of economic disparity and peace in separate letters: the Bishops' Peace Pastoral of 1983 *(The Challenge of Peace: God's Promise and Our Response)* and the Economics Pastoral of 1986 *(Economic Justice for All: Catholic Social Teaching and the U.S. Economy)*. De Berri and Hug describe how the letters were received by many as radical, especially in terms of the willingness to intervene in seemingly political and contemporary issues.[22] However, rather than a new calling for members of the Church to work for change within their societies, de Berri and Hug trace the deep roots of each document to the writings of popes, the Second Vatican Council, the Synods of Bishops, and many national conferences of bishops throughout the past decades.

The culmination of the Church's position on issues of social, economic, and political equality and dignity readily acknowledges its complexity. Typically, the written proclamations avoid political rhetoric or ideological justifications. Instead, there is a clear emphasis on the participation of its members. Pope Paul VI made this responsibility explicit on the eightieth anniversary of Pope Leo's *On the Condition of Labor*. As part of the responsibilities of being a *hearer* and a *doer*, Paul outlined an "incarnational" process, outlined by de Berri and Hug as:

1. Evaluation and analysis of their contemporary situation.
2. Prayer, discernment, and reflection, bringing the light of the Gospel and the teachings of the Church to bear on the situation.
3. Pastoral action which fights injustices and works for the transformation of society, thus laboring to make the "reign" of God a reality.[23]

The Second Vatican Council (1962–1965) reinforced that the members of the Church need to attend to the "signs of these times" and within these times to protect the dignity of the human person, the dignity of work, the common good, to lessen inequality, and to increase solidarity.

Prayerful thinking, action, and relationship are at the core of Catholic social teaching. Poorman draws upon these core principles in his description of pastoral responsibilities and interactional morality. Personal conscience and individual discernment cannot take place independent of a communal setting.[24] From a pastoral perspective, morality is not simply a matter of compliance with teachings, but rather, it is deeply rooted in relationships and our interactions around moral problems. Fitting in with my vision of social justice outlined throughout the book, the most deeply contentious and troubling aspects of our society cannot be regulated or imposed. From Thomas Aquinas, and more recently articulated by Pesch, many Catholic scholars approach social justice by emphasizing a process like "solidarism" as much as particular outcomes. We are responsible to each other, and we are moral and more fulfilled as individuals especially because we have communal accountability. Very much in line with social justice as it is conveyed in this book, engagement is a central feature of this process of communal responsibility and accountability. As described by Poorman:

> The sacred dignity of each person and the call to love one's neighbor as an essential element of one's love of God combine to demand that all differences be explored and all conflicts be addressed through respectful dialogue. This applies to religious differences as well as political, economic, social and cultural ones. Only through patient, respectful dialogue do people grow beyond the limitation of their experience, perceptions, opinions and values. Each person is a unique part of the tapestry of creation, of the mosaic of the human family. Only through dialogue can new levels of understanding and appreciation be achieved in the human community. The conditions for dialogue are destroyed and human dignity violated when demonizing rhetoric is used in times of conflict.[25]

So here embedded in Catholic traditions and teaching is the understanding that engagement is a critical part of social justice. We cannot settle on formulas or positions without defining them and redefining them in the public square.

Finally, rituals within the Catholic Church have been a central way to symbolize forgiveness. Reconciliation is not simply a matter of individual forgiveness, but rather, it acknowledges community accountability and through ceremony reintegrates the individual into the communal identity. The practice is repeated similarly across languages, cultures, and countries.

5. Rituals

Rituals and symbols are opportunities to connect past, present, and future into a seamless moment. They call forward the known as well as the unknown. And rituals are uniquely capable of bringing us together in shared communion while simultaneously respecting individual differences. Revelation, mystery, and forgiveness build bridges between individuals, strengthening communities. Rituals engage the other and invite those within and outside to think about engagement in nontraditional ways. Physical contact is one path of engagement, but religious traditions also emphasize prayer, meditation, and faith. Rituals and symbols can be concrete cues and central guides for these prayers, meditation, and faith. Religion can be a call to consider the importance of prayer, meditation, and faith not as practices defining the uniqueness of a community but rather as vehicles for engaging with others.

Religion is an invitation to consciousness. Each one of us hears a different answer to the questions of who we are and how we are in relation to our individual and collective identities. Rituals permit our different moments and personal meanings, but as shared experiences, they remind us that we are somehow together in communion and community. Major religions share the emphasis on ritual, empathy, and the individual quest for fulfillment. Each of these qualities is vital for the social justice project. While each religion conceptualizes these qualities more or less differently, the social justice project certainly depends upon these qualities. Each of the major religions described above has rituals that are practiced and that bring the individual in communion with others. Even where these rituals are performed individually, they involve texts, traditions, and ceremonies that bind individuals together. They are repeated in ways that bring familiarity and comfort. During times of stress or injustice, there is a shared understanding that rituals resonate that comfort and solidarity with those participating in the ritual. The practice and description of empathy varies very little across religions, and they share an emphasis on connecting with others. For all of the religions discussed in this chapter, social connection in service to others is an intrinsic part of individual fulfillment. From the perspective offered by these religions, it is entirely comfortable to view social justice as a necessary vehicle for individual fulfillment.

Ultimately, the goal of this reconceptualized social justice is to cultivate interconnectedness as a motivating value independent of economic and political interests. In terms of nurturing human connection values, social justice very much aligns with the ideal possibilities of religion in terms of carving out a space where individuals orient themselves toward each other. Meaning is more centrally defined by human interconnectedness rather than maximizing interests through strategic decision making and in the context of competition. Social justice and religion share this possibility with the fundamental difference that social justice does not depend upon a higher authority to justify, support, or explain those values.

CRITICISMS OF RELIGION

Returning to the heroes of activism described earlier in the chapter, each experienced a conversion and embraced formalized religion for a period of time. However much each was inspired by the study and mystical embrace of a particular religion, each ultimately turned away from the constraints and fallibilities of organized religion. Bonhoeffer rebelled against the Church and its unwillingness to take a more active role against Jewish persecution. Malcolm X turned away from Islam for a more tactical, confrontational approach to change, and while committed to peace, Aung San Suu Kyi turned much more of her attention to political institutions as the relevant focus for change. Religion became both a springboard and then a constraint for these social activists. Spiritual commitment gave way to social action, and ultimately, the tragedy and urgency of injustice broke through the formality and limits of any one organization. As articulated by an activist who both challenged and reformed his own understanding of faith and Church: "The Church, then, would betray its own love for God and its fidelity to the Gospel if it stopped being the 'voice for the voiceless,' a defender of the rights of the poor, a promoter of every just aspiration for liberation, a guide, an empowerer, a humanizer of every legitimate struggle to achieve a more just society, a society that prepares the way for the true kingdom of God in history."[26] Oscar Romero defined a responsibility for the Church to follow the problems of the current times, and the Church that must attend to worldly injustice or it risks becoming part of the injustice. For activists, there is no way that institutions, especially religious ones, with their potential energy and resources, can remain apart from the world or settle on theory and concepts in lieu of action. More generally, religion offers possibilities for social justice that are undeniable, but it can also present significant limitations and weaknesses that need to be addressed.

1. Faith and the Political Life

In *The Dignity of Difference*, Jonathan Sacks asserts that the great problem of the twentieth century was "when politics turned into a religion, when the nation (in the case of fascism) or system (communism) was absolutized and turned into a god."[27] For the twenty-first century, the greatest problem is this one turned on its head: "not when politics is religionized but when religion is politicized."[28] Whether the politicization of religion is in the form of theocracies or in the form of political advocacy, the result has been less space for religion to remain or to become the foundation of harmony and social connectedness.

To the extent that religious groups participate in the political sphere, they become tainted by the standards of politics. Where politics is about difference and distribution of outcomes, so too, religion becomes oriented around difference and distribution of outcomes. Participating in the political sphere is often portrayed as a defensive mechanism to protect rights around religion and religious practice. Protections through the political state may be important, but this protection comes with significant cost in terms of potential cooptation. The relationship between church and state needs to be revisited and reconsidered more carefully than suggested by the current context. With comingling of religion and politics, religions focus on government sanction rather than attending to community influence and individual virtue. The fact that the same religion becomes political and polarizing around an issue in some countries, but not others, reveals the impact and trend of politicization. Obviously, the variation across countries suggests that religious leaders and political leaders have choices about the comingling of their spheres of influence. While there is irresistible support that comes from the weight of the state supporting a particular religion, it may be a Faustian bargain. Once entangled in political language and the political process, it is difficult to disengage and even more difficult to appear neutral to the community.

In *Identity in Democracy*, Amy Gutmann addresses the tension between a state protecting religious freedom and a state potentially captured by religious interests: "Two-way protection" describes the ideal balance with a state, granting freedom of expression, activity, and organization to religious groups.[29] In return, religious groups permit a space that is protected and nurtured by the state, and it remains independent of religion and religious interests. In this way, minorities are protected from an encroaching majority exercise of influence. Tension is inevitable between the positive rights of religious groups and the rights of those who wish to be protected from others' religious expression. One of Gutmann's central claims is that there is not necessarily one clear distinction for liberal democracies. Liberal democracies vary across countries and across time, and each set of liberal democratic institutions needs to approach emerging groups and challenges. And while two-way protection addresses the relationship between the state and religion, Gutmann is clear that the state has an obligation to protect decisions made by citizens on the basis of conscience whether or not the individual justifies the decision through religious beliefs or not. Liberal democracies have slipped too frequently and too easily into granting special protection in the name of religion, which arguably undermines the integrity of state at the same time as it privileges religion over other types of conscientious expression. Rather than protecting particular religions or shoring up support for the state, this type of comingling increases the vulnerability of religion to political trends and politicization.

2. Declining Religiosity

In their book *American Grace*, Putnam and Campbell identify two aftershock periods with a discernible decline in religious participation in the United States. The 1960s encompassed a social phenomenon of sex, drugs, and rock 'n' roll that challenged religious values and raised the number of nonbelievers within the United States.[30] During the same time period, there was a new alignment of the religious with political interests embodied in the emerging social and political movement of the Religious Right.[31] The 1990s brought a second shock, both increasing the number of nonbelievers as well as declining religious attendance. According to Putnam and Campbell's research, the rise in individuals who do not affiliate with any religion corresponds with the increasing opposition to religious influence in politics.[32] While one can't sort out the causal connection definitively, we can speculate that the increasing politicization of religion has not benefitted religious groups in terms of increasing support or practices of the American public. Contrary to previous cohorts with approximately 5 percent expressing no religious affiliation, the contemporary cohort after 2000 reveals numbers more like 25 percent without religious affiliation. The decline in religiosity is concentrated among whites, among young people, and young men, in particular, but more generally, there is an increasing objection to the influence of religious leaders, and an increase in college-age estrangement from religious beliefs and practices.[33]

This is the current state of religion in the United States. Putnam and Campbell's survey of nonbelievers described their rejection of religion and "they became unaffiliated, at least in part, because they think of religious people as hypocritical, judgmental or insincere. Large numbers also say they became unaffiliated because they think that religious organizations focus too much on rules and not enough on spirituality."[34] Fewer people join and greater numbers are leaving. At the same time, within religions, many more consider themselves members without actually following doctrine: "Something had caused this younger generation to be more liberal on these moral issues, and those very same young people increasingly rejected organized religion."[35]

As summarized in the early part of this chapter, there are many virtues associated with religion, all religions. Especially because of its affinity with my reconceptualized social justice, it is disheartening to observe the trends of declining beliefs and practices. However, in light of these observations, social justice becomes even more necessary for fostering these virtues in place of organized religion. Religion can be an asset to the social justice project by fostering these values of empathy and self-fulfillment through engagement as well. In the current context of politicized religions, it is increasingly clear that social justice needs to be a foundation independent of religion. Just like democracy and capitalism, religion has become vulnerable to its misuse and its overuse.

3. Conflict between Religions

While the boundaries and divisions between secularists and those who practice faith are sharpening, conflict between particular religious groups has historically been responsible for some of the most violent wars and conflicts in human history. Many scholars, including Putnam and Campbell, confirm that the more interactions an individual has with those of another religion, the more tolerant he/she becomes toward that religion. The Dalai Lama quotes Thomas Merton that we "have reached a stage (long overdue) of religious maturity at which it may be possible for someone to remain perfectly faithful to a Christian and Western monastic commitment and yet to learn in depth from say a Buddhist discipline and experience."[36] From this perspective, modernity offers new opportunities for shared understandings and respect between religions.

However, the politics since September 11, 2001 reinforce the close association of politics and religion, and with the alignment, there are signs of much less tolerance between religions. Ayaan Hirsi Ali invokes the clash of civilizations thesis to emphasize the recent mosque controversy in New York City as part of a broader wave of religious division.[37] Ali says: "Americans have come to know and learn about Islam and Arabs through the prisms of terrorism and barbarism,"[38] with consequences for daily interaction. In addition to the formal institutional arms of security and surveillance, 9/11 nurtured a grassroots mobilization, which included attacks on the visible symbols of Islam, especially mosques. In their study of how Americans view other religions, Putnam and Campbell identify Muslims and Buddhists as the least popular among the considered religious groups. Given the unpopularity of these two religions in the United States, Putnam and Campbell weigh the support for building a Christian church compared to building a Buddhist temple. As many as 92 percent support or are not bothered by a Christian church and 76 percent of Americans do not have a problem with a Buddhist temple in their neighborhood. However, far fewer (15 percent) would explicitly welcome a Buddhist temple in their neighborhood. Perhaps surprisingly, the greatest opposition (50 percent) comes from the most religious, with secularists classified as marginally more approving.[39] Clearly being more religious does not suggest increasing tolerance toward other religious groups.

Very concretely, mosque controversies in the United States highlight the escalation of conflict between religions. The Council on American-Islamic Relations (CAIR) reports a trend of increasing attacks against Muslims with 602 civil rights complaints in 2002, to 1,522 civil rights complaints in 2004 to 2,728 in 2009.[40] The American Civil Liberties Union (ACLU) attests that there have been at least sixty-five distinct anti-mosque activities in the United States between 2008 and 2013. They include acts of vandalism, threats, racist comments by public officials, and the rejection of requests to rezone or build mosques. Whereas the increasing secularization of society might be a wake-up call for religious leaders to come together, the politicization of religion continues to divide rather than unify different religions.

SOCIAL JUSTICE AS THE FOUNDATION FOR RELIGION

I agree with Jonathan Sacks that "[I]t may well be that religious communities are one of the few environments in which these values are still sustained,"[41] but increasingly, spiritual values are segmented and serve as an addendum to the week rather than the central guiding orientation for life. This emphasis on values, whether religious or through a social justice process independent of religion, intends to put a sharp brake on the current trends where fewer participate in any religion. Even for those who maintain a spiritual dimension, it is the economic and political incentives that drive decisions and behavior. It may seem as though faith communities and social justice are so closely aligned that the social justice project should focus attention on making religion stronger, more autonomous, and more relevant—rather than forging new concepts and spaces for interrelating.

However, there are two critical differences that make social justice distinct from religion, and most significantly, for the exercise of interconnectedness.

First, and most importantly, social justice invites the nonreligious to the table with as much legitimacy and veracity as the religious. However, as much as the ideals of religion promote an underlying understanding of humanity, participation in a religion defines exclusivity. In very clear terms, social justice is not exclusive beyond the parameters of being human. Secondly, to the extent that there is a trend in religion becoming increasingly politicized, social justice presents a vehicle for rejuvenation of faith, independent of political rhetoric and policy victories. Rather than replacing religion, social justice has the restorative potential for religion just as articulated in the earlier chapters for democracy, capitalism, and technology:

> The move to a pluralist position of interchange with other religions by no means involves abandoning one's central commitment to one's own faith; it hugely enriches the understanding and practice of one's own religion, as Desideri argued. It allows one to see convergences with other religions, to sharpen one's grasp of one's own tradition by seeing its specific and distinctive characteristics by way of contrast, and to broaden one's respect for the extraordinary range and diversity of spiritual approaches developed by humankind entirely outside of one's faith tradition.[42]

The process of social justice advocated in this book institutionalizes the type of transparency and engagement described above. And by purposely removing policy outcomes from the social justice process, it enhances learning and collective possibilities.

IS RELIGION UNIQUE?

An important question is whether religion provides a set of values or organizations that are uniquely amenable to social justice. Is religion special in terms of its affinity with the social justice project? While religion does nurture qualities that are both fostered by and enhanced by social justice, it is in not unique in this capacity. As described above, the value of compassion runs through most major religions, but compassion centers many nonreligious movements as well.

The modern Humanist movement includes a group of accomplished scholars who vary in their attitude of religion as a potential source for moral society. The original Humanist Manifesto written by Sellars and Bragg (1933) cultivated principles and beliefs that they identified as a new religion. However, subsequent humanists explicitly turned away from religion, and in the second manifesto of 1973, Kurtz and Wilson clearly articulated that "No deity will save us; we must save ourselves."[43] While criticized by religious leaders, its purpose was less to alienate religion and much more importantly to emphasize collective responsibility in this world and for this world. Another iteration of the Humanist Manifesto was written in 2003. It emphasizes humans, independent of religious membership, but its principles fit within the reconceptualized social justice paradigm:

- Knowledge of the world is derived by observation, experimentation, and rational analysis.
- Humans are an integral part of nature, the result of unguided evolutionary process.
- Ethical values are derived from human need and interest as tested by experience.
- Life's fulfillment emerges from individual participation in the service of humane ideals.
- Humans are social by nature and find meaning in relationship.
- Working to benefit society maximizes individual happiness.
- Humanists are concerned for the well-being of all, are committed to diversity, and respect those of differing yet humane views.[44]

Supporting the legitimacy of the humanist alternative even further, evidence from recent research suggested that those who are highly religious are *less* motivated by compassion when they help others compared to less religious people, atheists and agnostics as well. The results suggest that those who are religious help people, but the reasons for helping involve other motivations, like moral obligation, reputation, identity, and doctrine.[45] From their study, nonbelievers are more likely to engage in random acts of kindness and they are more likely to be driven by compassion. Ultimately, the researchers conclude that although less religious people are less trusted, they are more likely to help others with the motivation of compassion than those who are religious.

These studies tell us nothing about the time or amount of assistance but rather focus on the motives for helping. In the context of social justice as interconnectedness, motivation matters very significantly. Highly religious people may provide more assistance to others, but it may be out of obligation and responsibilities within the faith, rather than out of compassion, human interconnectedness, and empathy. If these studies are generalizable, there is nothing uniquely capable about religion in terms of nurturing values amenable to social justice. Furthermore, the process of social justice described here may be more important and unique for nurturing a compassionate society.

From a very different perspective, literature can be a rich source of learning and developing empathy. John Horton and Andrea Baumeister's edited volume *Literature and the Political Imagination* outlines how "literature can provide more lifelike examples than the etiolated and simplistic illustrations typically employed by philosophers."[46] Without direct and personal experience, but also without religious doctrine, we learn about the other, and we can practice our own lives without the direct or personal consequences of mistakes. Complex understandings about motivation and human nature, unique possibilities, and contingent decisions emerge through the characters and novelists' observations. Insights challenge our assumptions and are ideals in a comfortable environment of meditation and contemplative rumination about potential realities.

Through fictional examples, novelists define, create, and capture preferences, behaviors, and outcomes in a way that emphasizes the universality of many of these preferences, especially under different regime types, while simultaneously defining the particularities and contingencies of experience. Arguably, enlightenment emerges from the act of reading widely. The specificity of the particular characters, settings, and dialogues invites generalization rooted in the explication of human connections. Through reading, we are invited into other people's lives. Across race, religion, gender, and economic boundaries we see ourselves and think deeply about our similarities as much as our differences. Liking a character, or even a part of a character, breaks down stereotypes and barriers, without direct contact or deep contact. Through novels, we learn about the human condition, and this learning invites shared understanding, and often compassion. So we can't conclude that religion is unique in terms of its affinity with the social justice project. Certainly, religion nurtures qualities that are both fostered by and enhanced by social justice, but religion cannot claim entirely unique legitimacy in the sphere of social justice.

NOTES

1. Message from John Adams to the Officers of the First Brigade of the Third Division of the Militia of Massachusetts October 11, 1798. http://www .beliefnet.com/resourcelib/docs/115/Message_from_John_Adams_to_the _Officers_of_the_First_Brigade_1.html Accessed July 26, 2013.
2. Curtiss Paul DeYoung, *Living Faith: How Faith Inspires Social Justice* (Minneapolis: Fortress Press, 2007), 151.
3. DeYoung, *Living Faith*, 19.
4. DeYoung, *Living Faith*, 25.
5. Jonathan Sacks, *The Dignity of Difference: How to Avoid the Clash of Civilizations* (New York: Continuum, 2003), 78.
6. Conn Iggulden, *Emperor: The Gates of Rome* (New York: Delacorte Press, 2004), 178.
7. DeYoung, *Living Faith*, 89.
8. Michael Sandel, *Justice: What's the Right Thing to Do?* (New York: Farrar, Straus and Giroux, 2009), 172–73.
9. The Dalai Lama, *Toward a True Kinship of Faiths: How the World's Religions Can Come Together* (New York: Doubleday Religion, 2010), xiii.
10. The Dalai Lama, *Toward a True Kinship of Faiths*, 112–13.
11. The Dalai Lama, *Toward a True Kinship of Faiths*, 44.
12. The Dalai Lama, *Toward a True Kinship of Faiths*, 54.
13. The Dalai Lama, *Toward a True Kinship of Faiths*, 54.
14. Phra Prayaudh Payutto, *Buddhadhamma: Natural Laws and Values for Life*, trans. Grant A. Olson in *Being Benevolence: The Social Ethics of Engaged Buddhism*, ed. Sallie B. King (Honolulu: University of Hawai'I Press, 2005), 93.

15. Sallie B. King, *Being Benevolence: The Social Ethics of Engaged Buddhism* (Honolulu: University of Hawai'I Press, 2005), 99.
16. King, *Being Benevolence*, 99.
17. King, *Being Benevolence*, 87.
18. Sayyid Qutb, *Selected Writings on Politics, Religion, and Society*, ed. Albert J. Bergesen (New York: Routledge, 2008), 154.
19. Qutb, *Selected Writings on Politics, Religion, and Society*, 156.
20. *Holy Bible*, New Revised Standard Version: Catholic Edition.
21. The Dalai Lama, *Toward a True Kinship of Faiths*, 102.
22. Edward DeBerri and James E. Hug, *Catholic Social Teaching: Our Best Kept Secret*, 8th ed. (New York: Orbis Books, 2012).
23. DeBerri and Hug, *Catholic Social Teaching*, 9.
24. Mark Poorman, *Interactional Morality: A Foundation for Moral Discernment in Catholic Pastoral Ministry* (Washington, DC: Georgetown University Press, 1993), 5.
25. Poorman, *Interactional Morality*, 21.
26. DeYoung, *Living Faith*, 57.
27. Sacks, *The Dignity of Difference*, 42.
28. Sacks, *The Dignity of Difference*, 42–43.
29. Amy Gutmann, *Identity in Democracy* (New Jersey: Princeton University Press, 2009).
30. Robert D. Putnam and David E. Campbell, *American Grace: How Religion Divides and Unites Us* (New York: Simon &Schuster, 2010), 122.
31. Putnam and Campbell, *American Grace*, 120.
32. Putnam and Campbell, *American Grace*, 131.
33. Putnam and Campbell, *American Grace*, 29.
34. Putnam and Campbell, *American Grace*, 131.
35. Putnam and Campbell, *American Grace*, 130.
36. The Dalai Lama, *Toward a True Kinship of Faiths*, 10.
37. Ayaan Hirsi Ali, "The New York Mosque is a Symptom of Civilizational Clash," *New Perspectives Quarterly* 27 (2010): 38–40.
38. Amaney Jamal, "The Racialization of Muslim Americans," in *Muslims in Western Politics*, ed. Sinno Abdulkader (Bloomington: Indiana University Press, 2009), 206.
39. Putnam and Campbell, *American Grace*, 513–14.
40. From CAIR 2005 and CAIR 2009 report quoted in Stephen Salisbury, "Mosque-mania Anti-Muslim fears and the far right," August 10, 2010. Accessed July 26, 2013. http://www.tomdispatch.com/post/175283/tomgram: _stephan_salisbury,_extremism_at_ground_zero_%28again%29__/.
41. Jonathan Sacks, *The Dignity of Difference*, 81.
42. The Dalai Lama, *Toward a True Kinship of Faiths*, 17–18.
43. "Humanism and its Aspirations," American Humanist Association, Accessed July 26, 2013. www.americanhumanist.org/Humanism/Humanist_Manifesto _III.
44. "Humanism and its Aspirations," American Humanist Association.
45. Yasmin Anwar, "Highly Religious People Are Less Motivated by Compassion Than are Non-Believers," *Media Relations*, April 30, 2012.
46. John Horton and Andrea T. Baumeister, eds., *Literature and the Political Imagination* (New York: Routledge, 1996), 13.

6 Implementing Social Justice

Men must be ready, they must pride themselves and be happy to sacrifice their private pleasures, passions and interests, nay, their private
friendships and dearest connections, when they stand in competition
with the rights of society.

—John Adams[1]

INTRODUCTION

While previous chapters present social justice as a valuable remedy for the
weaknesses in the central spheres of today's society, it is clearly important
to identify the ways in which social justice can be fostered. Success will be
most likely if current participants in the social justice project can reorient
their mobilization efforts and resources toward the goal of *social* justice
rather than *political* justice. The current social justice project has failed to
the extent that its current rhetoric is increasingly hollow. As discussed in
Chapter 2, while social justice advocates support types of change, the process of politicization can often lead groups further from that success. Clearly
there is "a tension between the inherently political nature of the institutionalization process and the social and institutional preconditions necessary
for that very process to be considered normatively legitimate."[2] I argue that
this social foundation needs to be built independent of the political system
of engagement in order to be truly effective.

Rather than changing policy, social justice needs to cultivate roots, consciously affecting individuals' values to be more social. These fostering
values can't be particular policies but rather a way of being together that
makes us more accountable to each other, more connected to each other, and
more deeply tolerant of each other. If social justice advocates joined together
to focus on these goals, even peripherally, there could be momentum around
creating and sustaining groups that bring together members of society who
have damaged each other in a way that is collectively relevant.

SOCIAL JUSTICE THROUGH INDIVIDUALISM

From the time of Plato, philosophers and political theorists have wrestled with the tension between the individual and community. While social justice orients the individual toward values that make the community central, we can't dismiss the current and important status of the individual. In the context of seemingly omnipotent individualism in U.S. society today, it is not surprising to receive a glassy-eyed disregard by many whenever someone mentions social justice. It is a label that often marginalizes those associated with social justice activities: do-gooders, idealists, tree huggers, granola munchers. From this perspective, you either fit the social justice mold or you don't. Also problematic, social justice often emerges as a rhetorical device simply to add legitimacy to a cause. Here it is a tag line to remind the target audience that the particular cause is an important one.

Instead of the alternatives of either self-sacrifice and idealism, or empty rhetoric, this book offers the idea of social justice as a process of engagement with and commitment to the collective. My conception promises to improve the political, economic, religious, and technology spheres, but its implementation also fits for the world as it is in twenty-first-century liberal capitalist democracies. Importantly, this reconceptualized social justice does not require people to turn away from liberalism and individualism. Social justice does not require "emptying" oneself in order to surrender to others. In fact, individualism prevails even along the journey to resurrect the significance of our collective identity:

> The only valid *we* is the *we* made up of real *I*'s, real subjects, who know their deepest subjectivity is engaged precisely in a relationship with others, a relationship that achieves a true and faithful saying of we, indeed a saying in which each *I* knows that there is no being an I unless I say *we* in this way.[3]

While there may be a natural intuition to collectivism, our society is saturated with self-interest individualism. We need mechanisms and spaces to re-entrench the collective intuition. I think that we fundamentally deny our potential as individuals when we abandon the relevance of our connections, when we turn our backs from deepening relationships with each other, and when we choose "I" over "we" instead of seeing the two as simultaneously and fully integrated. Taylor's discussion of authenticity describes a bold ethic with the individual and individualism at its source. He begins with the twenty-first-century Western liberal democracy world as it is and argues for a social ethic that is significantly centered upon the individual. After outlining the significant collective and individual malaises that follow from this entirely self-centered orientation, he does not reinvent the world, but through a slight shift, he reasserts the relevance of considering the "other" for one's own self-fulfillment. It is only through consideration of the other that we know ourselves. The ego demands that we fill ourselves up, but it is the connections with others that become a central vehicle for this fulfillment. The quest for individual authenticity requires interconnectedness in ways that fit with my version of social justice. There may be conflict, but through openness, we can achieve our authentic self. According to Charles Taylor,

> Authenticity (A) involves (i) creation and construction as well as discovery, (ii) originality, and frequently (iii) opposition to the rules of society and even potentially to what we recognize as morality. But it is also true, as we saw that it (B) requires (i) openness to horizons of significance (for otherwise the creation loses the background that can save it from insignificance) and (ii) a self-definition of dialogue.[4]

From Taylor's version of authenticity, I argue that the motivation for creating social justice as a process of engagement needs to be the individual as he or she is today. In return, social justice provides the vehicle for discovering our authentic selves in a way that conjoins us to others. It reinforces our harmony in a way that lets our individuality flourish. If we realize that we discover our individual selves through others, then we become bound to each other in an inextricably necessary and self-conscious way. If it is about individual self-fulfillment rather than surrender to others, then it is a much easier shift from today's political and economic context. Social justice for individual self-fulfillment can be very different from engaging individuals for instrumental purposes. If I need to know your identity as part of the process of figuring out my own identity, it is familiar but still quite distinct from a consumption orientation or from viewing relationships for their instrumental value. Just as the current malaise within our systems of democracy, capitalism, technology, and religion can be self-reinforcing, the renewed process of social engagement cultivates empathy, which can reinforce the collectivist orientation.

SOCIAL JUSTICE THROUGH SOCIAL MOVEMENTS

Social justice is a space where we remove blame and judgment from the individual and instead accept collective responsibility for the causes of polarization, alienation, and personal offenses of human dignity. Especially in the early stages, we heal as a community to go forward. While individuals and individualism prevail today as the foundation for emerging collectivism, we need to recognize that individualism emerged as part of a historically contingent shift in attitude and ideas. And if individualism is historically contingent, then we can admit the possibility of transformation again. Social movement theory provides a framework for understanding dramatic shifts in public opinion, often unanticipated and typically including far-reaching social, political, and economic change. Scholars studying interest groups recognize that expressive, transformative movements are not unfamiliar in U.S. political history. For example, in my work with Robert Salisbury,[5] we studied how a tidal wave of Christian coalitions and civil liberty groups descended upon the previously confined policy niche around funding for the arts. In our case study, issues became far removed from "politics as usual" with new coalitions and an incentive for individuals previously unaccustomed to participating in interest group politics, mobilizing around these new issues.

So in addition to the transformation of existing coalitions and groups within and across policy niches, expressive social movements can also become catalysts for new individuals and new groups to emerge. According to Loomis and Cigler, "[D]isturbances that act to trigger group formation need not be strictly economic or technological,"[6] and these disturbances can become a catalyst for potential new players to be brought into an emerging social movement. Dramatic shifts, like the fall of communism in the Soviet Union, suggest even more profoundly the possibility of transformation. As discussed in early chapters, Timur Kuran makes sense of the revolutionary change from communism to democratic capitalism by appealing to the distance between the preferences people articulate publicly and those that are carried privately. By accepting that individuals really preferred democratic capitalism and merely acted as though they supported communism, we appreciate the extent and speed of change. Similarly, I maintain that individuals carry stronger preferences for community connection and meaningful social relationships than exhibited by public activities and declarations. A social movement transformation is entirely plausible if there is even some public private disconnect between publicly articulated individualism and privately held preferences for more communitarian values and practices. Kuran's discussion of tipping points further suggests that frontrunners in terms of articulating and acting around different values can become the catalyst for those who will not necessarily mobilize first. While particular thresholds and timing are not entirely predictable, the potential change for social movement, including a movement around social justice, is well understood by social scientists.

SOCIAL JUSTICE THROUGH THE STATE

While social justice challenges politics and the state as a foundation for society, the state can nevertheless contribute to the transformation in making social justice a more relevant foundation. Of course, this raises a challenge. How does social justice reform the state if it is first and foremost emerging within a state and so to some extent a product of the state? There are two types of answers to this question: one emphasizes the possibilities emerging from top-down reform, and the other possibilities emerge from bottom-up lobbying. Political representatives in the United States have already moved one step in this direction with the immense popularity of town hall meetings. One significant difference between town hall meetings and these social justice meetings, however, is that people agree to meet again. Reiteration of the process is critical to social justice success.

While political representatives may not buy into the final outcomes of social justice for a reformed foundation and diminished relevance of the political system, they might be convinced to set up the initial conditions. Town hall meetings have demonstrated success in terms of connecting candidates with their constituents. Some of the most social revolutionary outcomes have emerged from the unintended consequences of decisions, often conservative decisions, to stall reform, taken by political representatives. I often invite my students to think much more creatively about politics in terms of unintended consequences. How did a conservative measure to pacify labor lead to revolutionary labor reform? How did a condition of depleted state resources from economic depression give birth to Keynesian commitments that began a welfare state? How did conservative reform of the Soviet State lead to the capitalist democratic wave?

The second type of answer returns to those current participants of the social justice project. Imagine if money and resources directed at particular policies by social justice advocates shifted focus to lobby for state supported (financed) town hall meetings. Currently, the state pays for parks for people to play in, it pays for food banks, and it pays for schools, so why can't it pay for meetings? Judges can be paid to mediate, clerics can be paid to record the testimonials, and identified leaders of current organizations as well as the public can be invited to participate. TV programs put together panels like this all the time. Like a town hall meeting, the only difference between the TV programs and the social justice intention is the requirement of repeated interaction. It is up to existing social justice advocates to reorient resources and strategies to lobby for these types of engagements. The rewards are not necessarily tangible in the short run, especially for any particular cause, but the possibilities for long-run transformative change should be evident, especially by those who have read diligently up to this point in the book. Social justice does not anticipate consensus as an outcome nor does it refuse conflict as part of its process. However, it does require that individuals disrobe some of their competition dominant in other spheres, such as politics and the economy. While disagreements will exist and may prevail, the expectation to win some particular outcome can be deinstitutionalized. The following three empirical examples illustrate how a more collective orientation can be institutionalized to transform communities previously characterized by competition, polarization, and injustice.

CASE 1: OREGON WINERIES, COMPETITION AND SOCIAL JUSTICE

A few years ago, I studied the wine industry[7] (*New England Journal of Entrepreneurship*) in Oregon and discovered the amazing but very real possibilities of individuals working against each other in a highly competitive market but coming together in community to share ideas, resources, and collective interests.

The concept of "green niche" provides an example of a sharp turn away from solely competitive market forces as the foundation for capitalism. The Oregon case of green-niche contributes to discussions of capitalism as potentially "relationally and communally constituted."[8] Focusing on capitalism as a societal phenomenon, Fletcher presented a framework identifying different theoretical types of relationality.[9] Here my case emphasizes *how* entrepreneurs transform into socially just communities and have a positive impact on collective possibilities for future change, especially environmental change.

COMPETITIVENESS THROUGH COLLABORATION

Oregon's wine industry is unique in terms of the number of wineries adopting sustainability practices. The emerging green niche is a model of social justice practices. Within the capitalist system, social justice does not replace profit as a motive for decisions. Rather, social justice practices become the foundation for decisions that affirm collective identity while also satisfying individual interests. Commitment to the green niche institutionalizes cooperation within a competitive market, and so this is an important example of social justice.

A prominent Oregon supplier of equipment and products and advisor to approximately 85 percent of all grape growers in the region estimates that more than 40 percent of Oregon's grape growers practice sustainability, even though only 25 percent adopt formal certification. Like many other agricultural crops, grape farming is commonly associated with herbicides, pesticides, and other chemical products throughout the growth cycle. The shift toward sustainability involves reducing or eliminating the use of these chemicals in an effort to restore the ecosystem within which the farm exists and also to restore the natural taste and nutrients of the particular crop. Central to the story among Oregon winery owners is the diversity in the adoption of sustainability practices: In the 1980s, Ted Casteel and Pat Dudley of Bethel Heights were looking for non-chemical solutions to the toughest problems of grape growing from mildew and weeds; Susan Sokol Blosser of Sokol Blosser winery attended a Natural Step training session in 1999 that initiated an entirely new vision for her life and the life of her business; when Josh Bergstrom of Bergstrom winery began farming grapes in Oregon in 1996, salesmen offered products to eradicate the weeds, and the herbicide was effective enough that the weeds died, but the chemicals also severely threatened his vines, most curiously leaving neon orange strips on them; Sam Tannahill is co-owner of the newly acclaimed largest winery in Oregon, AtoZ, and his early consciousness about sustainability focused on his family and personal food consumption, and in the process of cultivating a healthier life, he extended the values into his workplace; Kevin Chambers was a student at Berkeley North (University of Oregon), and in 1974, he was introduced to the "Earth First!" movement and carried these principles of organic and sustainability into his business; and for Stoller winery, it was the decision to build a winery in 2002 that led Bill and Cathy Stoller to hire premium architects who suggested LEED (Leadership in Energy and Environmental Design) certification as a possible direction.

With their sustainability practices, these Oregon winery owners defy the expectation that profit drives environmentalism. Josh Bergstrom of Bergstrom winery figures the biodynamic process adds costs of approximately $3,000 per acre. In spite of real costs that often are not returned, and far removed from the authority of government regulation, individual entrepreneurs in this region's wine industry are choosing sustainable practices. Oregon wineries are adopting environmental initiatives independent of government action, legislation, and regulation. In fact, all my interviews confirm that those adopting these environmental changes in the industry don't want government regulation or guidance toward sustainability. Nor are these vineyard and winery owners actively capturing the economic benefits of their green products. They express concern that government regulations may not be appropriate to distinct industries, and they all share a deep suspicion of the green market label—of "greenwashing"—cultivating or manipulating a product's origins solely to meet the appearance of green qualities for the consumer but at the expense of sacrificing quality.

For example, all three of the winery owners who farm biodynamically affirm the value of treating the vineyard like an ecosystem, but all are wary of associating their wines with this brand certification as opposed to the quality of the wine.[10] Each owner expressed strong concern that the consumer might be attracted to biodynamic as a brand and then taste a wine of less quality and forever associate biodynamic wines with poor quality. Whether correct or not, this perception is a driving force in their unwillingness to push the environmental association in a market context. And for many Oregon winery owners, quality-of-environment issues are about themselves and their relationship with each other as well as the farming process. Initially, this green niche community is not driven by profit interests. Over time, however, the creative ideas and collaboration that emerge from within the green niche do generate significant profitable outcomes.

In terms of collaboration and innovation, the community of Oregon wineries has become an example of experimentation through collective diversity, sharing, and cultivation of best practices. For example, members of the community experimented with organic wine production in addition to organic farming, and an emerging consensus dismissed it is as an unacceptable set of procedures for good wine. Regularly, Oregon State University scientists get together with a dozen winery owners to discuss ways to expand the technological frontier to make sustainability viable, available, and economical. It is the evidence of these types of spontaneous collective groups and their cooperation that define the green niche. For the Oregon green niche, its innovation is grassroots driven, but it is spurred by articulation and cooperation of community practices to groups outside of the green niche. The green niche has institutionalized diversity and individual creativity at the same time that it has cultivated shared values, community, and cooperation.

Innovation underlies competitive strategy, and it is also an important part of the green niche paradigm.[11] An interesting characteristic of the green niche entrepreneurship is how innovation emerges from the *interaction* between the deepening values within the community and the effort to extend those values to other groups. In the process of building bridges of values translated to the economy, wineries are developing unique grassroots-driven certifications and centers for grassroots research. The diversity of environmental practices fosters a community of experimentation with models of alternative paths to sustainability. The winery owners of Bethel Heights led a grassroots group, generating a new certification to include the diversity of sustainable practices. "Oregon Certified Sustainable" is pushing beyond the vineyard to include the winery and wine making processes. Within the wine industry, there are many different particular types of sustainable certifications. "Oregon Certified Sustainable" signifies and unifies all vineyards and wineries that have adopted the practices and performance criteria for any of the other sustainable certifications. There is much more marketing potential with one clear symbol that identifies the Oregon wine industry only and also represents a set of practices that foster sustainability. This new certification represents a shift from identity formation toward capturing the market benefits from these identities. Through the "Oregon Certified Sustainable" label, the community preserves its environmental diversity and competitiveness while articulating a vehicle for mainstream education and collective market potential.

Innovation as a green niche community emerges from the encouraged diversity of practices but also from the community's effort to coordinate and articulate their values to groups outside of the community. At the same time as the extension of values and the articulation of community pushes innovation, it is also shifting into more formalized political interests and profit-oriented marketization through "Oregon certified sustainable" as a uniform certification. In spite of the grist for innovation and deepening cooperation within the community, the emerging politicization and marketization also shows signs of tension with early motivating values. How this balance can be maintained—a balance of deepening values within the community and expanding influence of values beyond the community— depends upon leaders who both initiated community and continue to push their sustainability values in other sectors. In particular, the Oregon green niche shifts from propagating stronger identity-oriented values within the community toward a balance between goals—thicker environmental values and ties within the community but also widening influence through more formal interest-oriented politics and more marketable uniform certifications. Through leadership, nonmarket principles and early environmental decisions nurtured this green niche with a focus on the intrinsic benefits of the transformations. As the green niche extends the influence and relevance of these values into the broader political, economic, and cultural context, there is a feedback effect as the green-niche then responds to the changing broader context it helped to create.

The brand "Oregon Certified Sustainable" translates the diversity of good sustainability practices into a uniform brand for consumer education and recognition. The adoption of "Oregon Certified Sustainable" as a marketing label carries the possibility of enhancing the viability of Oregon wineries' sustainable practices. Particularly as the brand identification becomes a profit mechanism, the numbers and commitment of other wineries likely will increase. As a brand, it identifies independent certification (LIVE, organic, biodynamic certifications qualify), responsible agriculture, and responsible winemaking. Ted Farthing, executive director of the Oregon Wine Board (2004–2010), emphasized the importance of bringing together all the diverse practices into identifiable brand recognition. At this point, no wine region has captured a market-oriented environmental niche. Given the increasing number of Oregon wineries adopting these practices, sustainability seems a very promising area for regional recognition and association for consumers. At this point, however, the bargaining power resides with the consumers, and so there is a critical need to educate consumers about the meaning of sustainability in terms of wine. The Final Full Glass Research Oregon Wine Board Study 2007 revealed that many consumers are not sure what sustainable wine is, and whereas wine consumers tend to be more oriented toward sustainability purchases, this does not translate into the purchase of sustainable wine as a priority consideration. The creation of a uniform brand, even while environmental practices remain diverse, is a significant bridge moving from the green niche community of some Oregon wineries to more mainstream identification of greater numbers within the industry.

Oregon winery relationships with environmental groups can be characterized as much more of a partnership than an adversarial relationship, and this kind of alliance is unique compared to other regions. An interview with the Oregon Environmental Council confirmed the ways in which a significant state environmental lobbying group perceives the wine industry as a potential leader in adopting best practices. The Oregon Environmental Council identified a sharp divide within the industry that puts Oregon's wine industry on the right side of the environmental effort. Oregonians for Food and Shelter, Rural Coop utilities, Oregon's Cattleman Association, and Dairy Farmers of Oregon represent traditional farming in contrast with wine, representing a new direction and potential partner for sustainability. Oregon brings together entrepreneurs across sectors and industries, environmental groups, and government in partnership toward the goal of enhancing sustainability. In terms of a bridge from green niche community to mainstream recognition and influence, this model of partnership is critical for ongoing successful transformation in the wider state community. There are obvious possibilities for extending the relevance and influence of Oregon wineries as a model for social justice and sustainability.

The study of environmental values and the transformation toward sustainability practices offers a rich set of cases to emphasize social processes that underlay entrepreneurship more generally and model social justice possibilities. While the profitability of sustainability is not the focus, several relevant observations contribute to understanding the contrasting sources for profitability of the two paths. In Oregon, the green niche maximizes flexibility in terms of experimental farming, collaborative decision-making, and cultivating consumer demand toward sustainability while preserving the opportunities from traditional farming as well. The thick social relations characterizing the green niche, social capital, cannot be measured precisely, but some studies confirm that social capital gives business an edge in terms of investment opportunities and cost savings.[12] Finally, the culture of innovation surrounding the green niche continually pushes the production possibility curve and pushes forward cost-cutting possibilities to maximize the profitability of sustainability practices.

For many Oregon entrepreneurs, sustainability is an emerging issue of identity as much as interest. They reject government intervention as the solution to environmental degradation and as the foundation for rejuvenation. However, they also reject the market drive for sustainability, and they are reluctant to participate in the wave of green profits. Over time, however, "ecopreneurs" are organizing collectively in ways that transform small communities focused on intrinsic environmental values to more mainstream recognition and identification. This transformation entrenches cooperative values and diverse practices—in other words, social justice, into profitable and institutionalized, therefore viable, enduring sustainability.

CASE 2: MOSQUE CONTROVERSIES: POLITICIZATION, POLARIZATION, AND SOCIAL JUSTICE

After September 11, 2001, Muslim Americans and Arab Americans confronted a new political context within which their identity was recreated and imposed in terms of national security. Exclusion and racialization dominated much of the formal federal political legislation, while the national rhetoric of security framed these legislative and institutional changes. Evidence from neighborhood mosque controversies in DuPage County, Illinois confirms the impact of the national framing around terrorism and security. However, the neighborhood space also provided an unintended opportunity for emerging social justice. Transparency, intergroup sharing, and learning shifted debate from threat and terror to compatibility and religious pluralism.

NEIGHBORHOOD POLITICS: FROM SECURITY
TO RELIGIOUS PLURALISM

As mentioned in the previous chapter, across the country, the exclusion of Muslim Americans after September 11 transferred to the local level. The Council on American-Islamic Relations (CAIR) reports a trend of increasing attacks against Muslims with 602 civil rights complaints in 2002, to 1,522 civil rights complaints in 2004 to 2,728 in 2009.[13] The American Civil Liberties Union (ACLU) attests that there have been at least sixty-five distinct anti-mosque activities in the United States in the last five years. These activities include acts of vandalism, threats, racist comments by public officials, and the rejection of requests to rezone or to build mosques.

While security dragnets and national initiatives focused on catching terrorists, a process of exclusion confronted all Muslims. Parallel to policies of exclusion at the national level, "Americans have come to know and learn about Islam and Arabs through the prisms of terrorism and barbarism,"[14] with consequences for daily interaction. In addition to the formal institutional arms of security and surveillance, 9/11 nurtured a grassroots mobilization, which included attacks on the visible symbols of Islam, especially mosques. While security framed the national legislative discussion, religion and building mosques became another space subject to imposed and overlapping identities of Muslim, Arab, foreign, and terrorist. Initially, the debates around zoning laws for mosque building seemed to replicate the security frame, but then there was a discernible shift. Over time, a civil liberties and religious pluralism frame emerged, and the Muslim Arab American community became redefined away from speculative associations with terrorism and away from its presumed foreignness. Polarization gave way to learning, repeated interaction, and shared understandings in ways that offer another model of social justice.

Naperville and Willowbrook are two mosque controversies within the same county outside of Chicago, Illinois. The Irshad Learning Center in Naperville initially failed its attempt to receive county approval to build a mosque. However, months later and under the same county board, MECCA in Willowbrook was successful. Over the process of two mosque building controversies, the county community interacted in a way that looked a lot like my ideal version of social justice. Through social justice, the Muslim Arab American population became more deeply integrated into the community. Others eventually perceived the right to practice religion, Islam, as compatible with their own interests and the right to practice their own various religions. Most importantly, and arguably in a way that fits with the social justice project, the neighborhood space of contested identity shifted the groups within the community away from their previous status as unknown and unknowable.

NAPERVILLE, ILLINOIS

The Chicago area has close to 500,000 Muslims and approximately 100 mosques.[15] The Naperville mosque hearings took place between November 2008 and December 2009 and focused on obtaining a conditional use permit for the Irshad Learning Center. The Irshad Learning Center would serve approximately twenty-five families (anticipated 100 worshipers), and the proposal was that the mostly Iranian-born Muslims build a mosque and school. It was supported by four petitioners who are professors from the University of Illinois, Chicago, Northern Illinois University, and Elmhurst College. None of the petitioners spoke during the public hearings, and their silence was raised on several occasions as a rebuff of the community and the spirit of cooperation. Instead, their attorney spoke at the meetings on their behalf. However, in public conference interviews, the chairman summarized that upcoming elections played into a heightened anti-Muslim sentiment: "It is not a popular sentiment to be in favor of an application by Muslims, no matter how good the application is."[16] The Muslim leader interpreted the rejection in terms of anti-Muslim public opinion.

A representative for the neighborhood began his presentation with the claim that "none of us in any way begrudges the members of Irshad Learning Center the right to assemble and practice their faith according to the Constitutional Rights that we enjoy . . . at the same time we have and feel it's appropriate to reserve a right to enjoy the comfort and benefits of the properties we own without undue uses."[17] In response to the petitioners' assurances that noise and traffic would be limited, the neighborhood representative challenged the credibility and feasibility of limiting members, timing, and noise. They presented evidence that questioned the legitimacy of services ending by 10:30 p.m. and challenged the number of nights for these services. Further, neighborhood representatives raised the issue of enforcement. If neighbors were called upon to enforce the restrictions, it would undermine comfort and trust in the neighborhood community.

Neighbors were forthcoming about rejections on the grounds of neighborhood issues, like parking and late-night services: "our issues in intensity of use are number of nights, hours of operation, number of cars, number of people" (Wallace, neighborhood representative, 60). As an extension of neighborhood issues, one participant began with a focus on the timing of services but included: "I'm a Christian. I'm not here—I'm the president of the largest—one of the largest Greek orthodox churches in the Chicagoland area. I'm not against the Irshad Learning Center from a religious perspective. I am here representing my family. I'm the only one that is going to protect my children . . . One of these people are going to lose control, and they are going to crash into my property into the backyard where my children play."

Another neighbor suggested she learned about the property through the news coverage. In her testimony, she repeated the story that concerned the mortgage holder for the property, the Lavi foundation. The news story charged that the Lavi foundation had its assets seized by the government due to "alleged illegal ties to the Iranian government and funneling funds to nuclear development." The chairman of the foundation responded that he avoids media coverage of the particular buildings being considered by the County Board. Similarly, a member of the County Board explicitly denounced the relevance of the neighbors' claims about the group's association with terrorist organizations. Another neighborhood representative opposed the mosque and challenged the petitioner's appeal on the grounds of protection for religious institutions. "While the law does not permit the County to deny the petition as requested because they are a religious institution or in a manner that would substantially burden the practice of their religion, we do not believe it prevents the County from enforcing the requirements of its zoning ordinance related to approval of a conditional use."[18] Abiding by the requirements of a zoning ordinance, whether or not they are applied regularly or not, was not anti-Muslim from this perspective.

Building applications have to pass through several committees, including the Development Committee, the Zoning Board, and then finally, the County Board. In the final resolution, DuPage County Board officials denied the application of a conditional-use permit. This vote followed an earlier approval by the Development Committee. The Development Committee outlined twelve conditions, including noise limits, to shut down activities at 10:30 p.m., to restrict occupancy to 100, limit parking to twenty-seven spots, and to limit live-in maintenance to one caretaker.[19] Following the approval, the petition went to the Zoning Board where it was unanimously opposed. On April 8, 2010, the petitioners filed suit against all members of the Zoning Board and ten members of the County Board plus the chairman.[20] They were represented by an attorney for the Chicago office of The Council on American-Islamic Relations, who publicly stated that "a reasonable fact finder could plausibly find that the county treated ILC much less favorably than a secular comparator."[21] Their appeal claims that the County Board violated their first and fourteenth amendment rights and treated the petition unfairly. In particular, the ILC representatives raise the "speculative use" claims by the neighbors and board members as well as one board member's questions about potential "animal sacrifices."

WILLOWBROOK, ILLINOIS

Like the Irshad Learning Center, the Muslim Educational Cultural Center of America (MECCA) is within the DuPage County Board jurisdiction. MECCA was introduced as a facility to accommodate 30 to 40 people on a regular basis but up to 600 visitors and 230 parking spaces. Like Irshad, the process of approval involved the Zoning Committee, the Development Committee as well as the general board. At each stage, there was public participation from both proponents of the mosque as well as opponents.

Neighbors' claims focused primarily on nonreligious potential problems but sometimes invoked the particular religion as the cause. Opposition testimony came from the treasurer of a neighborhood civic association, who presented copies of 240 signatures. One member argued that the 600 occupancy limit would be overlooked: "Isn't it customary around the world and New York that they go out on the street? . . . Isn't it customary that they would go out on the streets and crowd the streets and prevent people from even entering their homes?"[22] Another witness articulated support for a pluralistic society and a diverse neighborhood but opposed the large presence of this particular structure: "All three of the other religious institutions have been good neighbors and we have no reason to believe the MECCA folks won't try to be good neighbors, too. However, even if our drainage problems are magically solved, parking never overflows and noise, lighting and traffic are maximally controlled, the existing proposal is still just too large for the property it's on."[23] Another neighbor called it a "masonry monster."

A commissioner quizzed Dr. Hamadeh (a medical doctor and president of the mosque) on the written petition. He asked about the Qur'an and questioned how the mosque can be a place for Islam as well as interfaith activities. Dr. Hamadeh reiterated support for the interfaith possibilities within a mosque with explicit evidence from the Qur'an. This same commissioner also addressed the meaninglessness of the minaret if there was not going to be someone calling them to prayer, at which point Dr. Hamadeh spoke about the symbolic significance of the minaret, like a church steeple. Other witnesses on behalf of the mosque included the architect who cited numerous modifications to accommodate potential concerns about traffic, water, parking, lighting, and landscaping. The landscape architect and various engineers also offered testimony. A real estate agent was brought in by the petitioner to comment on property value impact, and a member of the Zoning Board commented that MECAA "increases in what is my opinion a saturation of religious institutions into this specific area."[24]

Supporters invoked suspicions about motivation and potential religious bias. In particular, the denial of height variances fits within an existing 36 foot height limit outlined in the code, but one resident suggested that many churches are in excess of 35 feet.[25] In media interviews, a member of the Council on American-Islamic Relations (CAIR) referred to the Irshad case and publicly addressed concerns that the council is trying to limit religious institutions. Jane Ramsey, the executive director of the Jewish Council on Urban Affairs, spoke at the news conference and voiced solidarity against creeping anti-Muslim actions: "As a Jew, I am deeply troubled by the pattern across our Chicagoland and across America to deny Muslims houses of worship and community centers."[26] A local religious leader, Pastor Tim Casey, perceived an anti-Muslim bias. As pastor of the Good Shepherd United Methodist Church, he has opened up his church space for Muslims to hold Friday prayers: "Just because they are Islamic, people completely reject them," and "I find that attitude un-American as well as un-Christian."[27] Fitting into the emerging solidarity across religions, a local Islamic leader insisted it is not so much an anti-Muslim target as an "anti-religious" attack.[28]

The Development Committee voted 5–1 and the Zoning Committee voted 5–2 endorsing the application of the conditional use permit to build a mosque and school.

EMERGING SOCIAL JUSTICE: COMPARING PARTICIPANTS, RHETORIC, AND ALLIANCES

Both the Naperville and Willowbrook controversies brought testimony from neighbors. Both mosque controversies in Naperville and Willowbrook look similar in terms of participation by neighborhood associations. Both sets of hearings included testimonies of opposition by individual homeowners living in the immediate vicinity of the mosque. One striking contrast is the fact that the petitioner in Naperville did not speak to the board, using his lawyer to introduce the petition and to respond to questions. This was noted by the neighbors as a lack of good will. In contrast with Naperville, the president of the proposed mosque in Willowbrook provided extensive testimony. In his opening comments, he addressed that MECCA's goal was "to promote the practice of the Islamic religion in accordance with the American tradition. We promote tolerance between the Muslim faith and the other faith communities. We offer several services to the Muslim community as well as the surrounding communities."[29]

Also distinct, in Willowbrook, several individuals offered formal testimony supporting the mosque and acknowledging the importance of the United States in terms of religious freedom and the mosque for fulfilling their religious life. Whereas the testimony included some of these broader issues in Naperville, the board did not engage the arguments. They denied relevance of these types of claims in a way that dismissed the possibility of exchange. Without engaging the claims, the debates became tainted by the lingering sense of bias. One commissioner's exchange with the mosque president reveals the contrast in Willowbrook in terms of the willingness of participants to address the broader issues of security, diversity, and potential litigation. As briefly mentioned above, one of the commissioners asked about the interpretation of the Qur'an in terms of interfaith possibilities: "Now, the Qur'an wasn't written instantly; was it? . . . is it not proper interpretation of the Qur'an, if there are inconsistencies, to be governed by the latter writing . . . and what I'm trying to get into is how does Muslim religion square with your wanting to have interfaith gatherings? Isn't that contrary to the Qur'an?"[30] Rather than simply soap-box positions, the sides engaged with each other in terms of the meaning and myths about Islam. Dr. Hamadeh responded:

> Not at all. In fact, let me tell you something. When the Qur'an refers to the people of the book, which is Christians and Jews, the Abrahamic

faith, it uses the Arabic word "wit." Now "wit" in Arabic, if you translate it into English it's not friendship, it's much more than that. The Qur'an refers to the relationship between the children and their parents as wit, and that's the highest of relationship between a children and their respect to their parents. He uses the same phrase for Muslims to deal with the Christians and Jews which he uses for children to use with their parents. That's how important and—that's how important the Qur'an places on the relationship between the Muslim and non-Muslim faith.[31]

Through the arguments back and forth, information and the potential for new understandings begins to emerge. This is in sharp contrast with the controversy in Naperville where there was little depth beyond stating opposing positions, and there was an unwillingness to acknowledge any larger context of fear and racism. As part of the public testimony, Dr. Hamadeh addressed the context explicitly:

I mean, we all know the atmosphere around us and the talk about extremism and all these terms that are being used, unfortunately. I do think—the MECCA organization is a mainstream organization that promotes tolerance, promotes the assimilation of the Muslim community with a larger—the United States community, American community, our community. I think it is incumbent about civic organizations and civic authorities like your authority to encourage, not only allow us to exist, but encourage us because only by encouraging mainstream Muslim organizations that promote tolerance we defeat and we fight extremism and the other elements. At least in our view, this is a duty for all organizations, for all civil authorities to do, and it will be extremely helpful.[32]

Both of these controversies had different playing fields with one level of engagement taking place within the county board meetings and another level of engagement in the media.

The media story around Naperville emphasized how little commentary and discussion surrounded the County Board hearings. While a neighbor articulated concerns, including potential links to terrorism, a commissioner quickly denied the relevance and redirected the testimony. Rather than engaging with the fear directly and transparently, the board focused on the traffic and lighting issues. With only legal representation, the neighbors and board did not have an opportunity to hear from the leaders of the proposed mosque in a way that further stopped conversations about broader community issues.

However, the themes of fear and threat were conveyed in the media. Commentary included the defensive proposition of a member of Irshad asking, "Why have we been singled out, as if our activity should be restricted?"

Recall the media statement by the chairman of the Irshad board that "it is not a popular sentiment to be in favor of an application by Muslims, no matter how good the application is."[33] These concerns from both sides were announced in the media but were not engaged in the actual public hearings, limiting dialogue and the opportunity to shift misperceptions. In contrast the Willowbrook hearings demonstrate more participation and communication, the news coverage conveyed a Muslim neighbor modestly expressing some understanding about potential misperceptions, claiming that "It's partly our fault. We don't do enough to reach out to people," and he articulated the "lack of communication and fear of the unknown"[34] as the source for misperceptions. A local scholar clearly stated that "I don't see it as much of an anti-Muslim sentiment. . . . For now, I would say it's an anti-religious thing that's going on."[35] In another story, the journalist acknowledged that "The leaders (of MECCA in Willowbrook) have gone out of their way not to ascribe anti-Muslim motives to all this."[36] At the same time, an interview with a DuPage United representative confirmed the important role of non-Muslim support in contesting the assumed identities of Muslims as terrorists, while simultaneously not polarizing the groups with accusations. According to one community leader, opposition to the mosques is not necessarily anti-Muslim, but rather fear of the unknown. "It was helpful that we were not Muslims, showing that this issue mattered to more than the Muslim community."[37] Through their established strategies of informal listening sessions, Council members heard from members of the Muslim community directly. Through the non-Muslim organization but also from these personal and informal testimonies, Muslim identities shifted from the unknown to becoming personalized stories reinforcing the breadth and depth of their community ties.

On both occasions in Naperville and Willowbrook, a CAIR representative spoke in support of the mosque. Regarding Naperville, a CAIR representative expressed concern that "the board may have acted on improper factors in rejecting the Irshad Learning Center's permit."[38] For Willowbrook, CAIR addressed the concern about oversaturation and asked "How many mosques constitute an oversaturation in DuPage County or the unincorporated area of DuPage County?"[39] And while CAIR was the only emerging ally for supporters of the Naperville mosque, the Willowbrook media story included others, like the executive director of the Jewish Council on Urban Affairs and the Pastor of Good Shepherd United Methodist Church. The Willowbrook media story confirms the emergence of interfaith alliance with advocates purposely avoiding the accusations of anti-Muslim sentiment. According to the research about mosque controversies in Europe,[40] the framing in terms of antireligious rather than anti-Muslim rhetoric is not unique. Different from Naperville, Willowbrook and MECCA potentially opened the doors to more allies than in Naperville and Irshad where dialogue is limited and resistance framed as anti-Muslim. My interview with a DuPage county bureaucrat addressed the extent to which media learned about Islam.

When telephoned about MECCA, the reporter asked him about the minuet on top of the mosque. It was the bureaucrat's persistence that finally led the reporter to understand the importance of the minaret, not minuet for mosques.[41] Learning may not lead to immediate understanding, but for key players, like the reporter of the local newspaper, the process of learning about Islam is an essential step.

RESOLUTION

When conflict extends from the particular issue to capture the broader themes of opposition between groups, there is an opportunity to share information. In particular, the inclusion and engagement of expressive interests addresses Putnam and Campbell's expectation that more contact leads to more favorable opinion. Presumably, debates can move beyond argument and develop shared understandings in such a way that more positive interaction is possible in the future. Perhaps disagreement about the mosque remains, but it may also leave the increasing possibility of cooperation over other issues in the future.

With sharing information, there is the possibility of social justice through emerging understanding from these mosque controversies. Learning can be analyzed in terms of the exchange of information between the petitioner(s) and the commissioners. Evidence of learning emerged in Naperville when commissioners asked questions about Muslim practices. Also, learning seemed to take place when debates between petitioners and opponents moved beyond arguing positions and questioned perspectives. These exchanges were opportunities to clarify practices and beliefs in a way that suggested empathy and then understanding. There was little evidence of learning within the Naperville mosque controversy, but there were obvious shared insights evolving within the Willowbrook experience. Reinforcing the exchange between the president and a commissioner about the Qu'ran, commissioners asked questions about Islam that led to learning about practices such as masjid, the muezzin, and Eid.

In response to one opponent's inappropriate claims about property value decline, the petitioner's lawyer guided a discussion of block busting. Testimony for the petitioner included statements about a Chicago neighborhood that matched property values and built a mosque in a community with a shared ethnic identity: "what is very interesting is that this is an enclave of folks who principally I believe are members of this mosque based upon my observation of the people that are there plus an interesting article. It's not the Supreme answer, but Wikipedia, in fact mentions this particular neighborhood as being unique because there is an enclave of people of similar members of this institution who wish to live in the neighborhood, and you can tell from some of the names and from the way folks are dressed that they have created a wonderful enclave for their activities."[42] Addressing this commentary directly, the petitioner's lawyer asked if they knew about block-busting: "a practice where people in the real estate industry try to use various factors of race, ethnicity and so forth and so on in an attempt to change the people who are living in an area by making threats as to the value of their land changing because of changes in people who are coming into or leaving an area."[43] The witness retaliated, but the transparent engagement of expressive issues, such as diversity and threat, were important for undermining both his credibility and the seeming pretense that the neighbor was concerned about zoning. Arguably, engaging the claims directly, specifically, and at length revealed the hypocrisy of the opposition and potential sympathy for the petitioners.

Ultimately, the county that denied the Irshad request in Naperville approved MECCA in Willowbrook,[44] and by the process of social justice, the community moved forward. There are clear differences in the type of engagement in the two instances to suggest that the *process* of controversy around religion may have contributed to an emerging social justice community.

CASE 3: SOCIAL JUSTICE AFTER INJUSTICE

The documentary *Confronting the Truth* provides a cross-country overview of truth commissions that began in 1983 and now includes twenty countries.[45] From South Africa, Peru, East Timor, and Morocco, the process of truth commissions is painful, social, and healing for communities. In countries experiencing devastating civil war or formalized inequality, it is difficult, if not impossible, to create an institutional mechanism to locate and punish the guilty. Furthermore, punishing those who were guilty of perpetuating violence and crimes against others did so within a web of supporting institutionalized inequality. Putting the perpetrators in jail often means putting a greater percent of the population in jail than can be maintained. Also, putting the perpetrators in jail would diminish significantly the social capital necessary to introduce widespread reform, either because of the strains on the judicial system, or because those guilty too often include the economic, political, and social elite within the society. Truth commissions recognize that there may be a better way forward if some of the elite confront their guilt and take responsibility through a system parallel to the legal process.

According to the documentary, there are six characteristics that promote success. First, the truth commission process needs to be public and accessible. Secondly, its participant perpetrators need to tell authentic truths that are verified by others in the community. Thirdly, the process cannot become a witch hunt focused on shaming particular individuals. Fourthly, victims and perpetrators have to embrace the possibility of collective blame and collective responsibility. Fifthly, at all times, the truth commissions embody nonretributive justice and so revenge is never accepted as part of the motivation, process, or outcomes. Finally, the most successful truth commissions are characterized by leadership able and willing to embody these characteristics and to promote the collective healing of the community.

While the implementation of truth commissions varies across countries and contexts, generally, they are limited to the individuals who are not directly accused of a specific and violent crime. Rather, it is focused on truth-telling for victims, and then acknowledgement of responsibility for those who may not have perpetrated violence directly but may have turned away or participated through bureaucratic distancing. It is up to appointed members of the communities, not legal authorities, to judge the authenticity of confessions and to then offer the communal rituals for social healing. One of the most powerful mechanisms for social healing is the collection of evidence and recording of the testimonies by victims. These become the history and collective memory of the community in a way that respects the victims and often in ways that couldn't happen through the legal system because of limited evidence and rules about legal proceedings. However, overarching the particular cases and crimes, truth commissions privilege the community and the potential for social healing and progress.

In the current climate of polarization and rising tensions around identity and disagreement, setting up truth and reconciliation commission groups throughout the country could be politically advantageous. There is a tendency for Americans to look at the world, especially the developing world, as recipients of models of political and economic institutions rather than providing models for the United States. In this instance of social coordination, those countries recovering from far worse injustices and plagued by challenges of development, offer a rich model for social engagement that is exactly the type of model that can and should be transported to the U.S. context. In fact, not only can we draw from other countries' examples, but we can look to similar restorative justice principles that surround Native American councils as well. Native traditions and customs rely heavily on the principles of restorative justice, and with some freedom from the national court system, many First Nations have successfully implemented these principles.

The Mohawk Nation of Akwesasne covers land in Canada as well as the United States. Since 1995, United States federal funding and Ontario provincial government funding assisted this community to set up its own autonomous system of restorative justice. Particular cases include shoplifting, dangerous driving, assault, assault with a deadly weapon, and even vehicular homicide. Cases are presented to a council of community members and by the process of restorative justice, acknowledge the importance of spiritual healing and community harmony for justice. There are community rituals and opportunities to share emotions. The first step requires the offenders to open the hearing by giving respect to Mother Earth. Often this tradition dislodges any pretense and arrogance; it brings the offender into communion with the earth and reminds the community that we share the earth similarly. Then the hearing proceeds with each participating person telling his or her story and concluding with a precise answer how to bring balance and harmony to the situation. The underlying tradition emphasizes the intimate community responsibility to put someone back on track and reintegrate them into their community. On the Canadian side, the justice coordinator describes the following encounter:

> Thompson talked about facilitating a hearing for "a hard-core person in leather jeans and jacket, didn't give respect for anybody, had a lengthy record. He was advised by his lawyer to give this a try. [His charge was] assault with a weapon. We thought, How are we ever going to get through to this guy? We brought him in, treated him with respect, told him where his seat was. I asked him to read the opening address. He said, 'I have trouble reading.' I said, 'I'll sit beside you and help you.' So he read it and before he even got done he turned to his victim and said, 'I'm so sorry for what I did to you,' and started crying. My job was halfway done. Sometimes there is such a powerful aura around it that people go in there nervous, but when they get out of there they're so at peace."[46]

Often the rituals bring the transgressor into communion with the group in a way that elicits profound remorse. Things can be said in these proceedings that would not be included in a courtroom proceeding. As Thompson said about the person responsible for vehicular homicide, "the offender wanted to restore harmony and peace in the community. There's no mechanism in the courts to restore balance." Many of these moments and statements contribute significantly to the healing process for the victim, the offender, and the community.

With both judicial punishment and reconciliation, the following case shows the potential for adaptation of the truth and reconciliation model into our U.S. system. McBride's case also demonstrates how justice and punishment of the most heinous crimes can be complemented by a social justice or reconciliation process. Clearly, we can maximize punishment while simultaneously protecting human dignity and social healing in profound ways. In January 2013, the *New York Times* covered the crime committed by Conor McBride, a nineteen-year-old who shot his girlfriend of three years. In the thick of a three-day fight, Ann was the victim of McBride's gunfire, and she died in the hospital several days later. From this tragedy and from this violent irreparable social injustice, emerged a deep well of forgiveness and healing social justice. As described in the article: "Most modern justice systems focus on a crime, a lawbreaker and a punishment. But a concept called 'restorative justice' considers harm done and strives for agreement from all concerned—the victims, the offender and the community—on making amends. And it allows victims, who often feel shut out of the prosecutorial process, a way to be heard and participate."[47]

Not every crime is eligible or reasonable for social justice action. Typically, a facilitator determines the readiness of both victim and offender to meet without animosity. After this initial judgment, the case is then removed from the legal system and "into a parallel restorative-justice process. All parties—the offender, victim, facilitator and law enforcement—come together in a forum sometimes called a restorative-community conference." While the process of restorative justice is quite limited in the United States, it is usually reserved for petty crimes. Introducing restorative justice for murder was extremely unusual and possible only because the victims' parents were the key initiators of the process. Restorative justice does not replace the criminal justice process. Conor McBride received twenty years in prison plus ten years of probation. However, in this instance and most other cases of restorative justice, the criminal system acknowledges the relevance of the restorative justice process in determining the appropriate punishment. Restorative justice removes the entire burden of punishment. The defendant is evaluated both by the victims and a community representative in terms of his or her authenticity. There is a responsibility for the perpetrator to describe the crime and take responsibility for the anger and decisions that surrounded it. In this way, the restorative justice process broadens punishment into the realm of emotional and personal responsibility to the victims in particular. The process supplements crime and punishment with responsibility and forgiveness.[48]

EDUCATION

Green niches, the mosque controversies over time, and the cases of restorative justice are empirical examples of social justice envisioned by this book. Each one depended upon frontrunners who perceived the possibility of change, and in each example, the frontrunner embraced a collectivist solution. Without denying the relevance of democracy, capitalism, or religion, a stronger community was the focus and was built as the foundation for future engagement. And distinct from leaders who remain guided by their individual interests, frontrunners perceive the benefits of a more collectivist approach to their activities. It would be inappropriate to suggest that they deny their individualism or self-interest, but rather they perceive better outcomes with a collectivist foundation upon which to focus their individual activities.

Education is a final mechanism to foster the motivation and skills for increased social justice. Especially because of the number of social justice programs popping up across the country it is possible for these programs to become the hub of something that is academic and practice oriented. From my perspective, the classroom experience is potentially revolutionary. Introduction to social justice courses need to focus first on understanding these concepts of deliberation, transparency, authenticity, polarization, and engagement. Introduction to social justice can be an ideal interdisciplinary course, drawing upon analysis from political science, economics, communication studies, and theology. The introductory course can be a starting point for students to learn about examples that fit, applying the principles to improve the types of cases that don't fit. Students are captive, strategically tied to attendance, passionate, and diverse enough to make the experience a legitimate micro experiment. In many ways, freedom, diversity, and innovation depends upon also nurturing a good citizenry, and these have been the primary goal of the liberal education. Just like democracy in the United States, however, something has changed. Students aren't as open as we think they should be, and educators are focused on content over process. These days, and to our detriment, our education system replicates consumption and transaction more than enlightenment.

A college campus is fertile ground for pushing students beyond their comfort zone. At the same time, through new ideas and experiences, the undergraduate setting enhances the possibility of preparing students for life paths implementing social justice. Most students leave their homes and come to a new environment that provides experiences of social injustice as well as social justice. If successful, a college setting can shepherd a new generation where individuals see and act in a world with a solid foundation of social justice. By the end of four years, social justice can be closer to their way of being, and from this foundation, they can live within the market and democracy and utilize technology and they can be faithful to their religion as well. However, the critical distinction is that they will not "be" the market, nor will they let others be used as though they are market commodities. Similarly, socially just individuals work within democracy without letting the institutionalized competition that defines democracy then become their identities. Technology will continue to intrigue them, puzzle them, and mobilize them, but it will not define them. In this social justice realm, religion enhances and invigorates, but it does not carry the overwhelming capacity to exclude others. All of these arenas continue to exist as part of one's life, but if social justice becomes meaningful, it does not allow these other arenas to define who we are or will become entirely. We are part of a collective in a way that is at least as important as the individual pull against the collective, and we need to turn our attention to healing all of the damages these other realms have caused.

With a central foundation of social justice, we protect our collective identity, but we also nurture our individual selves and our individualism and the spheres within which we work and live. Rather than a trade-off, the healthy "I" and "we" create synergy. The market, the polity, and religion will become healthier spheres for our interactions because we are healthier with a foundation built of thick collective connections. For example, technology becomes more limited but likely much more powerful as a tool rather than a way of life. Religion is a place to thrive, and it can be as much a

significant part of individuals' lives as they want it to be but without sacrificing our collective identity that ought to expand beyond religion.

John Rees was a recent visitor to our campus, lecturing about shifts
within the World Bank development mission to recognize development more
holistically, including religion. His statement, "We don't live in an economy.
We live in a society" resonates clearly with the theme of this book, but I
would emphasize just as strongly other versions of this thinking.[49] We don't
live in an economy but nor do we live in politics, technology, or religion. We
live in a society. As the chapter on religion pointed out, the major religions
discussed in this book do place society and social connectedness at the center
of their religion. When religion is grounded in a socially just foundation, it
reinforces its central tenets about ways of living in the world. Perhaps most
importantly, when religion is grounded in a socially just foundation, then
like political and economic institutions, it can receive the benefit of a socially
just society.

A perception of relative equality is one of the qualities contributing to
the possibility of teaching and learning social justice; students arrive to
a new environment where they appear to live in similarly socioeconomic
ways. Also important, an ideal college experience for the goal of social
justice ensures diversity on many dimensions, including socioeconomic
status. Certainly there are inequities, but one of the positive aspects of
college is that socioeconomic disparities are not quite so grossly transparent compared to high school and living within their family communities.
Students are exposed to new people and new ideas in a concentrated space.
Especially on a smaller campus, they are likely to encounter each other
repeatedly over a four-year period. Another potentially potent ingredient
for social justice is that these students work and play together. From their
arrival on campus, there are group-oriented activities that bring them into
a collective that is very new but also focused explicitly on building solidarity. At the very least, students are required to participate in semester
or quarter length courses, which require regular attendance and repeated
interaction. It is in this type of environment that students can be shaken
out of their assumptions and familiar patterns of living. It is in this type of
environment that they can articulate a well-worn position conveyed within
their homes and realize that it sounds less comfortable, even ridiculous
and hurtful within a diverse community. It is here that they must confront
their individual selves rubbing up against others. Where a liberal education
emphasizes a live and let live approach to diversity, social justice demands
that we roll in the hurt of it. Liberalism was a hallmark of respecting
diversity, but its practice has deteriorated into respecting separate spaces.
Live and let live has evolved into separate quarters with sterile handshakes
in the public square followed by recriminating whispers among one's like-
minded individuals. In the next chapter, I explore teaching and concepts to
foster the practice of social justice at the same time as students study the
intellectual foundations for social justice.

NOTES

1. John Adams, Letter to Mercy Warren, April 16, 1776. http://patriotpost.us/ fqd/16934. Accessed July 26, 2013.
2. Jack Knight and James Johnson, *The Priority of Democracy: Political Conse- quences of Pragmatism* (New York: Russell Sage Foundation, 2011), 255.
3. Jeremy Driscoll, *A Monk's Alphabet: Moments of Stillness in a Turning World* (Boston New Seeds, 2007), 132.
4. Charles Taylor, *The Ethics of Authenticity* (Cambridge: Harvard University Press, 1991), 66.
5. Robert H. Salisbury and Lauretta Conklin Frederking, "Instrumental v. Expressive Group Politics: The National Endowment for the Arts," in *Inter- est Group Politics*, ed. Allan Cigler and Burdett Loomis, 5th ed. (Washington, DC: CQ Press, 1998), 283–303.
6. Allen Cigler and Burdett A. Loomis, eds. *Interest Group Politics* (Washing- ton, DC: CQ Press, 1998), 7.
7. This research on Oregon wineries was published originally in a compara- tive study of Oregon and British Columbia wineries. See Lauretta Conklin Frederking. "Getting to green: niche-driven or government-led entrepreneur- ship and sustainability in the wine industry" in *New England Journal of Entrepreneurship*, 14:1 (2011): 47–61.
8. Jerry Katz and Chris Steyaert, "Reclaiming the Space of Entrepreneurship in Society: Geographical, Discursive and Social Dimensions," *Entrepreneurship and Regional Development* 16 (2004): 179–96.
9. Denise Fletcher, "Entrepreneurial Processes and the Social Construction of Opportunity," *Entrepreneurship and Regional Development* 18 (2006): 421– 40.
10. AtoZ (Sam Tannahill); Bergstrom (Josh Bergstrom); Resonance (Kevin Cham- bers). I conducted these face-to-face interviews with Oregon winery owners during Spring, 2008.
11. Gill Seyfang and Adrian Smith, A. "Grassroots Innovations for Sustainable Development: Towards a New Research and Policy Agenda," *Environmental Politics* 16 (4), 584-603.
12. Lauretta Conklin Frederking, "A Cross-national Study of Culture, Organi- zation and Entrepreneurship in Three Neighbourhoods," *Entrepreneurship and Regional Development* 16 (2004): 197–215. Also see Lauretta Conklin Frederking, *Economic and Political Integration in Immigrant Neighbour- hoods: Trajectories of Virtuous and Vicious Cycles* (Selinsgrove: Susque- hanna University Press, 2007).
13. From CAIR 2005 and CAIR 2009 report quoted in Stephen Salisbury, "Mosque-mania Anti-Muslim fears and the far right," August 10, 2010. Accessed July 26, 2013.
14. Amaney Jamal, "The Racialization of Muslim Americans," in *Muslims in Western Politics*, ed. Abdulkader H. Sinno (Bloomington: Indiana University Press, 2009), 206.
15. Council of Islamic Organizations of Greater Chicago. http://www.ciogc.org/ Go.aspx?link=7654323.
16. Bob Goldsborough, "DuPage County Rejects Proposed Islamic Center," *Chi- cago Breaking News Center*, January 12, 2010.
17. Testimony from the public hearing.
18. DuPage County Board of Appeals Petition No. ???-???, May 14, 2009, 5.
19. Goldsborough, "DuPage County Rejects Proposed Islamic Center."
20. S. Carlman, "County Board Denies Mosque Tower, Delays Vote on Permit," *Couriernews*, February 8, 2011.

21. Carlman, "County Board Denies Mosque Tower, Delays Vote on Permit."
22. DuPage Country Board of Appeals Petition No. Z10–040, October 12, 2010, 72.
23. DuPage County Board of Appeals Petition No. Z10–040, October 12, 2010, 84.
24. S. Daniels and J. Ruzich, "Religious Leaders Urge Approval of DuPage Mosque," *Chicago Tribune*, January 19, 2011.
25. Carlman, "County Board Denies Mosque Tower, Delays Vote on Permit."
26. Daniels and Ruzich, "Religious Leaders Urge Approval of DuPage Mosque."
27. Daniels and Ruzich, "Religious Leaders Urge Approval of DuPage Mosque."
28. Daniels and Ruzich, "Religious Leaders Urge Approval of DuPage Mosque."
29. DuPage County Board of Appeals Petition No. Z10–040, September 20, 2010, 19–20.
30. DuPage County Board of Appeals Petition No. Z10–040, September 20, 2010, 30.
31. DuPage County Board of Appeals Petition No. Z10–040, September 20, 2010, 30.
32. DuPage County Board of Appeals Petition No. Z10–040, September 20, 2010, 32.
33. Goldsborough, "DuPage County Rejects Proposed Islamic Center."
34. S. Daniels and J. Gregory, "DuPage Board to Decide Today on Mosque," *Chicago Tribune*, February 7, 2011.
35. Daniels and Gregory, "DuPage Board to Decide Today on Mosque."
36. "In Good Faith," *Chicago Tribune Editorials*, February 17, 2011.
37. Amy Lawless Ayala, DuPage United Representative, in discussion with the author, Tuesday, August 14, 2012.
38. Goldsborough, "DuPage County Rejects Proposed Islamic Center."
39. Daniels and Ruzich, "Religious Leaders Urge Approval of DuPage Mosque."
40. Joel Fetzer and J. Soper, *Muslims and the State of Britain, France, and Germany* (Cambridge: Cambridge University Press, 2005).
41. DuPage County Representative, in discussion with the author, Thursday, June 28, 2012.
42. DuPage County Board of Appeals Petition No. Z10–040, November 9, 2010, 30–1.
43. DuPage County Board of Appeals Petition No. Z10–040, November 9, 2010, 92.
44. "On Friday, March 29, 2013, Judge Pallmeyer issued a 70-page decision granting judgment in favor of ILC on claims under RLUIPA's substantial burden provision, the First Amendment, the Illinois Religious Freedom Restoration Act, and state zoning law. Based on the detailed factual record, Judge Pallmeyer held that the Zoning Board of Appeals relied on, 'erroneous findings or impermissible speculation,' and the County's 'repeated errors, speculation, and refusal to impose conditions support an inference that the County subjected ILC to a substantial burden,' on its free exercise of religion. As a result, the court reversed the County Board's denial of a permit to ILC and ordered that the Board issue the permit, 'absent a material change in the circumstances.'" See "Cair-Chicago Wins Judgment for Muslim Center's Freedom of Religion," Cair Chicago, April 1, 2013. Accessed July 26, 2013. http://www.cairchicago.org/2013/04/01/cair-chicago-wins-judgment-for-muslim-centers-freedom-of-religion/.
45. Steve York, *Truth Commissions and Societies in Transition: Confronting the Truth* (Washington, DC: York Zimmerman, 2007), Documentary.

46. Laura Mirsky, "Restorative Justice Practices of Native American, First Nation and Other Indigenous People of North America: Part II," International Institute for Restorative Practices, Bethlehem, Pennsylvania, Posted May 26, 2004. Accessed July 26, 2013. http://www.iirp.edu/article_detail .php?article_id=NDA0.
47. Paul Tullis, "Can Forgiveness Play a Role in Criminal Justice?" *New York Times*, January 4, 2013.
48. As an example of new efforts to institutionalize the practice, a restorative justice initiative has been introduced at Marquette University Law School. See http://law.marquette.edu/rji/ for the program.
49. John Rees, Ph.D., Notre Dame Australia quoting Tim Costello, CEO of World Vision Australia. Lecture at the University of Portland, February 6, 2013.

7 Teaching and Living Social Justice

> Children should be educated and instructed in the principles of freedom.
>
> —John Adams[1]

INTRODUCTION

Several colleagues researched the different ways that students perceive social justice. Through questions about political association and then open-ended interpretations of social justice, they determined that students, regardless of how they position themselves as liberal or conservative, share a similar perspective of social justice. The shared interpretation includes "equal rights, basic needs, education, and community service." [2] There are small differences around environmental issues more prevalent for those who identify as liberal, and charity and just policy issues as more central issues for those who identify as conservative. From this data, which suggests some common ground, it is difficult to imagine the types of intractable problems or divisions that characterize mainstream society. In fact, recent national polls reveal that a great deal of consensus characterizes the United States more generally. The study cites a range of issues, including that seven out of ten people want to raise minimum wage, to support limits for Congress, to support building the Keystone pipeline, and to make preschool available.[3] From this perspective, political rhetoric purposely divides the nation rather than latent public opinion.

Certainly, at this stage of college life, perhaps there is more flexibility associated with political identities so that students have not yet squandered away this consensus, or alternatively, students prioritize certain issues over the established and acknowledged political divisions. At best, we can imagine optimistically that the larger population reflects this student sample and shares consensus around certain fundamental rights, needs, and opportunities for all people.

At the same time that there may be a shared foundation, we have to admit that societal forces regularly pull us far away from solidarity. Our collective "we" has been captured by assaulting arenas, like the market, the political system, technology, and religion. While we need to resurrect space for our socially just orientation, we have lost many of the intuitions, skills, and beliefs that make the socially just foundation desirable and rewarding. Our surrender to these political, economic, technological, and religious interests has reinforced these systems, and our central individualized role in them, as the relevant systems of being. We have lost our collective "we" in this bargain and adopted systems that celebrate individualism while they destroy a most critical and vital partner of individualism. For individualism to thrive and for us to thrive as individuals, we need to understand and explore our identities through social experiences, exchanged ideas, and emotional connections. The collective is an important part of each individual identity. While individualism accepts orientation around the individual, the individualizing process should be very much a social process. To become better individuals, more self-discerning and self-aware, we need to reinvigorate our social connectedness.

Many aspects of a college experience offer the unique opportunity to cultivate a new way of being for our young people. If they absorb these ways of thinking, believing, and experiencing, I expect that they will go into the postcollege world much healthier about themselves and much more optimistic about the collective within which they live. From the learned foundation of social justice, these young people are much more likely to "be the change" in their careers, in their families, and in their political parties, and the many other communities within which they live.

TRANSFORMATION OF THE INDIVIDUAL

Rather than merely respecting individual differences, social justice demands that we move to a deeper level of understanding, finding harmony with our differences. One of my senior students in a social justice capstone class commented that some of her roommates pegged her as a "tree-hugging granola." Regularly, she hears whispers as one reminds the other to avoid saying certain things around her because she is "into that kind of stuff." So when a roommate said she wouldn't get water for the others "because she wasn't a slave," they hushed when this particular student came into the room. We have become a culture in which individuals censor themselves, quickly figuring out who needs particular types of conversation. From one perspective, this is emblematic and potentially praiseworthy as part of civil society. However, it is difficult to move forward in terms of social justice with clever, strategic self-censors. Martin Luther King Jr. expressed a very different process of honest and open dialogue that rejects self-censorship and demands the greatest openness in terms of opposing views:

> Here is the true meaning and value of compassion and nonviolence when it helps us to see the enemy's point of view, to hear his questions,

to know his assessment of ourselves. For from his view we may indeed see the basic weaknesses of our own condition, and if we are mature, we may learn and grow and profit from the wisdom of the brothers who are called the opposition.[4]

Unfortunately, self-censorship may be a devastating hallmark of our heightened liberal society. We cater to our impressions of people and skate swiftly across the surfaces of social exchange. Rather than conversation and interactions from a place of integrity, we follow scripts. We are savvy, but we are also empty of authentic identity, and we are more isolated—all while we appear to participate in a more diverse and liberal society. So how can we break out of this scripted civility? If a course on social justice moves beyond learning about social justice to practicing social justice, it needs to break down the barriers of politicized rhetoric but also polite misrepresentation and silence.

Paulo Freire's seminal *Pedagogy of the Oppressed* juxtaposes the banking model of teaching, whereby teachers offer information about reality rather than a critical analysis of it. He argues that "the banking approach masks the effort to turn women and men into automatons,"[5] whereas he offers a different approach to teaching, "praxis," as the way forward to become more fully human. In referring to oppression and education, Friere states that "To no longer be prey to its force, one must emerge from it and turn upon it. This can be done only by means of praxis: reflection and action upon the world in order to transform it."[6] Education needs to be reflective, and individual reflection can be liberating, but only from a foundation that is social. Dialogue is the central prerequisite for individual liberation. In order to cultivate more spaces of social justice, young people need to be shaken out of their current ways of living politely and without authenticity. Until we find the relevance of our social engagements as the deeper and more meaningful way to discover ourselves, we remain disconnected. Freire's model of liberation from oppression is particularly apt for moving students toward a new way of engaging with each other authentically.

With the first conversations among my social justice students, they often agree that they are boxed in by their social justice identities. They feel unfairly pigeon-holed and resent being labeled or assumed in terms of their ideas or positions. Is it peculiar that the next stage of our conversations typically turns into their own assumptions about others? As a recent example, one student invited all of us to join her volunteer experience at a religious chapel. I mentioned in an earlier chapter that the way Bush's faith-based initiative plays out in American society, religious institutions receive support to provide services to the poor. As long as those services aren't attached to missionary appeals or contingencies, then religious organizations are able to provide extensive support to alleviate some of the poverty problem in the United States. This context becomes important for appreciating that one can work within the vehicle of religion without violating preferences or adherence to a strictly secular world. And while I was fully prepared for the other students in the senior social justice class to plea that they couldn't make time for a Saturday experience, their responses were much more unsettling. One student refused to attend because her version of social justice meant long-term relationship building, and it felt too intrusive and condescending to be offering support much more like an observer rather than in solidarity. Another student refused to attend because she wouldn't participate in anything supported by the Church, especially the Catholic Church. Now, if you have read this far in the book, I think it would strike you, as it did me, that my perspective of social justice as social engagement hadn't made much of an impact. What does it mean, and how are we to move forward, if the small group of social justice students cut each other off and purposely disengage when it doesn't fit their preferences or paradigm? We spent time beyond the initial rejection, sorting out the issues around the rejection, and while we didn't attend the service learning project together, we did move to a better place in terms of understanding. We became closer in spite of, or likely even because of, the conflict. So again and again, we need to divest students of their assumptions, but if the transformation is meaningful, we need to create an environment where it is comfortable enough for them to assert their deeply felt assumptions. We can be open to transformation only when we engage with each other authentically. This can be uncomfortable and rife with conflict, but the parameters nurture collective empathy while cultivating an inspired and protected individual identity.

Curtiss Paul DeYoung describes the pain and vulnerability associated with a very high-level, meaningful, authentic dialogue:

> Robert Kennedy asked for feedback from the margins in May of 1963, while serving as attorney general of the United States. He was raised in wealth and privilege with little awareness of poverty and racism. Yet President John F. Kennedy, Robert's brother, assigned him to interact with the Civil Rights Movement. Robert Kennedy invited noted social critic James Baldwin to assemble a group of African Americans to speak honestly to him about issues of race and poverty in the United States. A group that included sociologists, psychologists, activists, and artists met with Kennedy in New York City.
>
> The meeting began with a polite exchange on the state of racism. Robert Kennedy made comments about the positive role of the government in matters of civil rights. Jerome Smith was a young civil rights activist in attendance who had been brutalized and arrested several times. Listening to the comments, he exploded. He said he wanted to vomit just being in the same room with Robert Kennedy who had done so little to support the freedom struggle of African Americans. Singer Lena Horne described what happened next. "This boy [Smith] just put it like it was. He communicated the plain, basic suffering of being a Negro. The primeval memory of everyone in the room went to work

after that . . . He took us back to the common direct of our existence and rubbed our noses in it . . . You could not encompass his anger, his fury, in a set of statistics.

As Jerome Smith kept up his verbal assault of Kennedy, the attorney general turned away from Smith and ignored him. This made the others in the room even angrier, and they began to speak more bluntly too. Psychologist and educator Kenneth Clark recalled, "Bobby [Kennedy] became more silent and tense, and he sat immobile in the chair. He no longer continued to defend himself. He just sat, and you could see the tension and the pressure building in him." Clark reflected later that this was "the most intense, traumatic meeting in which I've ever taken part . . . the most unrestrained interchange among adults, head-to-head, no holds barred . . . the most dramatic experience I have ever had." Kennedy biographer Konstantin Sidorenko sums up the meeting:

It shook Robert Kennedy to the core of his beliefs. . . . It was the most important lesson any American public official had ever received on the anger and frustrations underlying segregation, poverty and the entire black experience. Most other prominent men might have walked out of the room quickly. Robert Kennedy stayed there until the meeting fizzled out three hours after it began. He was angry, hurt and disgusted with the entire process. His reaction could have been that the entire issue was futile and a waste of time. Something very different happened. Bobby changed.[7]

Quite aptly, DeYoung utilizes this story in his book about social justice heroes to emphasize the pain of the processes that are part of transformation: "Transformation requires the sacrifice of assumptions and humility of spirit . . . [and] will never be effective in deep social change without stripping off condescension and expanding a one-dimensional viewpoint."[8] Students can experience this type of transformation over a four-year period. It is up to teachers to provide the cases and discussions that cultivate honesty, curiosity, and complexity.

DIFFERENT TYPES OF JUSTICE

At the beginning of a course on social justice, it is important to place social justice within the broader discussions of justice. As Michael Sandel articulates the general parameters, justice is a way of distributing things we value, like income and wealth, duties and rights, power and opportunities, and offices and honors.[9] These are central concerns of justice, and certainly, these are central concerns of social justice as well. One primary difference is that justice focuses on decisions about how to distribute the things we value, whereas social justice is a priori to establish the foundation from which we should discuss how to distribute things we value. When thinking about the

U.S. context, our empirical system of justice draws from a broad band of ideals, including maximizing preferences, preserving rights, and promoting virtues. Our democratic process preserves the strongest vehicle for the utilitarian model of maximizing preferences. With its roots from Bentham and John Stuart Mill, democracy maintains the principle of autonomy and then both the freedom and equality of preferences. With an image of government as an arena, the voting mechanism defines the just collective will through the aggregation of preferences. Distinct from this system of aggregating preferences as a foundation for justice, there is a very broad range of political philosophers from Kant to Rawls to Nozick, who share a concern for the protection of inviolable individual rights. Whether in relation to government or each other, these philosophers emphasize justice in terms of rights.

However, it is apparent that the determination of rights, at least in the United States, is more often subject to contextual and nuanced interpretations in such a way that the manifestation or meaning of rights is settled by utilitarian mechanisms rather than fundamental principles. Education rights, safety rights, and freedom rights are increasingly decided and justified by the aggregation of preferences; a utilitarian, democratic process. With their different strengths and weaknesses, these versions of justice share the primary preexisting interests of the individual at the central core of justice.

While individualism is central to a good and just life, it cannot be the core of *social* justice. Equally fundamental is our social nature, and this needs to remain the focus of social justice as distinct from other types of justice that may be important in society. Aristotle offers a more transformational and social model to emphasize justice as the cultivation of virtue. Here justice includes responsibility to form the individual through good habits, which become good character, which becomes moral virtue. This Aristotelian version of justice moves us closer to social justice in terms of the emphasis on cultivating good citizenship. In fact, many of the characteristics that Aristotle associates with the political realm, I assert as important and vital but necessarily existing apart from the political realm, and instead within a social justice realm. There is a primary difference between social justice and the Aristotelian version of justice. For Aristotle, the source of virtue comes from the *polis*, whereas in the social justice model, virtues emerge from the grassroots social constitution and process of social justice.

It may be an unfortunate empirical outcome, but our political system no longer functions as the social glue for human goodness or collective responsibilities. Arguably, the political realm has become so tainted by individual interests and corruption that it cannot be even a potential source for realizing virtue of any kind. It is a small but important step to carry Aristotelian ideas into my vision of social justice because it cannot be found or cultivated within our modern liberal democracy. Being an ideal citizen doesn't mean that we share our preferences over most of our daily issues, but it does mean that we share understandings. Like Aristotle, I convey the importance of practice and habit, but whereas Aristotle placed practice and habit within the realm of the *polis*, I place the practice and habit of citizenship in terms of the realm of social justice.

The Rawlsian perspective around social justice emphasizes that an individual's status is much less about his or her abilities and much more about the systemic incentives and rewards that are both arbitrary and reinforcing. If we happen to live in a society that rewards excellence in sports, which we do, then someone who is very good in terms of these attributes receives significant financial rewards. However, if we live in this sports-crazed society, we shouldn't be surprised that someone who has expertise in pottery receives much less financial affirmation. I encourage students to think about the good luck, bad luck aspects of success. However, when they realize the arbitrariness, not necessarily the arbitrariness of their gifts, but of the fact that society rewards particular gifts over others, then they often are unsettled. What if societal rewards really are so random and without external validity?

I invite students to think about a radical starting point for secular social justice—that none of us is special. As conveyed by Michael McCollough's recent address to graduates of Wellesley High School,[10] if we are all special, then it is impossible for any one of us to be special. Students are pulled out of their comfort zone here. We are a society that raises our children to demi-God status. They are precious. It is jarring for them to consider what seems to be the antithesis—that they are entirely not special. Isn't this moving us to the heart of the social justice dilemma? Everywhere, we cultivate a sensation around individual talent and gifts, but we forget that our human nature is social as much as it is special in its individualism. If the fundamental core of each one of us is social, the tempering and even denial of individualism is as much a part of realizing our potential as the affirmation of it. Social justice is inherently and necessarily *social*, and it is the foundation upon which further discussions of justice in terms of distribution of goods and protections of rights must rest.

The frustration among students emerges frequently: "it feels hopeless, as though effort is much less important than the lottery of societal popularity." Michael Sandel includes a hypothetical letter to a student admitted to college. It emphasizes the randomness of criteria directing college admission and the systemic ways that reinforce particular arbitrarily defined assets:

Dear successful applicant,

We are pleased to inform you that your application for admission has been accepted. It turns out that you happen to have the traits that society needs at the moment, so we propose to exploit your assets for society's advantage by admitting you to the study of law.

You are to be congratulated, not in the sense that you deserve credit for having the qualities that led to your admission—you do not—but only in the sense that the winner of a lottery is to be congratulated. You are lucky to have come along with the right traits at the right moment. If you choose to accept our offer, you will ultimately be entitled to the benefits that attach to being used in this way. For this, you may properly celebrate.

You, or more likely your parents, may be tempted to celebrate in the further sense that you take this admission to reflect favorably, if not on your native endowments, then at least on the conscientious effort you have made to cultivate your abilities. But the notion that you deserve even the superior character necessary to your effort is equally problematic, for your character depends on fortunate circumstances of various kinds for which you can claim no credit.[11]

At this point, students typically feel disheartened, but I push them to reconsider. Instead of reinforcing helplessness, this case affirms the infinite possibilities for change. Recently, I read a copy of the newspaper article tracing the rise of popularized Judge Judy from cantankerous, reviled city judge to extraordinary celebrity.[12] I asked them what they thought about the story in light of our conversation. Several students responded that it made them even more depressed to think that the public sways of facile entertainment bring so much financial return. However, I remind them that the most amazing shifts in public opinion, status, and possibility are evident every day. Judge Judy is just one case of possibility, but a very different message is clear. Rather than cynicism, we can celebrate the vast potential for dramatic and profound change. Where so much change is possible, it should be inspiring to commit more effort not less, not to becoming the next Judge Judy, but to cultivating social justice communities. We spend time studying not only individual success stories but recalling the tidal wave shifts of anti-smoking, anti-drinking and driving, and environmental sensitivities. Change is everywhere, and it is dramatic, and it can reinforce our commitments to social justice.

The remaining part of this chapter addresses many concepts that I introduce in my social justice class. Each presents a unique perspective, often contrary to students' expectations, and the conversation of each brings students closer to awareness of social justice possibilities as an academic program and as a set of practices. Together, the concepts and the learning experience prepare students to implement their own communities of social justice. Recall the discussion of Dewey's distinction between epistemic and political democracy in Chapter 2. Epistemic democracy emphasizes a process of deliberation central to truth-seeking and beneficial to the formal political process. For Dewey, education is the critical catalyst for realizing deliberative democracy primarily because of "his belief that political democracy would not work well unless people learned to think about political questions the way scientists think about scientific ones—disinterestedly, intelligently, and empirically. He thought that ordinary people *could* learn to think this way but he was not optimistic."[13] Social justice here carries the values and goals of Dewey's epistemic democracy. However, rather than being a truth-seeking process in preparation for deliberative democracy as a more formal political process, social justice is the foundation for a healthier democracy, and also a healthier capitalism, religion, and technology.

1. Individual Justice v. Social Justice

On campuses across the United States, leadership is not only the buzz word but also the focus for new initiatives in academic programs and awards, the center of speeches, and the seeming panacea for the future. My students are amused whenever I tell them that Canadians are raised with the lesson that second place may be better than first; first place invites everyone's ire and jealousies, whereas second place is much better, earning much more support from the collective.

This is an interesting contrast between the United States and the more collective-oriented society in Canada. The individual who helps is more cherished than the one who leads. It is not surprising that the Canadian political system is more oriented around the collective, and over time, universal welfare policies have been supported by Canadian political culture. Regardless of the causal sequence to explain the Canadian context, my time living in the United States and raising two children here continually reminds me that other approaches and types of culture are nurtured in the United States. I couldn't quite believe the first soccer league game when parents had organized a bridge and banner of balloons for each child to run through individually and with the announcement of his or her name over the loud speaker. At the end of the season of every sport, each child receives a trophy with his or her name on it. Here, it seems as though from the very earliest stages, we raise our young people to imagine themselves as leaders or even superstars in training. We coddle, celebrate, and privilege our young people to the point where everyone believes he or she is meant to carry the torch and win gold medals. By definition, no one can be a leader if everyone is a leader, and yet we are multiplying the number of programs in college that emphasize leadership.

The critical question is how leadership can be part of the social justice project and whether the qualities of leadership are really the qualities that move the social justice project forward. With entitlement, we also nurture razor-sharp self-interest and arrogance but inevitable and proportionate disappointments. One of the most profound realizations as a mother was the fact that children and family life successfully couch disappointments. Personal disappointments can seem less severe just as any personal victory becomes less relevant. By extension, in community, we have more humility, but through these thick connections, we have more consistent relevance. A leader, like an entrepreneur, maximizes support, and this type of conceptualization presumes a driving self-interest on the part of the leaders. However, the version of social justice put forward in this book emphasizes the importance of building a foundation of civility and understanding in order to shore up support for the collective. In the words of activist Ella

Baker "strong people don't need strong leaders,"[14] and in the process of social justice this is especially true. However, how society thinks about social justice is largely path dependent. The Canadian system in many instances privileges collective rights—and perhaps social justice as it is conceptualized here as well—over individual rights in a way that contrasts with the American system.

The social justice umbrella is popularized in both contexts. However, as a Canadian-American teaching in a liberal arts college in the United States, I have learned how the difference is more deeply ingrained and potentially relevant than acknowledged by the shared social justice concept. In fact, I spend much time listening to American undergraduates, and through my foreigner lens, their vision of social justice corresponds much more clearly with a version of individual justice rather than social justice. Individual justice *for all* may be worthy as a goal, but it is not the same as social justice.

According to the vision in this book, the specific social justice outcomes are ongoing, and without a tangible, discernible reward for the leaders. It requires individuals to recognize their interests as necessarily vague and flexible in building the collective, not focusing on the alignment of specific interests with the appropriate leader and his or her goals.

2. Formal v. Informal

Students on campuses across the country demand recognition for rights (gay rights, minority rights, and political rights, for example) but the very pursuit of those rights may undermine the goals in two ways. First, rights are often inappropriately perceived as the vehicle for both recognition and acceptance within a community. However, the process of articulating and cultivating support can just as easily undermine the shared values they are seeking. It is not necessary to dissuade students from the fight to change rules and laws, but it is important to raise their consciousness that a change in laws does not necessarily move the collective circle closer together. Mobilizing and articulating goals and interests can break down cooperation just as it moves a group close to a goal. I traced this empirical and generalizable pattern in my study of social capital.[15] Just as groups become focused on a particular outcome, their more refined, individualized interests begin to surface. The energy of mobilization awakens people to the possibility of change and the possibility of satisfying particular interests. In a curious empirical twist, the very cause of group breakdown is the wave of social mobilization.

Rules and laws that proactively articulate individual rights may disassemble the cohesion of the broader community. Legal change does not always correspond with acceptance, and usually not acceptance in the ways that may be desired. If there is anything that colleges know well, the required courses are typically the least liked by students. Similarly, compelling individuals to particular treatment by the law certainly can improve the status of groups, but it can also limit the improvement just to the status demanded by the law. Claus Offe discussed this pattern in terms of labor mobilization and the victory of union recognition and representation. Instead of a meaningful and comprehensive victory of the oppressed, unions stunted the possibility of revolution.[16]

To instill a deeper understanding of both the possibilities but also the problems of change, it is helpful to draw on the many cross-country studies of revolutionary change that suggest cautionary tales about both the speed and formal institutionalization of rights. A broad brushstroke of examples can include the fall of the Soviet Union and the backlash following shock therapy changes. The feminist movement and its subsequent divisions provide insight into both the strengths and the weaknesses that come from targeting legislation over broader norm change.[17] In a parallel discussion around race, Tatum aptly describes a legitimized insipid and systemic racism that followed from laws that institutionalized equality but preserved the asymmetries of power.[18] From these very different examples, students are not pushed to avoid change, but they are encouraged to appreciate the complexity of goals and the potential unintended consequences of mobilization. As students, cases of mobilization and their consequences can be compared and analyzed through the social justice lens. What processes and outcomes correspond with solidarity in terms of shared understanding, and what processes and outcomes correspond with increasing polarization?

3. Process v. Outcomes

We love innovation and success, but as a society, we fail to nurture a mainstream understanding that the path of innovation and success is necessarily driven by failures and challenge. This sensibility that failure is an essential part of success is lost in our education standards and social norms. We educate students for the outcomes rather than the process. Young people think of social justice as a battle with winners and losers. In so many areas and ways, we have little passion for the process. To a large degree, my call for considering social justice in terms of its characteristics as *process* and distinctly *social* is part of a larger lament that collectively, in so many ways, we have forgotten the values of process and social connectedness more generally.

As soon as the conversation carries a tone of winning or losing, it is less likely a conversation promising social justice by the terms outlined here. According to Harford: "The everyday rituals of life are carefully designed to ensure that people experience the painful sensation of failure as rarely as possible."[19] While erasing failure is a chimerical goal, it also leads into a cycle of self-justification. As the *Financial Times* describes Carol Tavris and Elliot Aronson's book *Mistakes Were Made (but Not by Me)*, they offer new insights about the Milgram Experiment.

The Milgram Experiment was one of the most controversial and insightful social science experiments of the twentieth century. Milgram paired unknowing participants with research assistants. Under the pretense of an experiment about learning, the unknowing participant was designated as the teacher and was required to administer an electric shock to the "student." Amid fabricated screams of pain, an unexpectedly large number of participant teachers continued to administer increasing levels of shock. Tavris and Aronson analyze the experiment in new ways and suggest that beyond obedience, subjects of the Milgram Experiment revealed their unwillingness to admit mistakes. In spite of increasing intensities, subjects were unwilling to stop largely because they would rather repeat a mistake in a soothing process of self-justification.

What is it that makes some of us propelled by failure rather than defeated by it or determined to protect ourselves from it? Stanford psychologist Carol Dweck joins a cadre of researchers with her question: "what makes a really capable child give up in the face of failure, where other children may be motivated by the failure."[20] I don't think that it is mysterious. As educators, we can provide space for students to recover from failure. In their catalogue of failure, the *Financial Times* interviewed a choreographer who received sharp criticism of her Broadway ballet/musical. Tharp wrote a book called *The Creative Habit*, and the *Financial Times* outlined her processing of the failure: "she took the criticism on board, made the necessary changes to her show, and opened on Broadway to glowing reviews,"[21] conveys the importance of "an environment designed to allow that learning process" and subsequent transformative process. As educators, we need to reinforce failure as a critical step in the learning process in order to combat Dweck's observation that "students for whom performance is paramount want to look smart even if it means not learning a thing in the process."[22] Accepting failure in the cognitive realm is so important, but for social justice it is perhaps even more important for students to let each other make emotional mistakes. Our society is finely tuned around political correctness with the built-in shame, retreat and lies that follow.

4. Local v. Global

When one is alert to the plights of poverty, inequality, and suffering, the agenda for social justice seems appropriately vast and demanding. In teaching college students about social justice, it is clear that one of the least scrutinized areas is the prioritization between local and global social justice. College students are oriented to think globally these days. We wear the statistics about student participation in study abroad programs like a badge of honor. However, there are two issues that need to be unpacked in terms of the globalizing trend. First, there can be a clear trade-off between local and global social justice. For example, improving lives for individuals in U.S. society may come with the consequence of economic exploitation in other countries. As a flip-flop example, focusing resources on poverty across the world obviously raises eyebrows about those homeless on our own streets.

Linda Polman's *War Games* traces the pervasive corruption enveloping the globalized nonprofit industry.[23] Without certain commitments to the rule of law, war-torn societies are particularly vulnerable to vigilante intentions that are often misaligned in terms of the cultural and institutional context.

During a class focused on this dilemma, a woman from a food services provider led a discussion about gender discrimination and living in poverty. She shared her personal story of similar training and experience without equal compensation, and then her weekly pattern of donating plasma to pay bills. Swiftly and effectively, her story popped the pristine bubble of their college environment. While so many students jump into vans to head downtown and serve those in poverty, they return to the campus and overlook the potential struggle of those around them, including so many of the workers who serve them on a daily basis.

In her final summary, she addressed the workers' mobilization efforts around pay equity, but she didn't ask for students to join her effort. She simply asked that students be a little less rude to food servers, because while they may be at the front line of service,, they are likely also the most exploited. It is important for all of us to question what we are missing on our journey to fight for improved lives elsewhere. Elsewhere can be another country, another city, but just as importantly, it needs to be within our communities or even as closely located as within our own families.

Another layer of complexity emerges in solving social justice issues in other countries and other social contexts. For example, if I promote human rights in a foreign society, am I also undermining the social fabric or social capital that holds some communities together? This cultural version of Western imperialism is well-worn territory, recently summarized as the "white savior industrial complex."[24] Again, process over outcome is critical here. In terms of teaching social justice, we need to engage our students to think differently about social justice and our process of engagement much more than imposing particular standards. Social justice as engagement privileges relationships over solutions and long-run bonding over short-run victories.

5. Empathy v. Consensus

One of my senior social justice students observed that her social work capstone course had become an uncomfortable space. The sensitivity of social workers may be expected, but unexpectedly, half the class has turned into language police for the other half. From my student's perspective, this policing shut down communication. Bright people with interesting contributions remain quiet in the face of others' potential condemnation. For fear of offending someone, they say nothing. This seems problematic, and my student assures me that these tensions are replicated within the professional field as well.

If social justice moves us forward, we must remain vigilant about preserving openness, but also forgiveness. We can't walk away from the exchange in a moment of inappropriate language, or behavior, fearing that someone has finally shown their true intention. Our conversations can't be severed by political correctness or silence in the name of political correctness. It is an important process to be heard and to really hear oneself, and then to let the dialogue be a part of transforming understanding without intimidation. We rarely practice empathetic persuasion. It is an art with an important set of skills and commitments. In the classroom, even the best and the brightest seem hardwired to tread lightly. "Live and let live" is the motto described earlier in this chapter, and it has become a motto that chisels away at authenticity. Students have lost the art of civil discourse, which often requires disagreement as part of cultivating an authentic identity. It isn't enough to have an opinion. We need to practice articulating it, defending it, and discarding it in order to appreciate its value. There are uncomfortable stages that inevitably become part of the process. While I think that social justice can contribute to a better society, it is not intended to feel good. This is not an instant gratification model. It extends the family circle with the ideal that for better and worse, we are in this together. The problems don't go away, and declaring winners doesn't move us forward in terms of human connectedness. Consensus is not realistic, but this proposed understanding of social justice requires that we acknowledge and reaffirm what keeps us together, sharing political, economic, and social space. Through social justice, we affirm our social contract to generate healthier boundaries for our political and economic behavior and decisions.

Significantly, while students are more passive and coldly civil, the public image of the social justice advocate is less of a granola-munching tree-hugger and more of a violent anarchist.[25] This new framework for social justice compels participants to practice disagreement in ways that may limit recourse to violence, and it affirms that there has to be something in between passive, strategic silence and the righteous attack on others who do not share our views. There is value to sharing without convergence. Especially if the engagement is part of a reiterated process, then it can build identity around community as much as community is also an opportunity to explore one's own identity and interests.

6. Private Sphere v. Political Sphere

Social justice rhetoric brings the most private issues of identity into the public square. For example, few would disagree that gender and sexual identity are hot-button social justice themes on most academic campuses. However, in an effort to push forward political rights, the current social justice agenda slips into publicizing what could remain private. On the one hand, it used to be that individuals and communities functioned with much less government authority, supervision, or protection. Fitting into more of the classical liberal ideal, groups didn't focus expectations for opportunities and outcomes through government benefits. Instead, citizens were more self-reliant and restrained into terms of using the political arena to solve social problems. The sphere of private life was vast, with the exception of carving out a specialized critical and laudable space for public discernment and political decision-making. "Don't ask, don't tell" was the social norm for so much of our daily life, with muted attention and very limited consideration to a wide range of issues that comfortably fit into the private sphere.

The civil rights movement opened up the political domain as the central sphere to command recognition and protection. The political bargain expanded as individuals within the public sphere benefitted from the many ways that citizens were available for culling votes in return for promising a widening scope of enforcements. It is not surprising that today's political arena encroaches upon so many aspects of our private life that it is increasingly difficult to salvage a sense of a private life at all. Some might be hopeful that settling many of these issues in the political sphere will allow us to move beyond their relevance eventually. However, the current climate that pushes us to be public about our most intimate lives brings politics into our most private lives. Willingly, we have invited government to regulate, legislate, seemingly even to dictate the terms of our relationships. When did it happen that we value government approval and depend upon government recognition for legitimacy? Somehow, we need to reconsider the public-private balance and seriously weigh whether the value of a private life may be essential to a healthy public life. In this way, social justice can contribute to sorting out boundaries between what is private and what is social. Much like the effort to carve out distinct conceptual territory for social justice from political and economic justice, there may be collective losses when we teach our young people to blur private and public engagement indiscriminately.

7. Unintended Heroes of Social Justice

It is hard to fathom, but some of our greatest heroes for implementing measures of political, economic, and social justice are often those very leaders who sat on thrones of injustice. In line with thinking about social justice as a "battle" with winners and losers, or thinking about social justice in terms of "heroes" and "villains," we often think in binary terms about the presence or absence of social justice. For example, students look at an institution or community and conclude whether it is socially just or unjust. Even with narrower issues, like gender, students weigh the evidence: A university supports gender equality so it exhibits social justice, or it won't show the Vagina Monologues so it doesn't support social justice. A potential dynamic of social justice is missing from both casual and formal analysis, and so it is worthwhile to explore the many ways in which social injustice fosters social justice. I don't mean this observation in the pedestrian way that social justice is a remedy for social injustice. Rather, I mean to suggest that in the presence of great injustice are the moments when we often also see the best of solidarity and humanity emerge, not sequentially, but simultaneously.

History is filled with enough examples where an unexpected hero of social justice emerges, such as Bismarck, De Kleerk, or Nixon.[26] Whether because of a turn of heart and mind, or through a strategic maneuver, those who initiate change for the common good can't fit a cookie-cutter image. Many of those heroes of social justice that don't fit the mold credit the social context within which they made revolutionary decisions. Social justice as a process of engagement cultivates fertile ground for change so that even the most unusual heroes emerge from the fertile environment of social justice. Throughout the process of social justice, it is important to recognize that particular individuals capture imagination, attention, and potential. Whether it is because he or she makes a reasoned argument or an emotional plea, there are moments that put individuals in the spotlight. Conflict is not necessarily negative, but we do need to understand its boundaries when it can become toxic and when it can become a part of healing deeper fissures within communities.

8. Solidarity v. Diversity

In addition to Paolo Friere's seminal book on oppression, my senior social justice students read *Why are all the Black Kids Sitting together in the Cafeteria*.[27] Whereas Freire supports dialogue and praxis between the oppressed and the oppressors, Tatum emphasizes "within group" dialogue as well. Many of her observations are important, such as "where a person is a member of the dominant or advantaged social group, the category is usually not mentioned."[28] The oppressor group is normal or the baseline around which other groups are named and around which a system of racism is created. By practices of omission and assumption, young African Americans are caught in a smog of racialized discourse and practice, and Tatum catalogues its insipid quality. She recognizes the special place of her classroom to unpack these assumptions. Her final chapter meaningfully settles on support for cross-racial dialogue: "Segregation and inequality are strongly self-perpetuating, yet the ideal of democratic education is to create an environment in which such patterns can be interrupted. The first step in interrupting this cycle of inequity is mutual engagement."[29] The problems around race in the United States are evident, and Tatum's process for healing fits into the overarching perspective offered in this book. Engagement across boundaries is essential.

However, while Tatum is right to identify race as the critical cleavage in American society and dominant in terms of American political discourse, we miss the complexity as long as we define our oppression by this cleavage alone. "Kyriarchy" describes intersectionality and the ways in which we have many layers of oppression in society. On the one hand, more layers of oppression seem to suggest a more devastating situation. There are many more cleavages than race defining oppression in American society. Gender, sexuality, poverty, and nationality are pervasive identity issues that define oppressor and oppressed. But rather than deepening the fissures between people, or perhaps along with the deepening fissures in society, kyriarchy suggests that we are often both oppressor and oppressed depending upon the context. We have places where we identify as the oppressed, and then we also have contexts within which we identify as those who are oppressed, and these dual positions may actually open up opportunities for empathy. As part of the process of meaningful engagement, we need to tap into our understandings from both roles. Students need to raise their consciousness to the identities within which they are part of an oppressed group and those where they are not. This consciousness is sufficient to elevate engagement and push forward the social justice project.

While Tatum emphasizes the value of interracial group dialogue, she also, somewhat controversially, suggests that groups should self-select for dialogue within groups as well. At one of her conferences, an announcement invited African American participants to attend a breakfast. One disgruntled white person asked her how she would feel if Tatum attended a conference about race and all white people were invited to attend a breakfast. Tatum responded that it would be a good idea. This jarring response underlines her perspective that oppressors share a unique foundation, and exploring the issues around systemic racism need not include those who are oppressed and very familiar with the problems and frustrations. For the oppressed, forging a space independent of the racialized system is very important for raising confidence and building solidarity. I agree that intragroup dialogue, along the many different identities we deem relevant as individuals within today's society, is important. More generally, social justice dialogue will be better served if people leave their politicized identities at the door. There are systemic issues that need to be addressed through legislation, and while relevant for intergroup development, they are not the issues that should dominate social justice tables. Recognizing a political sphere that is distinct and an appropriate vehicle for mobilizing interests opens up the possibility that there can be a social justice space for a focus on bridge-building without the pressures of legislative success.

9. Emotions

Emotions can become a slippery slope. At the moments of a heightened emotional exchange, the dynamic between students and between students and the professor can become very confusing. From my own experience, I understand that students continue to treat me as the authority in the room, but too often they want me to utilize my authority to affirm their personal stories. Unfortunately, this is the realm of counseling, not higher education rigor, and most of us with Ph.D.'s should be honest in recognizing that we don't have the skills necessary to carry this individual and group dynamic successfully. Parameters need to be set.

One of my senior students guided me to a set of practices that I adopt to offer a place for personal reflection but still maintain focus around content and analysis. Social justice depends upon each student engaging with the other on the most controversial issues, but as a professor, it isn't my skill-set to validate emotions. While I can be an empathetic listener, and I want my students to practice social justice in the safe and meaningful environment of a classroom, it is also my job to return to the material, to ground the emotion in empirical cases and contexts, and to analyze ideas rather than pick sides within the context of a social justice debate. So a successful exercise has been to address an issue that typically divides students. Our campus offers a particularly robust set of opportunities. As a West Coast, liberal arts, Catholic University with an ROTC program, it isn't difficult to find issues that generate knee-jerk response and opinion. It takes very little to prompt a schism in the classroom that can create self-generating divisions among groups. A good exercise can be delineating the expected and likely opposing positions on an issue—a potential "for" and "against" scenario emerges regularly. Then students draw randomly an assigned position, as vague as "for" and "against," from which they work in small groups where two individuals have been assigned the "for" position and two individuals have been assigned the "against" position. After working together to form the arguments that support their position, they convey them to the other side. After hearing both sides and sets of claims, they need to move forward in some actionable way. I don't want to frame it in terms of compromise, nor do I want it to be in terms of policy solutions. If the classroom is the opportunity to practice my ideal conceptualization of social justice, then it is very unnecessary to conform to political solutions or solutions at all. If the conversations fit into the ideal model, there will be some expression and emblem of understanding. Of course, it may be more or less authentic in this type of contrived, lesson setting where positions were randomly selected. In the real world, people would be emotionally invested in their position. However, as much as college is a preparation for life, we do need to provide a safe place for students to explore what social justice as a process of engagement feels like, but then as institutions of higher learning, we need to return to rigorous and reasoned analysis.

Certainly, faculty teaching social justice courses need to negotiate the flow from emotion to reason to understanding. It is undeniable that there is something profound in terms of potential learning that emerges from a student's vulnerability and willingness to take a public risk. There are students who care deeply about an identity that has been marginalized by power systems within society. The spontaneous social justice engagements are the most profound as well as the most painful, and I suppose this is one of the enduring dilemmas of social justice. As a process, it cannot be controlled without undermining some of its transformative potential. We have to trust that transformation comes from intellectual and emotional stimulation. And whether it is the student coming out to the classroom community or whether it is a woman angry that she cannot become a priest, or someone at the lower end of socioeconomic status who is tired of the appearance of entitlement on campus, or a student offended that diversity in Oregon seems defined by terms other than race, it is the honest reflections that carry the most transformative potential.

In a class of social justice students at a Catholic university, religion is a repeatedly divisive cleavage. After it was clear that there was a distinction between those who were part of the church and those who were not, it seemed like any issue we discussed brought this particular cleavage to the surface. We had to unpack the cleavage to move forward, and while it was impossible to fully affirm everyone adequately, the added power dynamic of professor-student required my attention to students both individually and together. Students needed to know that their vulnerability was not affecting fair standards. I have had many students imply my beliefs in ways that drive their insecurity and then their anger towards me. Generally, I don't intervene when students begin to politicize or complain, and I rigidly limit my participation during the emotional moments precisely to affirm neutrality. However, I have come to realize that silence doesn't feel like neutrality to someone who is vulnerable. Students have taught me that it is an important step to affirm my empathy as an individual and to affirm their value as people in order to return to a normalized dynamic of professor-student learning. In these instances of heightened emotion, intellectual critique needs to be prefaced with formal acknowledgment (not necessarily agreement) in order to return to the normalized process of critique and exchange associated with ideas and learning.

10. Fact v. Fiction

Teaching a course on social justice requires different pedagogical skills compared to other social science courses. Quite naively, I was not prepared for the level of emotion described above and that I would navigate as part of the teaching process. By twenty-something, and perhaps largely because there is some process of self-selection into a social justice course, students feel the burdens of their personal experiences with injustice. As a social scientist, I approach social justice through an analytical lens. It makes sense to think about the particular issues in terms of interests, bargaining, risks, and potential outcomes. For many students coming into a social justice class, this lens is foreign to them. Social justice is the opportunity to delve into the thick layers of identity issues and to finally offload some of the pressures associated with power and perceived oppression. Inevitably, it feels personal for many of my students. After denying this layer of personal sharing that would often disrupt the course content, I realized that if I wanted to move forward with content, I needed to make space for personal reflection throughout. Students need to tell stories, and it is through their storytelling that I learned how stories are an effective mechanism for bringing us closer to the ideal practice of social justice.

Stories reveal life's complexity. Any position can be thwarted, challenged, and effectively reversed by the emotional potency of a life-changing event.

Sharing our stories opens us up to similar transformations. Of course, the emotional swells are uncomfortable from a social science perspective. After watching a documentary about mandatory deportation for permanent residents who have committed a felony, several students responded critically that it manipulated their views through emotion. The implication was that policy should not be based on emotion. From a discipline that is attached to the rational actor assumption, the student's observation sounds reasonable. Also to a large extent, media blitzes around favored topics have cautioned us against emotional energy as well. Increasingly, we sense we are being manipulated. However, emotions coming from sensationalized stories portrayed in the media are very different from interpersonal learning that emerges from shared experiences. While political scientists adopted the rational actor assumption model in order to generalize about behavior, it shouldn't carry too much normative relevance. Strategically motivated rational calculations as the basis for our policy can benefit from the thickness of human understanding about complexity and possibility that comes through storytelling and shared literature.

Creativity is a social experience that is often spurred by stories, and it is a central building block of the social justice project. Whether one is immersed in play, or productivity, or even if one has retreated into a studio space to paint or write in isolation, the act of creation is a response to engagement. Even while creative acts can be manifest individually as a rebellion against society, and while they can be expressed apart from society, the foundation remains social. In order to be most creative, we need to get beyond our individual self-interest. So often, our collective possibilities become dragged into immediate or short-run interests, whereas this social justice project requires tapping into the most creative connections. Stories, our own stories, and those provided by literature are a tremendous vehicle for moving individuals out of the realm of their self-interest and into the imaginary realm of creativity where the most potent possibilities for human connectedness lie.

Literature provides opportunities for people to deepen understanding around a shared human condition. Through novels, we share stories that are not our own and that can inspire us similarly. Through novels, we can join experiences that carry across generations, cultures, countries, and other barriers. Through the mythical truths offered by literature, we see ourselves in different ways and living different lives. This emotional and intellectual exercise prepares us for good citizenship, especially within a liberal democracy. Precisely because we are not vested in the outcomes of stories, we can be entertained, and simultaneously, we feel the lives of others. Arguably, these emotions generate connectedness and empathy that transfers well into the public square. From reading fiction, students learn about misunderstandings, tragedy, racism, sexism, love, jealousy, rage, forgiveness, and the list continues. From this emotional and intellectual place, we learn through the moral puzzles of others' lives, and we expand our own much more limited lives without the high costs of living other lives. Without multiple lives, we need ways to tap into other possible selves and the complexity of others that brings us into solidarity with them. Not only does literature inform our own sense of values, like freedom and equality, but it binds us together in solidarity and informs our civic virtues, like empathy, commitment, and creativity.

Art invites us to new ways of seeing politics, the economy, technology, religion, and each other. Richard Rorty defines the particular value of some literature as a central foundation of the process for cultivating justice. In my edited volume on Hemingway, Curtis quotes Rorty and the societal process of justice:

> of coming to see other human beings as "one of us" rather than as "them" [which] is a matter of detailed description of what unfamiliar people are like and of redescription of what we ourselves are like. This is not a task for theory but for genres such as ethnography, the journalist's report, the comic book, the docudrama, and, especially, the novel. Fiction like that of Dickens, Olive Schreiner, or Richard Wright gives us details about the kinds of suffering being endured by people to whom we had not previously attended.[30]

Similarly, social justice as a process of engagement can benefit from the expansive empathy that comes from understanding. Like social justice, and also as preparation for social justice engagement, literature prepares us for healthier political engagement while freeing us from the strategic mindset that plagues politicized rhetoric. Another important aspect of literature is its capacity as the source of solace or recovery from the political realm. Somehow, we need to return to the values of getting along well with each other, seeing each other as comrades at least as often as we see each other as competitors, and tapping into our collective synergy as much as our strength as individuals.

THE WAY FORWARD

For the United States, the path of social justice evokes a new social constitution around familiar ideals: "America has never been united by blood or birth or soil. We are bound by ideals that move us beyond our backgrounds, lift us above our interests and teach us what it means to be citizens. Every child must be taught these principles. Every citizen must uphold them. And every immigrant, by embracing these ideals, makes our country more, not less, America."[31] Like citizenship, but even more than citizenship, social justice and interpersonal engagement cannot be implied or assumed. It needs to be practiced. It needs to be respected institutionally, culturally, and strategically.

Within our political, economic, technological, and religious spheres today, we are oriented toward competition. With the justifications of individualism and freedom, the engine of competition is seductive. In the process and over time, cooperation and community have become increasingly compromised. We have fewer places where we experience, practice, and value the energy of community. Social justice is the mechanism to reenergize the population, not away from individualism, but toward a stronger foundation of community that inspires stable and sustaining individualism.

As outlined in this book, there are various ways to get there, and the best case scenario for success will bring together several types of efforts at once. There does not need to be a political or economic revolution of beliefs, preferences, or mobilization. The systems in place are good ones. However, the synergy is pushing away from the crucial balance of individualism from the context of community engagement. Community engagement is deteriorating by our own self-determined decisions. The trajectory could move us much farther away from our nature, which depends upon both individual and collective identity formation. The trajectory will chisel away not just at our collective identity, but at the balance essential for the very success of our individualist-oriented spheres of democracy and capitalism.

Reconceptualizing social justice was the primary purpose of this book. The United States was a focused example to highlight both the weaknesses of the current system as well as the possibilities with change. It has been beyond the scope of this book to translate these concepts to other regions and other countries. Many countries carry a much stronger orientation to the collective, either through the prevalence of traditionalism or institutionalized social democracy. More traditional countries, in terms of economic and political development and their social democracies, are moving away from this distinct emphasis on the collective. Further study needs to examine these different starting points and different trajectories, and to empirically test different ways of implementing social justice. In different ways, and to different degrees, exciting organizations outside of the university are successfully introducing measures to test many of the outcomes associated with aspects of this reconstructed social justice. Michael Porter's "Shared Value Initiative" offers consultation for companies to cultivate shared values in ways that fit with the reconceptualized social justice. The scholarly agenda for social justice programs in universities can be much wider than the corporate focus, but we can borrow tools and measures to test our broader hypotheses and cases.

Small shifts can cultivate the synergy that is more likely to sustain development. Social justice can save individualism from its worst manifestation, described by Hobbes as "solitary, poor, nasty, brutish, and short."[32] We don't necessarily need a Leviathan but we do need something. It invites academics to join the conceptually rich table of social justice that is far removed from the politicized jargon and ideologically biased activism currently associated with social justice. This book suggests our way forward both empirically and academically.

NOTES

1. John Adams, Defense of the Constitutions, 1787. The Patriot Post http://patriotpost.us/quotes Accessed July 26, 2013.
2. Andrew M. Guest, James Lies, Jeff Kerssen-Griep, and Thomas Frieberg, "Concepts of Social Justice as a Cultural Consensus: Starting Points for College Students of Different Political Persuasions," *Journal of College & Character* 6 (2009): 1.
3. Ninety percent agree on the following: they believe in God, are patriotic, consider preventing terrorism as a very important foreign policy goal, admire those who get rich by working hard, think society should ensure everyone has equal opportunity to succeed, believe it's important to get more than a high school education, favor teaching sex education in public school, find birth control morally acceptable, believe cloning humans would be morally wrong, believe it's wrong for married people to have affairs, and believe it's their duty to always vote. Connie Cass, "Maybe Americans Agree About More than They Know," *Associated Press*, May 12, 2013, 1.
4. Curtiss Paul DeYoung, *Living Faith: How Faith Inspires Social Justice* (Minneapolis: Fortress Press, 2007), 54.
5. Paulo Freire, *Pedagogy of the Oppressed* (New York: Continuum, 1970), 74.
6. Freire, *Pedagogy of the Oppressed*, 51.
7. DeYoung, *Living Faith*, 54–56.
8. DeYoung, *Living Faith*, 56.
9. Michael Sandel, *Justice: What's the Right Thing to Do?* (New York: Farrar, Straus and Giroux, 2009).
10. Michael McCollough, "You are not special commencement speech from Wellesley High School." Posted on June 7, 2012. Accessed July 26, 2013. http://www.youtube.com/watch?v=_lfxYhtf8o4.
11. Michael Sandel, *Justice: What's the Right Thing to Do?*, 180–81.
12. David Bauder, "The Evidence: Judge Judy Rules Daytime," *Oregonian*, Tuesday, February 12, 2013.
13. Richard A. Posner, *Law, Pragmatism, and Democracy* (Cambridge: Harvard University Press), 107.
14. Ella Baker, Posted on November 8, 2012. Accessed July 26, 2013. http://ellabakercenter.org/blog/2012/11/strong-people-dont-need-strong-leaders.
15. Lauretta Conklin Frederking, "Demystifying Social Capital Through Zola's *Germinal*," in *Teaching the Novel Across the Curriculum*, ed. Colin Irvine (Westport: Greenwood Press, 2008), 286–97.
16. Claus Offe, *Disorganized Capitalism* (Cambridge: The MIT Press, 1985).
17. Ariel Levy, "Life and Separate: Why is Feminism Still So Divisive?" *New Yorker*, November 16, 2009.
18. Beverly Daniel Tatum, *"Why are all the Black Kids Sitting Together in the Cafeteria?"* (New York: Basic Books, 1997).
19. Tim Harford, "Regrets? I've Had a Few," *Financial Times*, June 4/5, 2011, 4.
20. Carol Dweck, "The Effort Effect," *Stanford Alumni Association Publication*, March/April 2007, 50.
21. Harford, "Regrets?,"4.
22. Dweck, "The Effort Effect."
23. Linda Polman, *The Story of Aid and War in Modern Times* (New York: Penguin, 2010).
24. Teju Cole, "The White Savior Industrial Complex," *Atlantic*, March 21, 2012, comment on Kony 2012, http://www.theatlantic.com/international/archive/2012/03/the-white-savior-industrial-complex/254843.

25. The Occupy Movements are important both for their goals of social justice and for their means to achieve their goals, which are often violent. See "Occupy Oakland Protest Muted After Last Week's Arrests, *CNN*, February 5, 2012, http://edition.cnn.com/2012/02/05/us/occupy-protests/?hpt=us_c1; Patrick McGeehan, "Envelopes with White Powder Sent to Mayor and 6 Banks," *New York Times*, April 30, 2012, http://www.nytimes.com/2012/05/01/ nyregion/envelopes-with-white-powder-sent-to-bloomberg-and-6-banks .html?ref=occupywallstreet; and Kirk Johnson, "Occupy Protesters Regroup After Mass Arrests," *New York Times*, October 30, 2011, http://www .nytimes.com/2011/10/31/us/occupy-wall-street-protesters-arrested-in-denver -and-portland.html.
26. While Nixon was vilified for his personal behavior, Nixon was a champion of the environmental movement. According to J. B. Flippen, "No one remembers Richard M. Nixon as an environmental president, but a year into his presidency, he committed his administration to regulating and protecting the environment. The public outrage over the Santa Barbara oil spill in early 1969, culminating in the first Earth Day in 1970, convinced Nixon that American environmentalism now enjoyed extraordinary political currency," in Flippen, *Nixon and the Environment* (Albuquerque: University of New Mexico Press, 2000), Book Jacket.
27. Beverly Daniel Tatum, *"Why are all the Black Kids Sitting Together in the Cafeteria?"* (New York: Basic Books, 1997).
28. Tatum, 21.
29. Tatum, 212–13.
30. Rorty 1989, xvi in William Curtis, "Hemingway, Hopelessness, and Liberalism," in *Hemingway on Politics and Rebellion*, ed. Lauretta Conklin Frederking (New York: Routledge, 2010), 51.
31. George W. Bush, 2001.
32. Thomas Hobbes, *Leviathan* Part I, Chapter 3 [1651]. (New York: Penguin Classics, 1982).

Bibliography

Albert, Michel. *Capitalism vs. Capitalism*. New York: Four Wall Eight Windows, 1993.

Ali, Ayaan Hirsi. "The New York Mosque is a Symptom of Civilizational Clash." *New Perspectives Quarterly* 27 (2010): 38–40.

American Humanist Association, "Humanism and its Aspirations," www .americanhumanist.org/Humanism/Humanist_Manifesto_III. Accessed July 26, 2013.

Anderson, Alistair, and Robert Smith. "The Moral Space in Entrepreneurship: An Exploration of Ethical Imperatives and the Moral Legitimacy of Being Enterprising." *Entrepreneurship and Regional Development* 19 (2007): 479–97.

Anwar, Yasmin. "Highly Religious People Are Less Motivated by Compassion Than are Non-Believers." *Media Relations*, April 30, 2012.

Bankston, Carl L. "Social Justice: Cultural Origins of a Perspective and a Theory." *Independent Review* 15, no. 2 (Fall 2010): 165–78.

Barber, Tony. "Tensions Unveiled." *Financial Times*, November 16, 2010.

Baker, Ella. http://ellabakercenter.org/blog/2012/11/strong-people-dont-need-strong -leaders. Accessed July 26, 2013.

Bauder, David. "The Evidence: Judge Judy Rules Daytime." *Oregonian*, Tuesday, February 12, 2013.

Bauerlein, Mark (ed.). *The Digital Divide*. London: Penguin Books, 2011.

Baumol, William, Robert Litan, and Carl Schramm. *Good Capitalism, Bad Capitalism, and the Economics of Growth and Prosperity*. New Haven: Yale University Press, 2007.

BP. "Our Approach to Social Issues." BP. Sustainability Review, 2011. http://www .bp.com/content/dam/bp/pdf/sustainability/country-reports/bp_sustainability _review_2011.pdf Accessed July 26, 2013.

Briody, Dan. *The Iron Triangle: Inside the Secret World of the Carlyle Group*. Hoboken: Wiley, 2008.

Cair Chicago. "Cair-Chicago Wins Judgment for Muslim Center's Freedom of Religion," April 1, 2013. http://www.cairchicago.org/2013/04/01/cair-chicago -wins-judgment-for-muslim-centers-freedom-of-religion/. Accessed July 26, 2013.

Caldwell, Christopher. "Ivory Towers Will be Toppled by an Online 'Tsunami'." *Financial Times*, August 11/12, 2012.

Callan, Eamonn. *Creating Citizens: Political Education and Liberal Democracy*. Oxford: Clarendon Press, 1997.

Campaign Finance Institute. "The Cost of Winning an Election." http://www.cfinst .org/data/pdf/VitalStats_t1.pdf. Accessed July 26, 2013.

Cardoso, Fernando Enrique, and Faletto Enzo. *Dependency and Development in Latin America*. Berkeley: University of California Press, 1979.

Carlman, S. "County Board Denies Mosque Tower, Delays Vote on Permit." *Couriernews*, February 8, 2011.

Carr, Nicholas. "Is Google Making Us Stupid?" In *The Digital Divide*, edited by Mark Bauerlein, 63–75. London: Penguin Books, 2011.

———. *What the Internet is Doing to our Brains*. New York: W.W. Norton & Company, 2011.

Carroll, Rory. "US Chose to Ignore Rwandan Genocide." *Guardian*, March 31, 2004.

Cass, Connie. "Maybe Americans Agree About More Than They Know." *Associated Press*, May 12, 2013.

Center for Communication and Civic Engagement, "Primary Nike/Anti-Sweatshop Campaign Network Sites." http://depts.washington.edu/ccce/polcommcampaigns/nikecampaignsites.htm. Accessed July 26, 2013.

Chicago Tribune Editorials, "In Good Faith," February 17, 2011.

Cigler, Allan, and Burdett A. Loomis. "From Big Bird to Bill Gates: Organized Interests and the Emergence of Hyperpolitics." In *Interest Group Politics*, edited by Allen Cigler and Burdett A. Loomis, 389–405. Washington, DC: CQ Press, 1998.

Citizens United v. Federal Election Commission. Appeal from the United States District Court for the District of Columbia. No. 08–205. Argued March 24, 2009—Reargued September 9, 2009—Decided January 21, 2010.

CNN Wire Staff. "Occupy Oakland Protest Muted After Last Week's Arrests." *CNN*. Cable News Network, February 5, 2012. http://edition.cnn.com/2012/02/05/us/occupy-protests/?hpt=us_c1.

Cohen, Joshua. "The Importance of Philosophy: Reflections on John Rawls." *South African Journal of Philosophy* 23, no. 2 (2004): 114–19.

Cole, Teju. "The White Savior Industrial Complex." *Atlantic*, March 21, 2012.

Conklin, David. *Cases in the Environment of Business International Perspectives*. Thousand Oaks: Sage Publications, 2006.

———. *Reengineering to Compete*. Scarborough: Prentice-Hall, 1994.

Council of Islamic Organizations of Greater Chicago. http://www.ciogc.org/Go.aspx?link=7654323. Accessed July 26, 2013.

Crossette, Barbara. "Report Says U.S. and Others Allowed Rwanda Genocide." *New York Times*, July 8, 2000.

Curtis, William. "Hemingway, Hopelessness, and Liberalism." In *Hemingway on Politics and Rebellion*, edited by Lauretta Conklin Frederking, 50–74. New York: Routledge, 2010.

Dalai Lama. *Toward a True Kinship of Faiths: How the World's Religions Can Come Together*. New York: Doubleday Religion, 2010.

Daniels, Serena, and Ted Gregory. "DuPage Board to Decide Today on Mosque." *Chicago Tribune*, February 7, 2011.

Daniels, Serena, and Joe Ruzich. "Religious Leaders Urge Approval of DuPage Mosque." *Chicago Tribune*, January 19, 2011.

DeBerri, Edward, and James E. Hug. *Catholic Social Teaching: Our Best Kept Secret*. 8th ed. New York: Orbis Books, 2012.

DeYoung, Curtiss Paul. *Living Faith: How Faith Inspires Social Justice*. Minneapolis: Fortress Press, 2007.

Downs, Anthony. *An Economic Theory of Democracy*. New York: Harper Collins, 1957.

Driscoll, Jeremy. *A Monk's Alphabet: Moments of Stillness in a Turning World*. Boston: New Seeds, 2007.

DuPage County Board of Appeals Petition No. Z08–074, May 14, 2009, 5.

DuPage County Board of Appeals Petition No. Z10–040, September 20, 2010.

DuPage County Board of Appeals Petition No. Z10–040, October 12, 2010.

DuPage County Representative, in discussion with the author, Thursday, June 28, 2012.

Dweck, Carol. "The Effort Effect." *Stanford Alumni Association Publication*, 46–52, March/April 2007.

Economist (blog), "Market Troubles: Which Countries are Most in Favour of the Free Market," April 6, 2011. http://www.economist.com/blogs/dailychart/2011/04/public_opinion_capitalism.

Feminist Philosophers (blog), "Word of the Day: Kyriarchy," May 1, 2008. http://feministphilosophers.wordpress.com/2008/05/01/word-of-the-day-kyriarchy/. Accessed July 26, 2013.

Feser, Edward. "Hayek on Social Justice: Reply to Lukes and Johnston." *Critical Review: A Journal of Politics and Society* 11, no. 4 (1997): 581–606.

Fetzer, Joel, and J. Christopher Soper. *Muslims and the State of Britain, France, and Germany*. Cambridge: Cambridge University Press, 2005.

Fletcher, Denise. "Entrepreneurial Processes and the Social Construction of Opportunity." *Entrepreneurship and Regional Development* 18 (2006): 421–40.

Flippen, J. Brooks. *Nixon and the Environment*. Albuquerque: University of New Mexico Press, 2000.

Francisco, Valerie. "'The Internet is Magic': Technology, Intimacy and Transnational Families." *Critical Sociology*. Forthcoming in print. Online access April 30, 2013.

Frederking, Lauretta C. "A Cross-national Study of Culture, Organization and Entrepreneurship in Three Neighbourhoods." *Entrepreneurship and Regional Development* 16 (2004): 197–215.

———. *Economic and Political Integration in Immigrant Neighbourhoods: Trajectories of Virtuous and Vicious Cycles*. Selinsgrove: Susquehanna University Press, 2007.

———. "Demystifying Social Capital Through Zola's *Germinal*." In *Teaching the Novel Across the Curriculum*, edited by Colin Irvine, 286–97. Westport: Greenwood Press, 2008.

———. "Getting to Green: Niche-driven or Government-led Entrepreneurship and Sustainability in the Wine Industry." *New England Journal of Entrepreneurship* 14, no. 1 (2011): 47–61.

———. (ed.). *Hemingway on Politics and Rebellion*. New York: Routledge, 2010.

Freire, Paulo. *Pedagogy of the Oppressed*. New York: Continuum, 1970.

Friedman, Milton. *Capitalism and Freedom*. Chicago: University of Chicago Press, 1962.

Friedman, Thomas. *The World is Flat*. New York: Farrar, Straus and Giroux, 2005.

Gallup Economy, "U.S. Economic Confidence Retreats from Five-Year High," May 14, 2013, http://www.gallup.com/poll/162413/economic-confidence-retreats-five-year-high.aspx. Accessed July 26, 2013.

Gardner, David. "Abortion Clinics in US Get a Gun Guard After the Murder of Doctor." *Daily Mail*, June 2, 2009.

Gellner, Ernest. *Nations and Nationalism*. London: Blackwell, 1983.

Gerschenkron, Alexander. *Economic Backwardness in Historical Perspective*. Boston: Belknap Press of Harvard University Press, 1962.

Goldsborough, Bob. "DuPage County Rejects Proposed Islamic Center." *Chicago Breaking News Center*, January 12, 2010.

Goleman, Daniel. *Emotional Intelligence*. New York: Bantam Books, 1994.

Graeber, David. *Debt*. Brooklyn: Melville House, 2011.

Grusky, David B., Doug McAdam, Rob Reich, and Debra Satz, (eds). *Occupy the Future*. Cambridge: A Boston Review Book, 2013.

Guest, Andrew M., James Lies, Jeff Kerssen-Griep, and Thomas Frieberg. "Concepts of Social Justice as a Cultural Consensus: Starting Points for College Students of Different Political Persuasions." *Journal of College & Character* 6 (2009): 1–12.

Gutierrez, Gustavo. *Theology of Liberation: History, Politics, and Salvation*. Maryknoll, New York: Orbis Books, 1973.

Gutierrez, Gustavo, and Richard Shaull. *Liberation and Change*. Atlanta: John Knox Press, 1977.

Gutmann, Amy. *Identity in Democracy*. Princeton, New Jersey: Princeton University Press, 2003.

Gutmann, Amy, and Dennis Thompson. *Democracy and Disagreement*. Boston: Harvard University Press, 1998.

Harford, Tim. *Adapt: Why Success Always Starts With Failure*. New York: Farrar, Straus and Giroux, 2012.

———. "Regrets? I've Had a Few." *Financial Times*, June 4/5, 2011.

Hayek, Friedrich A. von. *The Constitution of Liberty*. Chicago: University of Chicago Press, 1960.

Hobbes, Thomas. *Leviathan*. New York: Penguin Classics, 1982.

Horton, John, and Andrea T. Baumeister, (eds). *Literature and the Political Imagination*. New York: Routledge, 1996.

Humphreys, Macartan, Jeffrey Sachs, and Joseph Stiglitz, eds. *Escaping the Resource Curse*. New York: Columbia University Press, 2007.

Iggulden, Conn. *Emperor: The Gates of Rome*. New York: Delacorte Press, 2004.

Ioffe, Julia. "The Blog Society." *Financial Times*, December 17/18, 2011.

Jackall, Robert. *Moral Mazes: The World of Corporate Managers*. Oxford: Oxford University Press, 1988.

Jamal, Amaney. "Civil Liberties and the Otherization of Arab and Muslim Americans." In *Race and Arab Americans Before and After 9/11*, edited by Amaney Jamal and Nadine Naber, 114–30. New York: Syracuse University Press, 2008.

Jamal, Amaney, and Nadine Naber, (eds). *Race and Arab Americans Before and After 9/11*, New York: Syracuse University Press, 2008.

Jamal, Amaney. "The Racialization of Muslim Americans." In *Muslims in Western Politics*, edited by Abdulkader H. Sinno, 200–19. Bloomington: Indiana University Press, 2009.

Johnson, Carrie, and Julie Tate. "New Interrogation Details Emerge." *Washington Post*, April 17, 2009.

Johnson, Kirk. "Occupy Protesters Regroup After Mass Arrests." New York Times, October 30, 2011.

Jones, Jeffrey. "U.S. Congress' Approval Rating at 21% Ahead of Elections," GALLUP Politics, http://www.gallup.com/poll/158372/congress-approval-rating-ahead-elections.aspx. Accessed on July 26, 2013.

Karl, Terry Lynn. *The Paradox of Plenty Oil Booms and Petro-States*. Berkeley: University of California Press, 1997.

Katz, Jerome, and Chris Steyaert. "Reclaiming the Space of Entrepreneurship in Society: Geographical, Discursive and Social Dimensions." *Entrepreneurship and Regional Development* 16 (2004): 179–96.

Keynes, John Maynard. *The General Theory of Employment, Interest, and Money*. New York: Harcourt Brace, 1936.

King, Sallie B. *Being Benevolence: The Social Ethics of Engaged Buddhism*. Honolulu: University of Hawai'I Press, 2005.

Knight, Jack. *Institutions and Social Conflict*. Cambridge: Cambridge University Press, 1992.

Knight, Jack, and James Johnson. *The Priority of Democracy: Political Consequences of Pragmatism*. New York: Russell Sage Foundation, 2011.

Knoke, David, Franz Urban Pappi, Jeffrey Broadbent, and Yutaka Tsujinaka. *Comparing Policy Networks: Labor Politics in the U.S., Germany, and Japan*. Cambridge: Cambridge University Press, 1996.

Kuran, Timur. *Private Truths, Public Lie: The Social Consequences of Preference Falsification*. Boston: Harvard University Press, 1997.

Kuttner, Robert. *Everything for Sale*. Chicago: University of Chicago Press, 1996.

LaFeber, Walter. *Michael Jordan and the New Global Capitalism*. New York: W. W. & Norton Company, 2002.

Levy, Ariel. "Lift and Separate: Why is Feminism Still so Divisive?" *New Yorker*, November 16, 2009.

Levy, David. "Interview with Milton Friedman." *Region*, June 1, 1992. http://www.minneapolisfed.org/publications_papers/pub_display.cfm?id=3748.

Lindlaw, Scott. "UAV Operators Suffer War Stress." *Associated Press*, August 7, 2008.

Manning, Jeff. "Legally Bound." *Oregonian*, August 5, 2012.

Marcuse, Herbert. *One-Dimensional Man*. Boston: Beacon Press, 1964.

McCollough, Michael. 2012. "You are not special commencement speech from Wellesley High School." Posted on June 7, 2012. http://www.youtube.com/watch?v=_lfxYhtf8o4 Accessed July 26, 2013.

McGeehan, Patrick. "Envelopes With White Powder Sent to Mayor and 6 Banks." *New York Times*, May 1, 2012.

Mirsky, Laura. "Restorative Justice Practices of Native American, First Nation and Other Indigenous People of North America: Part II." International Institute for Restorative Practices. Bethlehem, Pennsylvania. Posted May 26, 2004. http://www.iirp.edu/article_detail.php?article_id=NDA0. Accessed July 26, 2013.

Mojab, Shahrzad. "Theorizing the Politics of 'Islamic Feminism.'" In "Special Issue: The Realm of the Possible: Middle Eastern Women in Political and Social Spaces." Feminist Review 69, no. 1 (2001): 124–46.

Moyo, Dambisa. *Dead Aid: Why Aid is Not Working and How There is a Better Way for Africa*. New York: Farrar, Straus and Giroux, 2009.

Murray, Sarah. "Companies to Reduce Humanity's Footprint." *Financial Times*, Tuesday, April 24, 2012: 1.

National Survey of Homeless Assistance Providers and Clients. "Homelessness: Programs and the People They Serve." U.S. Department of Housing and Urban Development. 1999. Posted date October 20, 1999. http://www.huduser.org/portal/publications/homeless/homeless_tech.html. Accessed July 26, 2013.

North, Douglass. *Institutions, Institutional Change, and Economic Development*. Cambridge: Cambridge University Press, 1990.

North, Douglass C., and Barry R. Weingast. "Constitutions and Commitment: The Evolution of Institutional Governing Public Choice in Seventeenth-Century England." *Journal of Economic History* 49, no. 4 (1989): 803–32.

OECD (2012). PISA report. http://www.oecd.org/pisa/. Accessed July 26, 2013.

Offe, Claus. *Disorganized Capitalism*. Cambridge: The MIT Press, 1985.

Okun, Arthus M. *Equality and Efficiency: The Big Tradeoff*. Washington, DC: The Brookings Institution, 1975.

Olson, Mancur. *The Rise and Decline of Nations: Economic Growth, Stagflation and Social Rigidities*. New Haven: Yale University Press, 1984.

Payutto, Phra Prayaudh. *Buddhadhamma: Natural Laws and Values for Life*. Translated by Grant A. Olson. Albany: State University Press of New York, 1995.

Polman, Linda. *The Story of Aid and War in Modern Times*. New York: Penguin, 2010.

Poor Kids: An Intimate Portrait of America's Economic Crisis, Frontline (PBS, Posted November 20, 2012), Documentary, http://www.pbs.org/wgbh/pages/frontline/poor-kids/. Accessed July 26, 2013.

Poorman, Mark. *Interactional Morality: A Foundation for Moral Discernment in Catholic Pastoral Ministry*. Washington, DC: Georgetown University Press, 1993.

Porter, Michael, and Mark Kramer. "Creating Shared Value." *Harvard Business Review* Nos. 1–2, January/February 2011, 62–77.

————. *Strategy and Society: The Link Between Competitive Advantage and Corporate Social Responsibility*. Boston: Harvard Business Review, 2006.

Posner, Richard A. *Law, Pragmatism, and Democracy*. Cambridge: Harvard University Press, 2005.

Prensky, Marc. "Digital Natives, Digital Immigrants." In *The Digital Divide*, edited by Mark Bauerlein, 3–11. London: Penguin Books, 2011.

————. "Do They Really *Think* Differently?" In *The Digital Divide*, edited by Mark Bauerlein, 12–25. London: Penguin Books, 2011.

Putnam, Robert D., and David E. Campbell. *American Grace: How Religion Divides and Unites Us*. New York: Simon & Schuster, 2010.

Qutb, Sayyid. *Selected Writings on Politics, Religion, and Society*, edited by Albert J. Bergesen. New York: Routledge, 2008.

Rawls, John. *A Theory of Justice*. Revised ed. Cambridge: Harvard University Press, 1999.

Russell, Bertrand. "Philosophy for Laymen." In *Unpopular Essays*, 21–32. London and New York: Routledge, 1950.

Sacks, Jonathan. *The Dignity of Difference: How to Avoid the Clash of Civilizations*. New York: Continuum, 2003.

Salisbury, Robert H., and Lauretta Conklin Frederking. "Instrumental v. Expressive Group.

Politics: The National Endowment for the Arts." In *Interest Group Politics*, edited by Allan Cigler and Burdett Loomis, 283–303. 5th ed. Washington, DC: CQ Press, 1998.

Salisbury, Stephen. "Mosque-mania Anti-Muslim fears and the far right," August 10, 2010. http://www.tomdispatch.com/post/175283/tomgram:_stephan_salisbury,_extremism_at_ground_zero_%28again%29__/. Accessed July 26, 2013.

Sandel, Michael. *Justice: What's the Right Thing to Do?* New York: Farrar, Straus and Giroux, 2009.

————. *What Money Can't Buy*. New York: W. W. Norton & Company, 2012.

Sandler, Ronald D., and Phaedra C. Pezzullo. *Environmental Justice and Environmentalism: The Social Justice Challenge to the Environmental Movement*. Cambridge: MIT Press, 2007.

Schelling, Thomas. *Micromotives and Macrobehavior*. New York: W. W. Norton & Company, 1978.

Schumpeter, Joseph. *Capitalism, Socialism and Democracy*. New York: Harper & Brothers, 1943.

Seyfang, Gill, and Adrian Smith. "Grassroots Innovations for Sustainable Development: Towards a New Research and Policy Agenda." *Environmental Politics* 16, no.4 (2007): 584–603.

Shepsle, Kenneth A. "Institutional Arrangements and Equilibrium in Multidimensional Voting Models." *American Journal of Political Science* 23, no. 1 (1979): 27–59.

Sherman, Hugh. "A Topology of Strategic Management: Rational, Natural, and Ecological Approaches." *Journal of Management Science and Policy Analysis* 3–4 (1991): 332–45.

Sinno, Abulkader H. (ed.). *Muslims in Western Politics*. Bloomington: Indiana University Press, 2009.

Smith, Adam. *Theory of Moral Sentiments*. London: A. Millar, 1759.

Smith, Emmanuelle. "Won Over My Social Enterprise; Women at B-School; Increasing Numbers of Women are Being Drawn to MBAs that Offer a Strong Emphasis on Sustainability." *Financial Times*, March 26, 2012.

Solari, Stefano, and Daniele Corrado. "Social Justice and Economic Order According to Natural Law." *The Journal of Markets & Morality* 12, no. 1 (2009): 47–62.

Stiglitz, Joseph. *Globalization and Its Discontents.* New York: W.W. Norton & Company, 2002.

Strong Families, "Forward Together", http://forwardtogether.org/strong-families. Accessed on July 26, 2013.

Sunstein, Cass. *Republic.* Princeton: Princeton University Press, 2009.

Tapscott, Don. "The Eight Net Gen Norms." In *The Digital Divide*, edited by Mark Bauerlein, 130–59. London: Penguin Books, 2011.

Tatum, Beverly Daniel. *"Why Are All the Black Kids Sitting Together in the Cafeteria?"* New York: Basic Books, 1997.

Tax Policy Center. "The Numbers: How Do U.S. Taxes Compare Internationally?" http://www.taxpolicycenter.org/briefing-book/background/numbers/international .cfm. Accessed July 26, 2013.

Taylor, Charles. *The Ethics of Authenticity.* Cambridge: Harvard University Press, 1991.

Taylor, Michael. *Community, Anarchy and Liberty.* Cambridge: Cambridge University Press, 1982.

Tebble, Adam James. "Hayek and Social Justice: A Critique." *Critical Review of International Social & Political Philosophy* 12, no. 4. (Dec. 2009): 581–604.

Tullis, Paul. "Can Forgiveness Play a Role in Criminal Justice?" *New York Times*, January 4, 2013.

Turkle, Sherry. *Alone Together: Why We Expect More From Technology and Less From Each Other.* New York: Basic Books, 2011.

Tutu, Desmund, and Bettina Gronblom. "Camels Can Pass Through the Eye of a Needle." *Financial Times*, Thursday, April 5, 2012.

U.S. Department of Housing and Urban Development. "Homelessness: Programs and the People They Serve," Posted October 20, 1999. http://www.huduser.org/portal/publications/homeless/homeless_tech.html. Accessed July 26, 2013.

U.S. Environmental Protection Agency. "Environmental Justice." Environmental Protection Agency. http://www.epa.gov/environmentaljustice/. Accessed July 26, 2013.

Vogel, Steven, K. *Japan Remodeled: How Government and Industry are Reforming Japanese Capitalism.* Ithaca: Cornell University Press, 2006.

Weaver, Courtney, "The Philosophical Punks on Trial for Blaspheming Putin." *Financial Times*, August 19, 2012.

West, Peter J. "Social Justice and the Catholic Vote." *American Thinker*, March 16, 2012. http://www.americanthinker.com/2012/03/social_justice_and_the_catholic _vote.html. Accessed on July 26, 2013.

———. "Catholics and Voting Pro-Life: Social Justice Begins in the Womb." Life News. http://www.lifenews.com/2012/03/21/catholics-and-voting-pro-life-social -justice-begins-in-the-womb/. Accessed May 23, 2012.

White, Jenny B. "State Feminism, Modernization, and the Turkish Republican Woman." In "Special Issue: Gender and Modernism between the Wars, 1918–1939." National Women's Studies Association Journal 15, no. 3 (2003): 145–59.

York, Steve. *Truth Commissions and Societies in Transition: Confronting the Truth.* Documentary film. Washington, DC: York Zimmerman, 2007.

Zheng, Yuxing. "Public Officials Struggle to Reverse Tide of Political Incivility in Government." *Oregonian*, Sunday, August 19, 2012.

Index

For Product Safety Concerns and Information please contact our EU
representative GPSR@taylorandfrancis.com
Taylor & Francis Verlag GmbH, Kaufingerstraße 24, 80331 München, Germany